Riding with Reindeer

A Bicycle Odyssey through
Finland, Lapland, and Arctic Norway

Robert M. Goldstein

Published by Rivendell Publishing Northwest
Seattle, Washington

Rivendell Publishing Northwest, Seattle, Washington

Copyright © 2010 by Robert M. Goldstein

Published in the United States of America by
Rivendell Publishing Northwest, Seattle, Washington.

This book is a work of nonfiction.

Printed in the United States of America

Library of Congress Catalog Number 2009906998

Book and cover design by Liz Kingslien

Photos property of Robert M. Goldstein

First Edition, Third Printing

Publisher's Cataloging-in-Publication
   Goldstein, Robert M., 1955-
      Riding with reindeer : a bicycle odyssey through Finland, Lapland,
   and Arctic Norway / Robert M. Goldstein.
         p. cm.
      Includes bibliographical references.
      ISBN 978-0-9763288-1-0

   1. Goldstein, Robert M., 1955- Travel – Finland. 2. Goldstein, Robert
   M., 1955- Travel – Lapland. 3. Goldstein, Robert M., 1955- Travel –
   Norway. 4. Bicycle touring – Finland. 5. Bicycle touring – Lapland.
   6. Bicycle touring – Norway. 7. Finland – Description and travel. 8.
   Lapland – Description and travel. 9. Norway – Description and travel.

   914.897/04/34—dc22   2009906998

Contents

Presage

(Kuhmo, Eastern Finland)

"You are riding a bicycle, yes? And camping?"

I nod.

"You didn't ask about wolves."

"Wolves?" Like Little Red Riding Hood, I had not considered wolves.

"The wolves are a bigger problem than bears," she says, a hint of alarm in her voice. "They have attacked farmers' dogs and killed them."

The lilt in her accent falls neatly on the word *killed*, adding an emphasis that, intended or not, gets my attention.

The ranger explains that a bicycle might trigger the chase instinct inherent in the wolf pack; I begin having visions of a Jack London-like end to my trip.

Dedication

To my mother and father, who bought me my first bike,
which started this whole damn business

Note to Readers

READERS WHO ARE FLUENT IN FINNISH AND ENGLISH may find some of the conventions used to describe streets and geographic features rather odd. In Finnish the suffix designating a street, lake, river, or other geographic feature is attached to the end of the name. For example, Ounasjoki translates into English as "Ounas River," and Tehtaankatu is "Tehtaan Street." In many cases in this book, the object is obvious so I left the Finnish name as is. However, in a few cases where the object is not clear, I attached the English suffix, which means that Ounasjoki River would be read as "Ounas River River" in Finnish. (My apologies to Finnish speakers, but you have to admit your language presents some challenges.) With respect to place names, I relied on the Finnish spelling as noted on maps and other geographic references and not on English transliterations. When these sources were not available, I used the transliteration that made the most sense. In most cases I have converted euros, kilometers, and meters into their American equivalents.

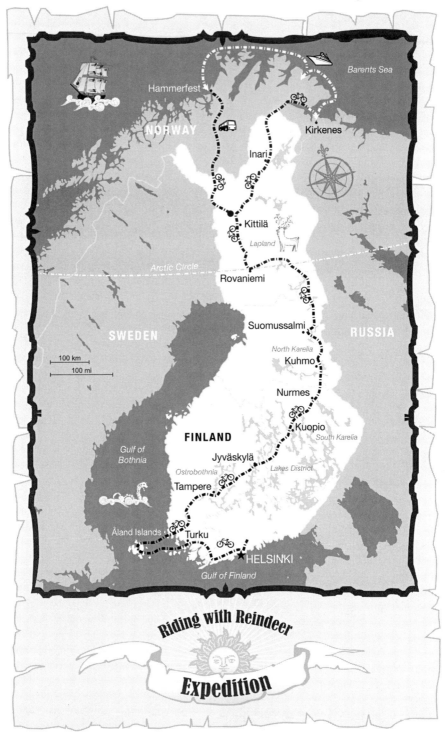

Preface

I LIKE BICYCLES. I like to ride bicycles. Sometimes, I like to ride bicycles great distances.

This passion began on my seventh birthday, when my parents bought me my first bike: a bright red J.C. Higgins one-speed. Multicolored tassels streamed from the ends of the handlebars. The machine's tremendous potential to propel me to faraway places soon became apparent—it was my means of exploration and escape, much as the horse was to early American explorers and pioneers. I ventured out on longer and longer forays into the unknown world, away from my little residential block of tract-home familiarity in Santa Clara, California. And as I grew older and bigger, a steady progression of bikes followed, each with more gears than the last.

The first expeditions I undertook as a preteenager were short reconnaissance missions. After I learned to read a map, my forays expanded—unbeknownst to my parents—in a 10-mile radius west to the Santa Cruz foothills, north to the Stanford University campus, and south to downtown San Jose.

When I was seventeen, I hatched a plan with my cousin Alan to ride during our summer vacation across the United States, a trip that would magically mix our shared passion for bikes and baseball. Our circuitous route would wind through almost every city in the northern United States that harbored a major league baseball team. We envisioned our final day as a triumphant ticker-tape ride down Madison Avenue in New York City, culminating with our arrival at Yankee Stadium, where we would throw out the first pitch.

Since neither of us had ridden our ten-speeds more than 30 miles in a day, much less fully loaded, we concluded that a shakedown voyage was in order. So in the spring of 1973, we rode our fully packed bikes out of my parents' driveway and headed north to Point Reyes National Park, our first planned overnight stop 75 miles away. I'll never forget wobbling down the driveway with our laden panniers hanging from rear racks, sleeping bags fastened on top. The bike felt as if a drunken fat man were sitting on the rear rack, shifting his weight at the smallest bump. I immediately thought: *What had I gotten myself into?*

We had started our trip with much aplomb, our parents and sisters waving good-bye from the driveway on a bright sunny morning. Neither of us would admit—at least not until many years afterward when the trip had become a legend—to feeling horrified and uncertain as we pedaled our ungainly machines out of sight. But we weren't about to turn back.

We wound down the traffic-choked hills of San Francisco, lunched with the hippies in Haight-Ashbury, crossed the Golden Gate Bridge, then serpentined up narrow Highway 1 to the crest of Mount Tamalpais before plunging down to the coast. This insane route planning was due to our naiveté and inexperience. Highway 1 at that time was (and probably still is) a busy two-lane road without shoulders. On narrow stretches on Mount Tamalpais we had to dismount and flatten ourselves against the roadside embankment to allow buses to pass. In spite of its dangers, the route was the only practical one to the coast. We lived that inaugural day of our first trip to the fullest, experiencing enough drama, uncertainty, disappointment, exhilaration, exhaustion, and pathos to fill a lifetime. Thirty-five years later, I still remember it vividly.

That was the first leg of a five-day sojourn that had the Russian River as its northernmost destination. On our return, we curled through the Napa Valley, then along the East Bay back to Santa Clara. Our adventures and misadventures were too numerous to chronicle here. Suffice to say, we encountered an assortment of characters, dealt with mishaps, and learned that the kindness of strangers was more than a cliché. Beginning a habit I would continue for life, I kept a meticulous journal. At the end of this record, I noted that the Russian River Expedition had spent a total of $5.41 on food and accommodations.

Alan and I never carried out our cross-country trip, which was probably a good thing since the tattered notes from our planning sessions showed an exceedingly ambitious schedule, with multiple hundred-mile days across some of the meanest land the American West had to offer.

In the intervening years I became an adult, with a job and responsibilities, though I did not follow the typical path of my peers and lock away my bike in a dark corner of the garage, a victim of the nine-to-five routine. I kept riding regularly, for pleasure and for basic transportation. By the time I reached middle age, I was among a handful of hardy souls who commuted to work by bicycle—winter, spring, summer, and fall. Perhaps in homage to that long-ago-planned journey with my cousin, I even ventured out on my bike for vacations: I bike toured in China in 1982 (dubbed the Sino-Seattle Bicycle Expedition), when the streets of Beijing and Shanghai were still choked with workers in Mao suits pedaling Flying Pigeons, the one-speed black bike that seemingly everyone owned. Nineteen years later, I rode a bike from Nanning, China, over the hills of North Vietnam to Hanoi, the final destination of the Sino-Vietnam Expedition.

The bicycle, as I learned by personal experience, is the perfect way to explore a country. You see the land, feel its undulations, and experience the region's weather. You are out there with the people and critters, not enclosed in composite plastic and glass, shooting through the countryside at blur speed. Bicycle journeys are not always pleasant, but they are always an experience—and to me, "experience" means being alive, feeling both the wind in your face and the pain in your butt.

But times had changed since my first transoceanic forays, when airlines did not charge $100 or more to ship a bike. It became clear that this next trip would require a special bike—one that I could literally pack into a standard-sized suitcase, check as baggage, and build when I got to my destination. Enter the folding bike: in my opinion the greatest innovation for bicycles since inflatable tires. Since my earlier trips, the folding bicycle had improved to the point where such a vehicle was now a realistic alternative to the hassle of shipping a full-sized touring bike.

My bike of choice was the New World Tourist (NWT), a sturdy 27-speed manufactured by the Green Gear Cycle, Inc. of Eugene, Oregon. The NWT is part of a line of folding bikes known as Bike Fridays, and is specifically designed for the type of long arduous journey I was planning. The bike has 20-inch wheels (circumference) as opposed to the standard 27 inches on road bikes. The small wheels and innovative design allow the Bike Friday to fold neatly into a special suitcase that is accepted by the airlines as checked baggage. The case is converted into a wagon by attaching a collapsible axle and small lawnmower-sized inflatable tires. This setup would allow me to be completely self-sufficient. I could stuff my gear in the wagon—the ultimate in sustainable, self-propelled travel.

In 2007, I was ready for a new adventure, new experiences, and perhaps my last shot at an epic journey. The fates had dished up Finland of all places as my destination, and my goal was to bike from Helsinki to the Barents Sea, a self-supported trip of roughly 2,000 miles, depending on the route. The distance far surpassed the mileage of my other trips. Why I chose Finland, or rather why Finland chose me, is the subject of the following chapters. Thus began the Riding with Reindeer Expedition.

Why Finland?

TUCKED AWAY ON THE EASTERN EDGE OF SCANDINAVIA, Finland is the proverbial "wallflower country"—overshadowed by the deep fjords and soaring mountains of Norway, the legendary blondes of Sweden, the volcanoes of Iceland, and the pastries of Denmark. Among her Nordic sisters, Finland is like the smart, introspective girl: cute in a non-flashy way yet tinged with an aura of mystery, perhaps a bit rustic, waiting awkwardly in her sensible shoes for someone to ask her to dance.

Almost no one knows who this shy girl is, particularly Americans. She has no well-known landmarks, boasts no wonders of the world, and she is flat. Finland's primary geographic feature is her 188,000 lakes—and thus there are also a lot of fish and fishermen. The remnants of ancient civilizations are not found in her bounteous forests; nor did the Romans stray this far. She gratefully missed the action during the Dark and Middle Ages, and got only a touch of the Renaissance. The country's one city of renown, Helsinki, sits on the same latitude as southern Alaska—a geographical location that rules it out as a surfing and beach holiday destination.

I am almost certain that Finland has never been mentioned within the following context: "Martha and I are heading to Hawaii next week for our vacation." You can substitute Paris, the Grand Canyon, or Manhattan for Hawaii without diminishing the impact of the statement; the vacationers are going somewhere to relax or have fun. Plop in Finland and you shock your listener to attention.

"You are going *where?*" was the common refrain I got when I told friends where I was headed.

There has to be a good reason to ride a bicycle through Finland: either you really enjoy bicycle riding through forests or you have to be slightly insane—both arguably true in my case.

Finland staked out a niche in my subconscious early in life. I don't remember specifically when the conversation occurred, perhaps in grade school as I was beginning to become aware of the larger world around me. One evening at dinner my father observed that Finland was the only country that had repaid its World War II debt to the United States, unlike the Soviet Union.* Why I would remember this tidbit of conversation and not thousands of others that transpired around our dinner table is a mystery left to those who study the human mind. This singular declaration produced in my head an image of a country of hard-working, honest, debt-paying citizens—an oasis of integrity among a fraternity of nations that sloughed off their financial responsibilities. The impression lay tucked away in some unused portion of my developing brain for many years, awaiting the chance for recall when it might be useful.

At about the same time, my parents gave me an album and a bag of postage stamps from around the world. If they had hoped this would kindle an interest in world geography, they were not disappointed. I soon knew the name of every British and French colony, their capitals, and locations, as well as the names and fates of extinct sovereign regions (Newfoundland and British Columbia once issued their own postage stamps) and territories (the Kingdom of Hawaii). Since countries inscribed stamps in their own language and script, I received tiny linguistic lessons ranging from Cyrillic to Japanese. One day I found a stamp from *Suomi. Where was Suomi?* I wondered. Suomi stamps were rather unassuming, with early issues featuring a stylized lion—which seemed to place Suomi somewhere in Africa. *Somalia, perhaps?*

---

* My father was correct that Finland did repay its war debt, but he was confused about which war they'd been incurred. Loans were made to European allies during and in the aftermath of World War 1. The loans were renegotiated in 1922 by the World War Foreign Debt Commission. Finland was the only country out of fifteen to repay its loans in full. After World War II, the Finns paid war reparations to the Soviet Union ahead of schedule.

Suomi is what the Finns call their country in Finnish, a seemingly incomprehensible language with mysterious Siberian origins. The literal meaning of *Suomi* is "end of the land"—quite fitting, as I would later discover. Suomi stamps were modest and didn't call attention to themselves, unlike those issued by her neighbor, the Soviet Union, whose flashy and numerous issues served as convenient propaganda tools. Finland's stamps appeared to be designed for the mundane purpose of paying for the delivery of mail. Whoever was in charge of the Suomi postal system seemed down-to-earth and, above all, sensible.

Finland did not enter my world again until 1987, when I was thirty-two and undertook a dubious solo trip across the Soviet Union aboard the Trans-Siberian Express. The trip was a disaster from the start. Prying a visa and train tickets from the Soviet bureaucracy was maddening. My flustered travel agent in Seattle put me in touch with a Helsinki travel expert, telling me that if anyone could finagle a visa and tickets away from the Soviets it was the Finns; they knew how to do such things. Twenty-four hours after my dossier was turned over to her, Hanna in Helsinki called my London bed-and-breakfast and told me not to worry; everything was in order. My visa and tickets arrived by express mail a day before my scheduled departure for Moscow.

The trip ended up being a fiasco anyway, thanks to my own ineptness and a series of misfortunes that probably could never be replicated. It did not help that my train tickets were issued in Helsinki. The Soviet authorities who were to meet me in Novosibirsk and Irkutsk thought I was Finnish, which is ridiculous because I look as Finnish as Pancho Villa. But that didn't matter. My minders greeted me at my train stations as "the gentleman from Finland" and peppered me with questions about the weather in Helsinki and reindeer husbandry. In Novosibirsk, a Soviet woman befriended me and helped get me on the right train.

"They expected someone from Finland," she told me, sternly.

"I don't look like a Finn," I replied.

"I know, but they don't know that. Your train vouchers were issued in Finland."

"But any idiot can see that I am not Finnish," I said. "Look at me."

I puffed up my five-foot, seven-inch frame and turned my head to give her a profile of my dark complexion, inherited from my Oaxacan maternal grandfather.

"Don't try to be rational," she snapped. "You are in the Soviet Union. Your vouchers were issued in Finland. Therefore you are a Finn."

From that moment I became an accidental Finn, unbeknownst to the government of Finland.

The trip uncovered one more crucial link to Finland. I learned afterwards from my Aunt Frances and Uncle Bernie that a long-lost great-grandmother of mine was actually from Helsinki. She had left there for the Russian Empire's Jewish Pale of Settlement in search of a husband, probably in the latter part of the nineteenth century when Finland was still part of the empire. So, as luck would have it, I really *was* the gentleman from Finland.

In 2005, I published *The Gentleman from Finland—Adventures on the Trans-Siberian Express,* which retells the story of my misadventures on that journey. During a promotional tour, I encountered some true Finns who had settled in the U.S., blending in seamlessly with their flawless English and WASPish appearance. As I signed her book, one of these Suomi expatriates told me she was disappointed the book was not really about Finland.

"No one ever writes travel books about Finland," she said sadly. Without thinking, I quipped that my next book was going to be on Finland, though this was the first time it had seriously occurred to me.

So Finland, long dormant in my mind, was rapidly making its way to the top of my consciousness as a travel destination. But I needed one more push. That came soon enough, and it had nothing to do with Finland.

I was fifty-one years old by the time *The Gentleman from Finland* hit the bookstores, and was in my sixth year as chief financial officer of the Seattle Public Library. At the beginning of my tenure, the library had embarked on a massive building project—at the time, it was the largest publically financed library construction program in the United States.

Then the recession that hit the country after the September 11th terrorist attacks resulted in years of budget cutbacks, layoffs, and service reductions that added untold stress to my job. By 2005, these events had worn me out. Friends told me I looked exhausted and haggard. My hair turned gray. I was irritable. From my eleventh-floor office in downtown Seattle, I would look out the window and think of myself as a prisoner: my nerves frayed and my emotions dulled by the monotonous routine of my job, with its endless nonsensical meetings.

I wanted to live life fully again, and I wanted to do so while I was still reasonably young. If it meant forfeiting the high salary of a stable government job, so be it. The trade-off seemed like a no-brainer: be free or work a few more years at a job I had come to hate. If I continued on the latter track, I believed I would likely soon drop dead.

So I concocted an escape plan. I had always wanted to go on a grand expedition. (Remember those cross-country plans I had as a seventeen-year-old?) I assumed that the market for fifty-one-year-old former CFOs as expedition members was rather slim. Who would take me? Besides, I wasn't interested in freezing to death on Mount Everest. Why not go to Finland, the place that kept popping up on my radar? I began seriously mulling it over. I could form my own expedition, organized around *my* abilities and tolerance for risk and anxiety. Who says an expedition has to involve climbing impossibly tall mountains or visiting a penguin rookery in the middle of the Antarctic winter? An expedition, in my mind, is a voyage of discovery—undertaking the unknown. For the housebound, a trip to the store is an expedition. Finland certainly seemed unknown; for me, terra incognita.

Truth be told, Finland became less of a terra incognita as I prepared for the trip. I learned that Finland had risen from the devastation of World War II, when most of its cities had been bombed and thousands of civilians were homeless, to become, by many international standards, one of the world's most well-off countries in terms of the health, education, and general welfare of its citizens. It accomplished this while being regularly ranked one of the least-corrupt countries in the world.[1]

Not only did this confirm my childhood notion that Finland was chock full of honest people, but this ranking made Finland a nirvana for someone who spent the better part of his career working in local and state government. The Finns actually respected their government and its officials.

I was sold. I bought a used NWT folding bicycle for $800 and planned my ride from Helsinki to the Barents Sea, through Lapland and Arctic Norway. It was a long way, 2,000 miles, through forests and desolate moors populated mainly by reindeer. The trip would take me far beyond the Arctic Circle and into the Sami-speaking[2] regions of Lapland. This would certainly satisfy my vision of a personal epic adventure.

I would take my time, absorb all that Finland had to offer, and learn about its history, culture, and people. I would zigzag my way along an improbable, illogical course—propelled by my own power, hauling my own stuff, and without touching an automobile or burning a single gallon of gas.

And that is how the Riding with Reindeer Expedition came to be. In the summer of 2007, I asked Finland to be my date for the summer dance. It turns out I have a weakness for that kind of girl, especially if she is wearing sensible shoes.

Helsinki

"WHERE IS EVERYONE?" I ask my airport shuttle driver.

I am forming my first impression of Helsinki as we head down nearly empty streets lined with stately neoclassical buildings. The only sounds are the cawing of gulls and clickity-clack of the green and gold trams trundling down the middle of wide boulevards. Breaking through the morning fog, the sun shines brightly on grassy parks, blossoming gardens, and the white tower of Helsinki's stadium, built for the 1952 Summer Olympics and a symbol of Finland's emergence from the dark days of World War II.

"Everyone has left for the summer holiday," explains the driver. "The entire city empties. Everyone goes to their summer cabins by the coast or by a lake."

Of course—it's July 1. The unofficial start of the summer holiday season, when most Finns take advantage of the generous four to six weeks of annual vacation that is their birthright. I wonder who's left behind to run the country, drive the trams, or check me into the hostel where I will spend the next five nights.

"Today is my last day," continues the driver to me, his only passenger. "Tomorrow I'm going fishing."

When I mention I'm from Seattle, he says, "That Bill Gates is some guy." Yes, I reply, but eager to show I've done my homework, I mention Linus Torvalds, the brilliant young Finn who invented the rival Linux computer operating system. The driver is unimpressed with his countryman. "But he gave it away for free," he scoffs.[3] My second impression of

Helsinki is that it is a bicycle rider's paradise, at least compared to cities in the United States.

Shortly after the shuttle van scooped me up at the airport and merged onto a freeway, I noticed the slender, paved cycling paths on their own dedicated rights of way paralleling the main road. Once among the curving hodgepodge of the city's streets, the paths continue as separate rights of way or join the street and are marked with green paint. I did not know it at the time, but I was only glimpsing a sliver of the more than 685 miles of bicycle paths that crisscross the city. The bike is clearly king in Helsinki. With great satisfaction, I realized that I had come to the right place to start my long ride to the Barents Sea.

Stowed in the back of the van is a black Samsonite suitcase carrying the pieces of my 27-speed folding bike. Next to the suitcase is a large, green duffel with all my other gear, including the parts that convert the suitcase into a wagon.

When the shuttle stops at the Hostel Academica, the driver wishes me well on my journey. "You know it is a very long way to Lapland," he says. I shrug. What can I say? I know Lapland is a long way. But from the mouth of a native Finn, it seems even longer.

Helsinki is not cheap. A stay in a conventional hotel, along with meals, can easily cost $300 a day. The unsponsored *Riding with Reindeer Expedition* does not have that kind of money. The Expedition's bare-bones budget of $70 per day must last two months. Thus, the hostel is the utmost luxury it can afford. While it is possible that someone else has already pedaled a folding bike self-supported from Helsinki via the Åland Islands to the Barents Sea, I suspect that it is highly unlikely anyone pulled off this feat on such a paltry allowance. The free fall of the greenback against the euro—Finland is a member of the European Union—adds to the austerity, diminishing the Expedition's purchasing power daily. Did I mention that this trip has *many* challenges?

So in keeping with the budget, I am taking advantage of the conversion of university dormitories to hotel rooms during the summer vacation. The Hostel Academica on Hietaniemenkatu, which normally houses students attending the Helsinki College of Economics, meets my standards for cheapness and location. This is my only reserved accommodation. After Helsinki I will need to hunt for lodging on the go. My gear includes a tent, stove, and sleeping bag. I expect to camp a lot.

New arrivals from around the world crowd around the reception desk. The line overflows into the lobby. In front of me, a Russian film crew, their equipment spread over the floor, is trying to check in or out; I can't tell which, and neither can the reception clerk. A gaggle of girls who are liberally tattooed and dressed in black leather stands behind the Russians. Their belts, which appear to be slotted with bullets, hang loosely around their thin waists. They tote motorcycle helmets adorned with skulls and crossbones. To my right is a woman, I think, who sports a shockingly pink ridge of hair on an otherwise shaved skull. The style reminds me of a stegosaurus. Another woman dressed in black leather with metal spikes protruding from the shoulders of her jacket queues up behind me. I give her a wide berth. Injury by impalement would be an unfortunate setback this early in the Expedition. A babble of Russian, Finnish, German, and English fills the room.

As a middle-aged American male who possesses neither pirate garb nor a dinosaur-style hairdo, I feel distinctly out of place. *Should I have checked into a hotel more consistent with my age and hairstyle?* I worry. *Damn my measly budget!* But I quickly vanquish these disruptive thoughts. *Get used to it,* I tell myself. *This is how epics start.* Encounters with strange characters in a foreign place are standard epic stuff.

I reach the front of the line only to be told that my room is not ready, so I roll my encased bike and lug the duffel with the rest of my gear into an adjacent area that is a combination kitchen, library, and television room. I join two petite Japanese girls who appear as dazed by the diverse jumble of humanity in the lobby as I am. In the kitchen, a young man carefully wedges a frozen pizza into a microwave. The inside of the oven is splattered with red, the remains of a previous user's sloppy cooking.

The room is ready as promised at two o'clock, but alas, the elevator is out of order. So I lug my gear up two flights of stairs, through two heavy steel doors with locks that look like they belong in a medium-security prison, and down a corridor to my room. This display of security is puzzling, given Finland's remarkably low crime rate.

I lean into the heavy metal door of my room, but instead of a cell-like space I am pleasantly surprised to see a large chamber. Sun streaks in from big windows. A narrow bed is tucked against the wall. There is a kitchen with a range, sink, and large refrigerator. A door leads to a bathroom with a shower and towel-heating racks. I congratulate myself, thinking, *Not bad for $51. If I am reincarnated, I want to come back as a Finnish college student.* I roll the suitcase into a corner and declare that the Riding with Reindeer Expedition has officially landed. Then I plop onto the bed for a nap.

◊◊◊   ◊◊◊   ◊◊◊

I cannot sleep. Outside my window, workers hammer on rebar protruding from the supporting columns of an addition to the College of Economics. It's Sunday afternoon, but apparently these construction workers will take summer vacation in the winter. My plan had been to rest, vanquish the jet lag, and explore tomorrow. But why wait?

An hour later after assembling my bike, I walk past a fresh cadre of leather-clad, dinosaur-haired people milling around reception. They take no notice of the guy rolling his little bike down the hallway into the street.

I have no idea where to go. I just want to christen the trip and feel what it is like to ride in Finland. I push open the door, walk the bike down the street, and cross the tram tracks. I hop on the seat and pedal along the red-green paved lane bordering Mechelininkatu.*

At first, cycling in Finland feels no different than it does in my hometown of Seattle. The asphalt looks the same, as do the cars, though the Finnish signs with their long strings of seemingly random letters will take some getting used to. But there are some not-so-obvious differences. I feel a little like I have been transported to a parallel universe, but a

---

* Per my earlier "Note to Readers," *katu* means "street" in Finnish.

friendly one—not the science fiction movie kind where the family strolling with a baby carriage suddenly transforms into flesh-eating zombies. Everything here is the same. Yet everything is somehow different.

I ride a few blocks, skirting the city cemetery, and merge with locals, many of whom are riding one-speed Helkamas, a sturdy bike built for city errands and armed with a chain guard, heavy-duty fenders, and a wand-like device with a reflector that juts out at a right angle from the rear carrier. I pedal on, stopping at a munchkin-sized traffic light for bicycles, then cross under a turnpike and into an industrial area.

After traveling for nearly twenty-four hours, I expected to be exhausted. But I have energy. The discombobulating effect of journeying halfway around the world is offset by the simple pleasure of riding a bike and feeling the city unfold at a leisurely pace. I have transformed from spectator to participant.

I have a map, but stopping to read it is too much of a hassle, which leads me to wonder what really did happen to me on the flight over. *Was I sprinkled with magic dust?* I am someone who always likes to know what's going to happen. *No map? What's gotten into me?* I cycle on, carefree. The bicycle paths unfold like a magic carpet before me in the bright afternoon sun—which will circumnavigate most of the horizon before reluctantly sinking sometime after midnight. Dealing with nearly twenty hours of daylight will be interesting, I realize.

I wend past sidewalk cafés, ice cream stands, and sandy beaches where pale Finns baste after suffering through the long dark winter. *How lost can I possibly get?*

I curve through a shipping terminal dotted with restaurants and sleek new waterfront hotels. The path wedges between warehouses and empties onto a beautiful beach filled with frolicking children. Sailboats fleck the bay, and stout little ferries prepare to carry folks to the islands visible from shore. I drift along a tree-lined promenade, passing a marina and more open-air cafés. The city is like a gigantic waterfront park, a place for an endless idyll, a nap, or a good read on one of the park benches positioned every twenty feet or so.

As I ride, soaking in this unfolding pleasantness, I face a plethora of choices about where to turn. Routes zip off at all angles. Signs pointing to mysterious neighborhoods await exploration for another day.

A cyclist heads to Helsinki's outdoor market.

I stick by the bay and round a point that seems to set me on a course for the city center. I pass a massive ocean liner of the Silja Line. It is preparing to cross the Gulf of Finland for the two-hour trip to Tallinn, the capital of Estonia. Further on is the Kauppatori, the city's fish market. After that I arrive at an open-air market with stalls selling fresh fruit, vegetables, pastries, and souvenirs. Across the cobblestone street at the end of a long line of stately neoclassical buildings is the Presidential Palace. Presiding over the city center's eastern flank is the brick-red Uspenski Cathedral, its gold onion domes shimmering, a reminder of Finland's time as part of the Russian Empire.

I follow a canal under the shadow of the cathedral and find myself at another bay with shipyards and a power-generating plant in the distance. I curl back into the city center, toward the railroad station whose entrance is guarded by two giant, stone god-like figures holding globes, then past a teeming commercial district and promenade. I find more evidence of the bicycle's supremacy as I pick my way around bike stands clustered with hundreds of parked bikes. Where there are no empty slots, bikes that could not find a spot are cabled to handrails, trees—anything that is stationary. Finding a place to park might be a challenge, I realize.

After gliding past the offices of Finland's largest newspaper, the *Helsingin Sanomat* (Sanomat means newspaper in Finnish), I stop next to a gleaming white modern building, its end designed so that it juts into the plaza like the prow of a ship. This is the Kiasma Museum of Contemporary Art. Its sleek design and blindingly white facade loudly proclaim that Finland has arrived in the modern world.

Presiding over the plaza in front of the Kiasma is a statue of a distinguished-looking man from the bygone era of gallant cavalry charges. High atop the marble pedestal, he sits ramrod straight on his horse, saber at his side, gazing down the street that bears his name. I back away to get a better look, dodging picture-snapping tourists and young skateboarders, who rocket irreverently by on the red paving stones.

This is Carl Gustaf Emil Mannerheim, who, perhaps more than any other Finn, was responsible for saving the country from the clutches of the Bolsheviks in 1918 during Finland's civil war, and from annihilation by the invading Russians in the Winter War of 1939–40. If there had been no Mannerheim, it is likely there would have been no Kiasma, nor any of the other evidence of prosperity that just passed before my eyes. Finland would have been just another Baltic country only now rebuilding its economy after the long suffocation of Soviet dominance.

If I wanted to know more about Finland, its tumultuous past, the brutal war that ravaged the now quiet forests of Karelia (eastern Finland)[4] and bogs of Lapland, I would need to learn more about this man and his time.

Statue of Carl Gustaf Mannerheim at the Kiasma Museum of Contemporary Art

The Marshal of Finland

ON A CRISP MORNING A FEW DAYS AFTER MY ARRIVAL I retrace my inaugural route that bordered the Gulf of Finland. I turn into a tree-shaded lane within Kaivo Park, then grind up a hill into a leafy conclave of mansions and sprawling compounds with country flags indicating various embassies and consulates. When I reach Kalliolinnantie, I scan the addresses for Number 14.

I have come here to learn more about the man on the cavalry horse. Number 14 was his home. It is now a museum, Finland's equivalent of Mount Vernon. I expect to easily spot it amid tour buses and curious pedestrians.

I pedal to the end of Kalliolinnantie. Seeing nothing that would designate the landmark, I turn around and slowly retrace my path, peering intently at house numbers while glancing at a brochure showing the house. *Shouldn't there be a large sign?* Finally, by process of elimination, I turn into a driveway that leads me to a modest two-story white villa with a red-tiled roof. The only vehicle present is a red Vespa parked near the front door. There are no guards. *There is more security when I visit my parents at their gated community in California,* I think. I hoist my bike onto the stone front porch, lean it against the house's outer wall, apply the chain lock, and walk into the home of Carl Gustaf Emil Mannerheim, the father of modern Finland.

My initial encounter with Mannerheim is fitting because his path to becoming a Finnish national military hero was as circuitous as my planned trip through his country. Born on June 4, 1867, into an aristocratic family with deep roots in Russian and Swedish society, Mannerheim's pedigree provided few hints of what was to come. His great-grandfather, a count, was a renowned collector of beetles, and also president of the Viipuri Court of Appeals. His father, Robert, a playwright, would have been wise to continue in entomology. To generate more income, he turned to business. His subsequent bankruptcy due to ineptness may have convinced young Gustaf that a military career was the path for him. His father fled to Paris. His mother died soon after, and the family descended into poverty.

After being expelled from Finnish cadet school for an unexcused absence, Mannerheim's only remaining option for a military career was to leave Finland—then a grand duchy of the Russian Empire—and join the Russian army. The strategy worked. He shed his youthful belligerence and rose through the ranks to become a Chevalier, a personal guard to Maria Feodorovna,[5] Empress Consort of Russia, and mother of the country's last czar, Nicholas II. In 1892, Mannerheim married Anastasia Arapov, a relative of the great Russian writer, Alexander Pushkin. The arranged marriage, while it lasted, produced two daughters. A son died at birth. The couple separated after seven years and was divorced in 1919.

While Mannerheim's marriage floundered, his military career flourished. He was one of the empire's few bright spots during the otherwise disastrous war with Japan in 1904–05. Afterwards, he undertook a two-year scientific expedition through Central Asia, Tibet, and China. During World War I, he distinguished himself as a field commander holding together the wavering Russian fronts in Poland and Transylvania.

By the end of 1917, Mannerheim was fifty years old and had already served thirty years in the Russian army. He wanted to retire and return to Finland, but when he arrived in Helsinki on a wet miserable December day, Mannerheim found his homeland gripped in the same revolutionary fervor that had toppled the czar. The Finns, long restless under Russian rule, clamored for independence. Two weeks after Mannerheim got home, the Finns got their wish. The new Bolshevik leader, Vladimir Lenin, granted Finland its freedom. Lenin, who was preoccupied with consolidating Bolshevik rule in Russia, believed that it was only a matter of time before Finland's burgeoning communist movement would overthrow the new republican government and create a sister socialist state.

Finland plunged into a bloody civil war. Communist forces, with the aid of Russian troops still stationed in the country, occupied Tampere and other industrial cities in central Finland, then captured Helsinki in January of 1918. Desperate to find a commander with battle experience to lead their rapidly disintegrating forces, the fledging government summoned Mannerheim to Vaasa, the temporary capital on Finland's west coast. Mannerheim quickly transformed the ragtag force into a formidable army, which recaptured central and northern Finland, then swept the Bolsheviks from Helsinki and Karelia. By May 1918 the war was over. After a failed attempt to become Finland's first president, Mannerheim temporarily retreated from political and military life to work for various humanitarian causes.

During this period, Mannerheim lived in a variety of rented quarters, a vagabond-like existence that Finland's business leaders thought unseemly for the country's greatest military hero. In the early 1920s, the Finnish candy king, Karl Fazer, persuaded Mannerheim to take the villa he owned at Number 14. It was love at first sight, and in 1924, Mannerheim moved into his new abode.

With culinary habits and etiquette shaped by the royal Russian court, Mannerheim's dinner parties at Number 14 became legendary. The house's expansive dining room hosted a who's who of Finnish and foreign political and business dignitaries, with Mannerheim himself fussing over the guest lists and menu.

By the late 1930s, Finland's fledging republic had stabilized, but its existence, along with those of other new democracies in the Baltic region, was becoming more precarious as Adolph Hilter's Germany grew more powerful. Finland also faced the threat of a vengeful Soviet Union, still smarting over the failure of Finland to transform into a communist state. The Finns desperately wanted to stay out of a war that seemed inevitable, but the diplomatic balancing act between Germany and the Soviet Union was becoming almost impossible to manage.

Soviet strongman Joseph Stalin insisted that Finland exchange a large part of Karelia, the Hanko Peninsula, and islands in the Gulf of Finland for trackless wilderness in northwest Russia. Stalin wanted the additional territory to act as a buffer around Leningrad (now St. Petersburg), which at that time was only 20 miles from the Finnish border. It wasn't the Finns he feared, but the Germans, should they invade Finland.

Initial negotiations were cordial, but the Finns' stubborn refusal to acquiesce tested Stalin's patience. By the fall of 1939, Stalin and his foreign minister, Vyacheslav Molotov, had had enough of the pesky Finns. If they wouldn't trade their territory, he would seize it by force.[6] Stalin's advisors estimated that the 600,000 troops, 3,000 tanks, and 1,200 planes mobilized along the Finnish border could crush the little country in ten days—two weeks tops.

In the Karelian Isthmus, the critical area near Leningrad, 20,000 Finns hunkered down in a jumble of concrete bunkers and barriers that would soon be known as the Mannerheim Line. In North Karelia, Soviet troops, their columns massed along the few forest roads that led into Finland, faced a handful of border guards and civil defense companies, who drilled with wooden guns because real ones were in short supply. Altogether, Finland, with a pre-World War II population of three million, could only muster 180,000 troops, no tanks, a few aging antitank guns, and 41 operational planes. It seemed like no contest.

But the Russians had miscalculated.

Long before the Russians had assembled their troops, Mannerheim had received the title of Field Marshal of Finland and was named head of the National Defense Council. Continually frustrated with skimpy military budgets and what he perceived as the government's failure to fully recognize the growing military threat posed by the Soviet Union, Mannerheim had repeatedly threatened to resign and retire permanently from military life. But as the autumn of 1939 dragged on, and with Russian troops massed on the border, Mannerheim rescinded the last in a series of resignation letters and took command of the Finnish army. He did so reluctantly, noting in a letter to his daughter Sophie that he "had not wanted to undertake the responsibility of commander in chief, as my age and my health entitled me, but I had to yield to appeals from the President of the Republic and the government, and now for the fourth time I am at war." He was seventy-two.

On November 30, 1939, the Soviet army attacked. Helsinki was bombed. Russian tanks, trucks, and foot soldiers crowded onto the few roads leading into Finland, providing an easy target for Finnish defenders hidden in the forests. Finnish soldiers snuck up to the ponderous Soviet tanks, pried off the treads with crowbars, then tossed gasoline-filled liquor bottles at them—a technique first used during the Spanish Civil War earlier that decade. The Finns christened the new weapon the "Molotov cocktail," a dubious honor for the Soviet foreign minister that would stick for all time. As more tanks rumbled across the frontier, the Finnish Liquor Board rushed 40,000 more empty liquor bottles to the front.

By mid-December, it was clear that the Russians would not waltz into Helsinki. Soviet armies stalled along the entire front. Continued frontal assaults along the Mannerheim Line were rebuffed by withering Finnish artillery and machine-gun fire. So disturbing were the relentless Russian attacks and subsequent slaughter that some Finnish machine-gunners begged to be reassigned. The Isthmus became a grisly killing field strewn with the frozen bodies of thousands of Russian dead amid the smoldering ruins of tanks and trucks.

By the end of December, the Winter War, as the conflict came to be called, was shaping up to be a massive embarrassment for the Soviet Union. Finland became the darling of the Western Allies—its tiny army holding off massive Soviet forces during the coldest winter in memory. The Allies, led by Great Britain and France, plotted ways to get reinforcements to Finland without nudging Nazi Germany into the war.

A stylized portrait of Mannerheim graced the cover of *Time* magazine in February 1940. The cover story gushed, "Foreigners in Helsinki, who doubted that the Finns could resist a determined drive to flank the Mannerheim Line, were amazed at the strength of the Finnish mobile defense."[7]

Despite the heroic stand, Mannerheim knew it was only a matter of time before the Soviets, with their almost unlimited manpower, would finally overwhelm the exhausted Finnish defenders. In February, the Russians finally broke through the remnants of the Mannerheim Line. The Finns fell back to secondary positions, hanging on for dear life as Mannerheim committed his last reserve troops to plug the holes.

On March 12, 1940, the Finns signed an armistice with the Soviet Union, which ceded most of Karelia, the Rybachi Peninsula—Finland's only access to the Barents Sea—and granted the Soviets a base on the Hanko Peninsula. It was a bitter pill for the Finns and Mannerheim to swallow. But it was the price of freedom. As he signed the agreement, Finnish President Kyösti Kallio quoted bitterly from the Old Testament: "may the hand wither that is forced to sign such a paper."[8] A few months later Kallio suffered a stroke, paralyzing that same hand and arm. He died soon thereafter, adding yet another war casualty to the 25,000 Finnish dead and 44,000 wounded—a staggering 40 percent of all men under arms when the war began.[9] Another 400,000 Finns fled their homes when Karelia was turned over to the Soviet Union.

The country's travails were hardly over. Fifteen months later Finland would find itself at war with Russia again. On June 22, 1941, Germany launched Operation Barbarossa, sending three million soldiers to attack the Soviet Union. Four days later, Mannerheim issued orders for the revamped and re-equipped Finnish army to attack the Russian lines to regain territory lost during the Winter War. Finland, the underdog hero of the Western Allies in 1939, now found itself in league with Nazi Germany.

From the beginning it was an uneasy association. The Finns made it clear they were not in a political alliance with Germany and that their only military goal was to reclaim territory lost during the Winter War.[10] The Finnish government refused to let Germany intervene in Finnish domestic affairs, thus protecting Finland's tiny Jewish population from Europe's Holocaust.[11] Mannerheim took this one step further, allowing Jews who served in the Finnish army, along with captured Russian-Jewish prisoners, to conduct religious services at the front under the noses of German liaison officers.

Unlike the Winter War, when the Finns were on the defensive, the outbreak of the Continuation War, as this new conflict was called, saw an explosive offensive that quickly overwhelmed Russian lines. By December of 1941, the Finns had retaken all of the Karelian Isthmus and were 20 miles from Leningrad. But the advance came at a price: another 25,000 Finns dead and 50,000 wounded.

When the German high command demanded that the Finns attack Leningrad from the north and east, while they attacked from the south, Mannerheim refused, replying that Finland had achieved its military goal. The Finns dug into defensive positions. Reserves were allowed to go home. Perhaps Mannerheim knew that the Russian Bear would reawaken with a vengeance; there was no need to provoke her further. Hitler, however, was furious with Mannerheim's refusal to press the attack.

In the spring of 1944, the Russian Bear awoke. The Soviet army, its lessons learned from the Winter War disaster, launched a ferocious attack across the Karelian Isthmus that threatened to overrun Finland. Finland wanted out of the war, but Stalin would not negotiate with the Finnish government in power.

Once again, Finland turned to the man who had saved them during the civil war. Tired and suffering from rheumatism, Mannerheim reluctantly agreed to add the job of president to his military duties, following the resignation of the incumbent, Risto Ryti. He quickly concluded an armistice with the Soviets, who demanded war reparations, most of Karelia, and the long-term lease of the Porkkala Peninsula for use as a military base.[12]

But the most difficult condition demanded by a vengeful Stalin was that Finland drive the German army out of Lapland. Mannerheim ordered his weary troops to attack the German Mountain Corps entrenched in Lapland. Thus began the country's third war in five years.

When it ended less than a year later, Finland was a land of internal refugees. Its economy was devastated, its cities in ruins. But unlike the once-free democracies of Eastern Europe and the Baltic states of Estonia, Latvia, and Lithuania—all of which had fallen under Soviet domination—Finland was still free.

The wars and their unrelenting stress had taken a huge toll on Mannerheim, who was by then seventy-eight. A photo of him during his presidency shows that his once robust body with its chiseled features had withered into a scarecrow frame with sunken cheeks and tired eyes. His health deteriorating, Mannerheim resigned as president in 1946.

He never returned to Number 14. Instead, he bought a house in Lohja, 20 miles west of Helsinki, where he intended to rest, write his memoirs, and reunite with old friends. The next year, following the advice of doctors, he moved to the Valmont Sanatorium in Montreux, Switzerland.

Mannerheim spent his final four years away from the country that claimed him as its greatest hero. He died at the age of eighty-two on January 28, 1951, in Switzerland. A few days later, Gustaf Mannerheim came home to Finland for the last time. A horse-drawn caisson bore his coffin along the streets of Helsinki. He was buried in the city cemetery on a small hillock surrounded by the graves of the thousands of soldiers who served under his command.

                              ᭡ᢩ   ᭡ᢩ   ᭡ᢩ

When I open the door and step inside the hallowed house, it's clear that I am the first visitor this morning. The receptionist in the front room fetches me an English-speaking docent after issuing me a pair of plastic booties, the type worn by medical staff in operating rooms. My guide, Peter, a tall, clean-shaven young man, dressed in a crisp blue suit leads me into the dining room where a full-bodied portrait of Mannerheim is propped on a chair. This is not the thin and tired post-war Mannerheim, but a robust aristocrat, smartly dressed in a waistcoat with a white vest accented by a sliver of gold sash. At six-feet, three-inches tall, Mannerheim, with a neatly trimmed mustache, stands at attention, his dark penetrating eyes staring ahead. He looks like Douglas Fairbanks Sr.

Peter explains that the furnishings are largely untouched from the day Mannerheim left in 1939 to take command of the Finnish army on the eve of the Winter War. We snake our way through the richly toned interior to the study.

"This was his favorite room," says Peter.

Paneled in dark wood, the walls are lined with tiers of bookshelves. The books are in an array of languages: English, German, Russian, Finnish, Swedish, and French, among others. Mannerheim spoke and read them all fluently. Ironically, it was Finnish that gave him the most trouble. But Peter sets me straight on rumors that Mannerheim, who grew up in the Swedish speaking part of Finland, could not speak his country's predominant language.[13]

"Not true," he says. "As a child, he learned to speak Finnish in school, but I am sure he had forgotten a lot after spending thirty years in Russia, before returning home. After all, no one speaks Finnish outside of Finland."

Two large tiger skins are splayed on the floor, heads tilted up, fangs bared. Mannerheim loved to hunt. These specimens were shot during a trip to Nepal in 1937. On another wall hang richly decorated thangkas, meticulously hand-painted cloth banners depicting Buddhist deities, collected by Mannerheim during his travels in Tibet. Before me is an exquisite captain's desk with inlaid wood of different hues. But it's a small oil painting tucked away in a dimly lit corner of the room that catches my attention. Amid a dark impressionistic forest are white, ghost-like figures on skis: soldiers.

"When do you think this was painted?" asks Peter, noticing my focus on the painting.

"It had to be after the Winter War," I reply.

"That's what everyone thinks. You might find this hard to believe, but this was painted by Akseli Gallen-Kallela in 1899.[14] He had this dream about soldiers dressed in white, skiing through the forest. You have to remember that in 1899 there were no ski soldiers, and no one had thought of using white camouflage to blend in with the snow. That would not happen until 1939, during the Winter War."

"You mean the dream was a premonition?" I ask.

"Maybe," says Peter. "Gallen-Kallela kept the painting for nineteen years. After the Civil War, he gave it to Mannerheim. But I agree with you. I think it was a premonition of what would happen forty years later."

We climb the stairs to the second-floor bedroom, which probably reveals more about Mannerheim than any other part of the house. Although a leading figure in Finnish social as well as civil society, not to mention dashing if not downright handsome, Mannerheim's private life following his divorce in 1919 remains largely a closed book. In his memoir, Mannerheim devotes only a single sentence to his married life. The décor of the bedroom suggests the habits of an ascetic with a penchant for communication. It holds a simple cot, where he slept to ease chronic rheumatism that first developed after his service in the Russo-Japanese War. Next to the cot, on a bed stand, is an intercom bell and a phone. Mannerheim slept only five to six hours a night. He was usually up at 7 a.m. and didn't retire until after midnight.

"What was he like?" I ask, as Peter sets up a projector to show me slides taken by Mannerheim during his 1906–1908 assignment to Central Asia.

"He was very kind to his soldiers in the field. But he was demanding and hard on the officers who reported directly to him. Some would describe him as difficult to deal with."

Initially Mannerheim was not keen on traipsing across Central Asia, a trip that he correctly guessed was no more than a spying mission. But the Russians persisted, framing the trip as a scientific and ethnological survey. He traveled with a Finnish passport, which made passage through territory controlled by China easier.

In the summer of 1906, he set out with a handful of Cossacks following the path of the Silk Road through Samarkand, Kashgar, Tibet, and finally into Beijing. Amongst his gear was a box camera. If Mannerheim had never made it as a political and military leader, he showed promise as a photographer. The photos—which range from the everyday life of Tibetan peasants, silk weavers at their looms, Chinese opera, old men, and nobles in all their finery to sweeping landscapes of the Tian Shan Mountains—are remarkable in their composition and clarity.

In the Mongolian city of Utaishan, Mannerheim met the thirteenth Dalai Llama, a meeting the Chinese were not keen on allowing, given the tension between China and Tibet, and Tibet's flirtation with Russia. Mannerheim wrote in his memoirs that his visit was monitored by a Chinese "pidgin English-speaking official … sent to the monastery to shadow me." When the visit concluded, Mannerheim demonstrated and presented the Dalai Llama with a Browning pistol. "I apologized for the humble gift, regretting that after such a long journey nothing more worthy of the recipient remained, but added that times were such that there were occasions when even a holy man might find a weapon more effective than a prayer wheel," recalled Mannerheim.

Mannerheim completed his monumental trip in 1908 in Japan. He recrossed Russia on the newly built Trans-Siberian railroad line, a trip I had taken in the opposite direction twenty years before this journey to Finland. I hoped his rail journey was more pleasant than mine.

Peter leaves me in the same small reception area I entered an hour ago, and I slip out the door into the dappled sunshine of the quiet leafy neighborhood.

As I close the door, I feel like I have been through a time warp: one of gourmet meals served to men in tailcoats and women in elegant gowns, a time of horrible wars with ghosts of white-cloaked ski soldiers gliding through the forest. I return to another world: one of quiet streets lined by stately buildings, of trams rattling down cobbled streets and pensioners walking their dogs in the park. I unlock my bike and coast down the hill, thinking that I will no doubt encounter the legacy of Mannerheim many times as I pedal through the country he saved.

Masha

THE PLEASANTLY SUNNY DAYS IN HELSINKI SLIP AWAY. After three days here, I have grown comfortable in my routine of cooking breakfast, then venturing onto the city's streets and shopping in the markets, where I puzzle out Finnish and Swedish food labels. The warm weather—the temperature ranges from the high seventies to low eighties—draws throngs of sunbathers to Hietaranta Beach. The sidewalk café on Aleksantennkatu and at Esplanad Park are packed by midafternoon. Helsinki seems like a giant summer holiday camp for city dwellers.

I want to plop myself down on the beach or in a café, but there is work to do. This is, after all, an epic—preparations must be made for the trials that surely loom ahead. There is precious little time for goofing off. Besides the tasks of learning some local history, collecting supplies, and preparing the bike and wagon, I am left with some unfinished business concerning my mysterious great-grandmother, who wandered these streets more than a hundred years ago.

I know little about Masha Raisal. She had lived in Helsinki and had moved to the Jewish Pale[15] in what is now modern-day Poland. There she met and married my great-grandfather, Abraham. They had five children, the second-youngest being my grandmother, Ethel. Somewhere between 1903 and 1905, traveling either alone or in pairs, the family emigrated to the United States. Family legend has it that Masha came last with Ethel, but they were turned away at Ellis Island in New York City because Ethel had an eye infection. Somehow, the two made it to Montreal, and then finally reunited with the rest of the family on New York's Lower East Side. Masha died a few years later.

Events of the twentieth century—the Great Depression, two World Wars, and the dissolution of my grandmother's part of the family—helped pulverize the shards of my family history. My father, along with his brother and sister, grew up in a Denver orphanage—the National Home for Jewish Children—and by the time I came along, there was little left to go on.

No one remembers where Masha was buried, let alone where she had spent her childhood. An uncle advised me that her purported last name, "Raisal," might be a middle name common among Yiddish speakers at that time.[16] One piece of physical evidence that confirms Masha's existence is a faded family photograph taken shortly after the family reunited in New York City. Masha sits next to Abraham, her hair in a bun. She wears a long flowing dress, neatly pleated in front. Unlike the distrustful melancholy evinced by my great-grandfather, she smiles wanly, perhaps relieved to have arrived on a friendly shore after the difficult voyage across the North Atlantic and subsequent deportation to Canada. At least we have that picture, but tracing Masha back to Finnish soil will be a challenge.

The Finns, mostly through the Lutheran Church, have maintained remarkable records for tracing family roots. A Seattle friend of Finnish ancestry told me that she could trace her lineage back to the Middle Ages. I am afraid that my task will be more difficult, if not impossible. For starters, Masha was Jewish, not Lutheran. The first Jews did not arrive until after Sweden ceded Finland to Russia in 1809 after the culmination of a bloody war. But unlike other Russian territories, Finland was allowed a good deal of autonomy within the empire, becoming a grand duchy with its own Diet, or legislative assembly. The first Jewish residents of Helsinki were retired soldiers who had fulfilled their thirty years of service in the Czarist army. They were allowed to settle anywhere in the empire, while their brethren were confined to the Jewish Pale in western Russia. Many chose Helsinki because it was relatively free of the virulent anti-Semitism in Russia. But like Jews elsewhere in the empire, the retired soldiers faced restrictions. A Czarist decree in 1869 allowed Jews to engage in only one business activity: the buying and selling of old clothes. They were barred from traveling or attending festivals. The children of Jewish families could only stay in Finland if they were not married.

The last restriction provides a clue as to why Masha left Finland for Russia. Assuming she was a young woman in her late teens or early twenties, she had no choice but to leave Finland or face spinsterhood. The trip would have occurred sometime in the 1880s. These are my only clues. It isn't much: a name that may not even be a full name, no address other than Helsinki, and the knowledge that I have descended from soldiers and secondhand clothes dealers.

∿∿ ∿∿ ∿∿

On the fourth morning after my arrival in Finland, I pedal to 26 Malinkatu, the address of Helsinki's hundred-year-old synagogue. Both the domed synagogue and a newer community center are tucked away in a gated compound. A kosher butcher shop is next door. I am met at the gate by a short, swarthy man with twinkling eyes and a neatly trimmed mustache. He wears a baseball cap. I initially mistake him for a caretaker, but no, this is Andre Zweig, Finland's one and only cantor and unofficial spokesman for Helsinki's Jewish community.

"You are going to ride to Lapland on that thing?" asks Andre, as I park my bike at a rack inside the compound. "Oy vey."

Stripped of its racks and shorn of its wagon, the bike, I admit, looks like something that belongs in a circus. I shrug and mumble something about the bike's sturdy design. Frankly, I am more worried about my body making it to Lapland than the bike. I explain the circumstances of my great-grandmother's sketchy existence in Helsinki.

"You don't know where she lived? Are there any relatives left here? Have you checked the Jewish cemetery for the same last name?" Andre asks.

Although I admit my genealogical search skills are minimal, I have checked all the names in the Jewish section of the city's Hietaniemi cemetery. Raisal was not among the names listed on the cemetery's Web site, an absence that seems to give greater credence to the theory that it was a middle name and not a surname. Andre takes me to the synagogue's archivist, but he only nods his head sadly after I tell him my story.

"This synagogue was built in 1906, so our records only go back to that date. If she left Helsinki around 1880, we probably have no records of her. Back then, people came and went; Finland was part of Russia. Who knows where they went?"

The trail, if there ever was one, has disappeared again. I suspect that long-lost relatives lay buried in the cemetery, but without a proper last name and dates I have little hope of ever finding them. One other thread remains, which will be explored in another week when I reach the ruins of a Russian fort in the Åland Islands. I was told that Jewish soldiers were among the garrison in the mid-1800s. Some of them brought their families. The decaying gravestones of a cemetery in the forest surrounding the ruined fortress might be worth checking.

"I guess that's it," I tell Andre, who offers to show me around the compound and take me to the sanctuary where the Torah is kept.

Andre tells me he was not born in Finland, but in Transylvania, Romania. His family moved to Israel, where he grew up. He eventually served as a tank driver in the Israeli army. A veteran of the Six-Day and Yom Kippur Wars, Andre's talent for playing the guitar—both classical and folk—proved more useful than his tank driving. Soon he was leading the army's entertainment division. Eventually, the government sent him to Scandinavia to promote tourism to Israel. In Finland, he was interviewed by a young, attractive Finnish journalist, who would become his wife. He stayed in Finland, eventually becoming the synagogue's cantor, a position he has held for twenty-four years. Now divorced, with his son grown and working in the U.S., Andre tells me he is thinking of returning to Israel.

That would not be unusual for Helsinki's Jewish community, whose Orthodox members once numbered about 2,000. Immigration to Israel, intermarriage, and integration into broader Finnish society, though, have reduced the community to half that size today.

When we reach the synagogue's office, I notice a black-and-white photo of Gustaf Mannerheim dated from 1944, the darkest hour of Finnish history when the revitalized Soviet army threatened to overrun the country's exhausted defenders. Mannerheim is presenting a wreath to the Helsinki Jewish community's leaders.

Andre Zweig, cantor of Helsinki's synagogue

"Mannerheim came here from the front to thank the community for its support of the war," says Andre. "Twenty-three of our members who were soldiers in the Finnish army died during the war. Not everyone was found. Some are buried in common graves with the other Finnish soldiers in the Karelian forests."

Andre says Mannerheim appreciated how difficult the war was for the community due to one of history's bizarre ironies, which saw Jewish soldiers fighting on the same side as the Nazis. Andre tells me of a Jewish soldier who dodged enemy fire to rescue a squad of SS soldiers. The Germans awarded him the Iron Cross, but he refused to accept it.

I thank Andre for his time and buy a copy of his CD, *My Yiddish Soul*. A Jewish friend of mine in Seattle had given me a dollar and asked that it be donated to the Helsinki synagogue. He told me that this contribution was symbolic and would "ensure a safe journey." I do so, and add a ten euro note to bulk up the insurance policy.

The Unfinished Symphony

I HAVE PUTZED AROUND HELSINKI and its pleasant environs long enough. It is time to try something more ambitious: a shakedown cruise for the long rides that lie ahead.

Thirty miles to the north, tucked away in the Finnish countryside beyond the ring of Helsinki's freeways and suburbs, stands the home of Jean Sibelius, Finland's greatest composer. While Gustaf Mannerheim holds the honor of Finland's principal military hero, Sibelius claims that title in the realm of classical music.

The 25-mile route looks straightforward enough once I clear the dense tangle of Helsinki's bike paths. What better way to test my stamina and the bike, and to learn something about this musical enigma whose prodigious output during the first half of his life contrasted with the procrastination of his last thirty years, as his promoters and friends waited patiently for him to finish his potentially greatest work—the 8th Symphony.

I make quick progress skirting the industrial section of Helsinki Bay, passing the Arabia dishware manufacturing plant, then following a trail that parallels the lazy waters of the Vantaajoki. The city gradually gives way to open fields, vegetable plots, and pine forests. The suburban homes and apartments transform into wood homes and barns almost all painted a dark reddish-brown with white trim. Flowering lupines, columbines, yarrow, and purple fireweed line the path, which crosses the river on delicately engineered bridges, then flits under and over freeways and major arterials. Most of the route along the first dozen miles is lined by streetlights, so it can double as a cross-country ski path during winter's dark months.

For the first 15 miles I ride on a dedicated cycling path, wondering if I will ever touch a real road. I encounter only a handful of other riders, but am astounded by the feverish activity to keep the bicycle trail infrastructure in good working order. Every few miles I pass workers shoring up the path, mowing the right of way, fixing cracks, filling potholes, or cleaning drains.

I soon learn the meaning of "flat" in Finland. North of Helsinki is not flat, at least not in the sense that Kansas is flat. Retreating glaciers ground most of Finland into a series of low hills, probably imperceptible to motorists whizzing by on the Tuusula Motorway, but they slowly begin taking a toll on my legs. Getting my bearings is also a challenge. Landmarks are hard to discern because even hillocks are covered in forests that block the vista. This, combined with the circular path of the sun, causes mayhem with my usually good sense of direction.

Soon after reaching the city of Tuusula, I veer off in the wrong direction because what I think is north is not north, but one of the other three directions. I am not sure which one. For two hours I ride aimlessly in the forests near Tuusula, hoping to catch sight of a massive lake north of the city. I consult my map, but I am uncertain of which road I'm even on. My compass gives bizarre readings. The needle lurches wildly between north and south. "I will deal with you later," I chide the malfunctioning gizmo.

I backtrack to Tuusula and am about ready to give up on my quest to learn about the mysterious 8th Symphony when I accidently find the path that leads out of town and follows the lakeshore highway. I pedal into an area of rich farmland sprinkled with forests. A tiny sign posted near an underpass points me to the Sibelius house, Ainola, perched on a forested bluff overlooking a well-tended garden.

In contrast to Mannerheim's house, which reflected the refined tastes of a well-traveled aristocrat-soldier, Sibelius's house is the ultimate Finnish country hideaway. The two-storied, wood-framed house boasts magnificent exposed fir beams. The curve of massive logs is visible in the walls. A striking green-tiled fireplace dominates one corner of the dining room, a reminder that Sibelius associated colors with various musical keys (he thought green represented F major) and that Ainola lacked central heating and plumbing throughout his lifetime.

Ainola, the country home of Jean Sibelius

Sibelius and his wife, Aino (the namesake of the house), and their three daughters moved here in 1904. Sibelius, then a robust thirty-eight years old, had grown weary of Helsinki and thought he could work better in the silence of the countryside. Indeed, his most productive period ensued shortly after moving here, although he had already contributed significantly to the musical world and to the revolutionary fervor gripping his homeland. In the 1890s, Sibelius's compositions based on the *Kalevala*, Finland's national epic poem, gained him international recognition. In 1899, Sibelius completed *Finland Awakes*, later changed to *Finlandia*, which became the country's unofficial anthem. When first performed, however, the title was listed as the innocuous *Impromptu for Orchestra* to appease Russian officials, who no doubt would have been alarmed at its original nationalist title and the passion it stoked in Finnish audiences.

By the early 1920s, Sibelius had composed seven full symphonies, along with scores of other compositions. He was a master of the tone poem, a composition style that portrays, through musical expression, the folk legends and moods depicted in the *Kalevala*.

Sibelius lived life to the fullest. He drank. He smoked. He lived beyond his means and, starting early in life, was perpetually in debt. He suffered from extreme bouts of depression and anxiety, complaining of a weird metallic taste in his mouth that strangely occurred when he visited his banker. If not for Aino—the daughter of a Finnish senator, fluent in five languages, and the composer's one solid anchor besides the house in the woods—one wonders if Sibelius would have self-destructed shortly after Finland achieved its long-sought independence in 1917. Despite his transgressions, she loyally stuck with him.

In the mid-1920s, Sibelius began composing a new symphony. The work seemed to progress rapidly at first. In the autumn of 1927, he enthusiastically told a friend, the American music critic Olin Downes, that two movements were finished.[17] Later, Sibelius went to Berlin to continue work on what he told friends would be his greatest symphony. But as time progressed and no symphony was forthcoming, the composer's responses to inquiries regarding its progress grew more inconsistent and evasive, perhaps a reflection of his mercurial mood swings and his inability to perfect the score. Sibelius optimistically agreed to conduct the symphony's première in Boston during the 1930–31 season. But as the deadline approached, he confided to friends that the symphony was not finished. By 1933, his sponsors had given up, though Sibelius notes in his journal that he continued to work on the first movement.

Tidbits of evidence suggest that this, his "greatest" symphony, did exist. A 1938 invoice to Sibelius from a Berlin copy shop reveals a work order to copy and bind a "symphonie." But an invoice is not a symphony.

During a visit to Ainola, the Finnish conductor Nils-Eric Fougstedt reported seeing on a shelf the 8th Symphony score with several choral parts. Aino recalled that sometime between 1944 and 1945 "my husband had collected a lot of manuscripts in a laundry basket and burned them in the dining room fireplace." The only surviving evidence today is tucked away at the University of Helsinki. It is a single page with a few notes and some unidentified sketches in G minor, which possibly could have been for the 8th Symphony.[18]

Perhaps the most intriguing clue involves Akseli Gallen-Kallela, the Finnish artist who presented Mannerheim with the painting of the white-camouflaged ski soldiers that seemed to be a premonition of the Winter War. He was also a friend of Sibelius. When Gallen-Kallela died in 1931, Sibelius composed an organ composition in his friend's honor—described as "strange and inexplicable"—that some musicologists believe may have been the template for the 8th Symphony.

〰〰〰 〰〰〰 〰〰〰

Visitors are free to wander through Ainola at their leisure. Although its wood interior is naturally dark, the house faces south, filling the main rooms with light as I look down on an expansive garden brimming with fruit and vegetables, as well as a rainbow of roses, peonies, poppies, and fuchsias. The garden was more than just an ornament. During the World War II shortages, the produce was needed to feed the family.

In the living room sits a Steinway grand piano, a gift for Sibelius's fiftieth birthday. He seldom used it, though, preferring to compose in his head before committing notes to manuscript paper. A number of striking paintings hang throughout the house, almost all of which are composed in somber colors. One portrait labeled "Death of a Child" by Oscar Parviainen, a family friend, shows Aino hunched over the body of their infant daughter Kirsti as the angel of death looms in the background.

Like Mannerheim, Sibelius's favorite room was the library, where he could be found in the evenings smoking a cigar in the green chair near the entrance. A portrait on the back wall shows a young, dashing Sibelius, with a full head of hair and a debonair, full-brushed mustache. This is markedly different from photos of him later in life. All physical appearances change with age, but the transformation of Sibelius from a handsome youth to a stout, bald-headed gnome whose features look like they were chiseled from white granite, is striking because there is no hint of resemblance between the young and old Sibelius. It is as if they are two different men. His sensitivity to criticism, internal angst, and years of depression over his inability to create one last masterpiece clearly took their toll. Toward the end of his life, it reportedly pained him to even talk about music.

Outside, about fifty yards east of the house, amid a grove of fir, lies a giant stone slab inscribed with Sibelius's name. He died on September 20, 1957, at the age of ninety-one. Aino lived for another twelve years before she passed away in 1969 at age ninety-seven. Her name, in much smaller script, was added to the bottom corner of the monument. The stone, perhaps by design or perhaps by fate, has a green tint, leaving Finland's greatest composer and his wife in a final repose of F major.

ww   ww   ww

Toward midafternoon I pry myself away from the tranquil loveliness of Ainola and begin the ride back to Helsinki. I am pleased with the day. Not only have I made my first significant foray outside of Helsinki, but I actually found Ainola despite some rather grievous navigational errors. I figure I'll make it back to Helsinki in less than three hours. My confidence is such that I do not bother to top off my water bottle or stop for a snack in Tuusula.

Soon storm clouds begin to gather to the east, and I hear the subtle tympani of distant thunder. Overhead the sun still shines. *It will be an easy ride back*, I think: straight down the path paralleling the Tuusula Motorway, along the river, through the woods and farms, straight into Helsinki—a no-brainer. Reveling in my newly enhanced navigational skill I decide to take what I think is a shortcut across a park. An hour later, I find myself hopelessly lost among a tangle of suburban streets. I am out of water. The sun shines with a vengeance. I am lost.

I stop to reconnoiter, realizing that getting lost in the Helsinki suburbs is not exactly a good precedent for a trip that is supposed to navigate through Lapland and end at the Barents Sea. At this exact moment I am thinking that I have embarked on the lamest expedition ever conceived.

Wanting desperately to avoid ignominy, I stop and pull out a magnifying glass so I can read the microscopic print on the gargantuan city bike route map issued by the Helsinki information office. Tracing the route on the map isn't easy because several of the major street names have been obliterated by the folds.

While studying the map, I smell smoke. I look up but see no obvious source. I return my attention to the map, but soon wisps of smoke are drifting by. I glance back at the map and see that the concentrated sunbeam of the glass has ignited the map! I snuff out the flame and am relieved that the burned hole lies somewhere east of my present location. Still, it is clear that I have moved a step closer to the Lame Expedition Hall of Fame.

A middle-aged man who happens to be walking by stops to help. His nose twitches like a mouse scenting cheese.

"Do you smell smoke?" he asks.

"No," I deadpan. "I don't smell anything."

I've had enough humiliation for one afternoon. I hand him the map. After carefully scrutinizing the roads, he at last informs me that I have reached the town of Malm. He says I am heading in the opposite direction of Helsinki. He cheerily points out the right way and instructs me that when I reach the railroad tracks, I should follow the road that parallels them. That will lead me to Helsinki.

I follow his directions, but when I reach the tracks I can find no obvious way to exit the overpass. I continue along the road thinking that it too will parallel the railroad. It does not, but instead curves through a forest and into another suburb. Forty-five minutes later I concede that I am lost again. I stand at a crossroads hopelessly studying my map while trying not to set it on fire this time.

I flag down a tall, blonde woman who has just disembarked from a bus. I ask if she could tell me the way to Helsinki. My request puzzles her.

"You are going to Helsinki?" she asks. "It's a long way." She mentions that I am approaching a town whose name did not sound familiar.

"If you continue in this direction, you will end up in Russia," she says. I hope this is a joke.

"But I don't want to go to Russia." My reply is more of a whimper than a declarative statement, another black eye for the Expedition. I have been to Russia and didn't have a good time.

The woman, who looks like she could have just strolled off a fashion runway in New York City—she has that leggy, model bearing—seems to sense that I really need to be pointed in the right direction or perhaps taken home and given a bowl of soup. The latter is not going to happen, but she takes the map and begins pondering its many lines, politely ignoring the burned hole on the eastern quadrant. The Finns know the Russians well. They wouldn't knowingly send me there. This I have faith in.

Many minutes pass before she turns to me brightly and describes a route she says will return me to Helsinki. I listen carefully, but soon realize I have no hope of remembering these directions. Not wanting to impose on her kindness further, I thank her, turn the bike around so I will not go to Russia, and retrace my path through the forest and the suburb back across the overpass. I then wind my way down to the railroad tracks on a road I had not seen the first time I crossed.

By now my sense of direction is completely discombobulated. I stop another passerby and ask the way to Helsinki. She points down a road that follows the tracks. Slowly, I make my way into familiar territory, finally intersecting with the trail that parallels the Vantaajoki. It is nearly eight at night when I wearily pull the bike up to the hostel. The now-familiar crowd of leather-spiked people mills around on the outside steps in the warm evening. It feels like home.

Somehow I had transformed what was supposed to be a 50-mile trial jaunt into a 70-mile ordeal. Worse yet, the very feature that I found thrilling about riding in Finland—the overabundance of dedicated bike paths—proved to be my undoing. *I had better scout the route out of town,* I realize. *Otherwise, I might spend my entire summer cycling in circles around Helsinki.*

Is the President of Finland Really Conan O'Brien?

THE OFFICIAL START OF THE EXPEDITION is now only a day away. To avoid frittering away more time getting lost and found in Helsinki, I turn my attention to the serious business of buying supplies and surveying a route out of the city.

I stock up on cheese, salami, eggs, crackers, bananas, and flat bread. I buy a portable stove (a self-lighting Primus) at Stockman's department store, along with a canister of butane; now I have two stoves. I cannot find the proper fuel canister for the stove I hauled from home anywhere in Helsinki. I buy the complete series of six ridiculously detailed maps denoting the country's primary national bike routes in blue and secondary routes in red, along with topographic and geographic landmarks identified in three languages, including English.[19] Now I have no excuse for getting lost.

By the end of the shopping spree, I am in a state of financial numbness. At $24 each, the maps alone put a big early dent in the Expedition's budget. I cannot bring myself to fork over another $30 for a Finnish-English dictionary (and add another pound of weight). I decide I can wing Finnish with the few pages of translations in the back of my Lonely Planet guidebook. Sadly, I would pay dearly for this moment of budget austerity many times in the ensuing weeks. Finnish, I would discover, is a language that cannot be finessed with a few cheeky cognates like "el checko por favor."

For now, though, I calculate that I have most everything I need, including a mobile phone for emergencies. My only luxuries are a portable shortwave radio, a copy of the book *The Race for Timbuktu,* which describes early attempts by European explorers to reach the fabled city, and a recent edition of *The Economist.* The latter made the final cut more as an aid to induce sleep than because of my need to know about the currency crisis in Zimbabwe.

Finland is a long country with a narrow waist. I always thought it resembled a poodle sitting on its hind legs, with its head representing Lapland and its hindquarters the wider south. I have about sixty days to complete what I estimated to be a 2,000-mile trip, though I need to get to the Arctic with enough time to take a train or bus back to Helsinki to catch my September 4th flight back to Seattle. The overall plan is to actually begin by heading south, then start northeast, cutting across the Lake District to North Karelia. Once in Lapland, I would veer west to Rovaniemi, then turn north to the Barents Sea.

My immediate plan is to ride for two days to reach Ekenäs, Finland's southernmost point. Another two days would get me to my first layover in Turku, 150 miles to the west. It would also be the jump-off point to the Åland Islands, 50 miles off the tip of mainland Finland and reachable by ship.

But first I need to figure out how to wind my way through the tangle of bike routes in Helsinki and its western suburbs. One of the new maps shows that National Bike Route 1, which runs a block from the hostel, heads exactly where I want to go.

I decide to try it out. I cycle across a causeway to Lauttasaari, an island suburb, which connects via another causeway to Espoo, headquarters of Nokia. The route winds in and out of parks and greenbelts, bumps along on dirt along the bay, and bisects leafy neighborhoods of homes and apartments that meld into the landscape. At times the path skirts the Gulf of Finland, filled with sailboats, then cuts into groves of trees and grassy meadows. Flowers bloom in profusion. For scenic beauty within an urban setting—Espoo is Finland's second largest city by population— this ranks as one of the best day rides I have ever taken. For nearly 20 miles until I ride onto the last causeway that breaks free from the city and crosses the marshes into southwestern Finland, I never touch a road. It is all dedicated bikeway.

But from the viewpoint of the full-fledged Riding with Reindeer Expedition, now burdened with two stoves and enough maps to wallpaper my hostel room, this route is an accident waiting to happen. The numerous turns—sudden grades up pleasantly wooded hills followed by plunging gravel paths leading straight to the sea before veering off at a sharp right angle to follow the coast—are too dangerous for a bike pulling a wagon. I return via a less scenic route, following a series of interconnected paths that parallel the freeway, which cuts straight as a knife's edge through Espoo back to Helsinki. This will do.

In the early evening, I take another break from packing and ride out to the Folk Arts Center located adjacent to Seurasaari, another of the many islands connected to Helsinki by bridge. At home in Seattle, I have been known to attend folk dances sponsored by local groups that want to keep their traditions alive. Basic steps for many Eastern European, Scandinavian, Gypsy, and Israeli dances are easy to learn, but more importantly, once learned they serve as a sort of international language; thus community dance groups thrive worldwide. The Internet makes it easy for folk dancers to connect with sister organizations across the globe. I have found that it's a great way to meet the locals when I visit a foreign country. Prior to leaving for Finland, I had corresponded with Paivi Karvila, a member of the Helsinki folk dance group. She sent me directions to the Folk Arts Center.

I find the center nestled in a grove of trees. Entering through a gate, I pass a garden and a large wooden house, then head down a hill to an open-air amphitheatre surrounded by a forest dolloped with wildflowers sprouting in its sunny openings. On the stage about twenty-five people link hands in a circle and step to a tune I recognize as Macedonian. The music emanates from a portable compact disc player. The sun slants in and shines on the stage like a giant spotlight. The dance leader, a tall, thin man in the middle of the circle, demonstrates the proper steps. I find a seat on one of the log benches, but no sooner have I made myself comfortable than the leader waves for me to join the circle.

Within thirty minutes I have made a dozen new friends. Not everyone speaks English or is comfortable speaking it, but a few do. These include Wim, the instructor, and Paivi, who glides over to introduce herself once word of my origin spreads. I ask a nearby woman if they perform any Finnish folk dances, but she replies that no one knows any.

"We do mostly dances from the Balkan countries, plus some Russian and Israeli," she tells me.

Later Paivi invites me to join her, Wim, and some of her friends for coffee at a bayside café about a mile away. It's after nine at night, but the sun is still high in the sky. I follow Paivi, who rides a sturdy Finnish-made, one-speed bicycle. She guides me by tree-shaded parks, past more gardens, and along expanses of freshly cut grass. Entering a leafy residential area, she points to a large house partially hidden by trees.

"That's where the president lives," she says.

"The president of what?"

"The president of Finland," she replies. "She's not home right now. She's at her summer cottage in Naantali."

Had the president been home, I wonder if Paivi would have pedaled right up to the front door, knocked, and introduced me. It just seems like that kind of country. Finland's president is Tarja Halonen, the country's first female head of state, who was first elected in 2000. She is indeed known for her approachability and is often referred to as "Moominmama," a lovable yet wise character from a popular Finnish children's book. Halonen inadvertently gained popularity in the United States in 2006 when the late-night television talk show host Conan O'Brien told his viewers one night that a Finnish visitor had told him he resembled their president. Perhaps testimony to a combination of a quirky national sense of humor and political savvy, Finnish supporters of Halonen, who was then fighting for a second term, aired campaign ads during O'Brien's show, which was popular in Finland. O'Brien even did mock campaign ads for Halonen, which may have helped her get reelected. The Finns clearly love a good laugh—and, by Jove, if their president could stand up to a joke, then she deserved a second term.

Later, O'Brien was invited to do his show in Finland, where he finally met Halonen. While the two sat comfortably before cameras, Halonen, not one to miss a good opportunity, told O'Brien that the mystery of whether Conan was really moonlighting as the president of Finland could finally be put to rest. "You have also made a great favor for us, because I think that at least now quite many more Americans know where Finland is," she quipped.

"The prime minister lives here," says Paivi, waving to another home, which seems next door to that of the president, though it is hard to tell given the park-like setting, which obscures property boundaries. I wonder to myself if the prime minister looks like Jay Leno.

"He's not home either," she says in a tone that leads me to think that perhaps the president and prime minister notify their countrymen when they leave town so the garbage can be put out and the mail picked up.

"Who's running the country?" I ask.

"I don't know," she says. "It's summer—not much is happening. I think maybe the foreign minister."

I feel sorry for the foreign minister, who has to actually work during this paradise-like season, while the rest of the country frolics at summer homes on lakes brimming with trout. We bike onto a grassy peninsula, past a marina bursting with boats, to a crowded bike rack in front of a little red hut—the Regatta Café.

Late-night coffee is about as normal in Finland as early-morning coffee is in the United States. The Finns love coffee, a point that statistics confirm: Finns are the world's leading coffee drinkers on a per capita basis. I, like many Seattleites, enjoy a good cup of joe, too, but not necessarily on the eve of departure for my adventure. I am planning to rise early tomorrow, and the last thing I need before going to bed is a jolt of caffeine. On the other hand, I do not want to squander this opportunity to mingle with my newfound Helsinki folk dance friends. When in Finland, do as the Finns.

The author (right) enjoys a midsummer night's coffee break with folk dance friends.

I order coffee and a pastry. Tomorrow is a long way away.

After I explain my plans to bike the length of Finland, Wim tells me that years ago another American bicycle rider had visited their group and befriended one of their women. "They both rode off. I'm not sure where, but we never heard from her again," he says.

I explain that I depart early tomorrow—so there is barely time to finish packing, let alone fall in love with someone from the group, then haul her off to Lapland with me. I tell them Finland seems like a good country to cycle in because of its relative flatness and that so far I have been impressed with the expansive network of dedicated bike trails in the Helsinki area.

"You think it is good?" says Paivi. "I think the bicycle path system can be improved. They say it isn't as good as the systems in countries in the European Union."

I do not have the benefit of this comparison, but clearly every person sitting at the table would be horrified if they were to fly to John F.

Kennedy International Airport and try to cycle into Manhattan. I suppose it is a matter of perspective, but nothing could persuade me that the hundreds of miles of paths that crisscross greater Helsinki are anything short of a cyclist's paradise.

An older woman sitting next to me offers some advice for my trip: she says that Finnish people are rather shy—not greeters like Americans, but not unfriendly.

"Just ask if you need help," she says, adding that the populace's taciturn behavior is changing rapidly, with almost all young Finns learning to speak some English.

"My son speaks English," she says. "He never took a class. He learned from computer programming and from American movies, which are not dubbed in Finnish. His English is very strange, like a techno English."

When I tell the group of my plan to ride to Ekenäs tomorrow on National Bike Route 1, Wim pipes up that he lives on a farm along Route 1 near Inkoo. He explains that the highway at that point is called the old King's Road, a reference to the time of Swedish rule, when the road served as a major courier and transportation route between the countries.

"Look for a pair of wooden shoes hanging from a post by the road. He's from Holland," says Vivica, a woman sitting next to Wim. "My husband and I live next door. The farms are at a place called Marieberg."

By the time we say our good-byes, I have an invitation to spend the evening at Marieberg. At least my first night on the road will be among friends.

Helsinki to North Karelia

The Epic Begins, Really It Does

MY FIRST THOUGHTS OF THE MORNING are not publishable, as I half bounce, half carry the heavy wagon down the stairs of the hostel.

Last night, after my coffee social, I spent considerable time trying to stuff gear, food, maps, and my two stoves into the wagon, which is about the size of a large suitcase on its side. Not everything would fit. The tools, spare tire, guidebook, compass, lunch, and maps are stuffed into the front carrier. The sleeping bag and tent are strapped to the rear rack. Still, there is not enough room. So clothes and whatever else I cannot get into the wagon are jammed into a daypack, which is then stuffed into a big duffel. This, in turn, is fastened to the top of the wagon by bungee cords whose ends hook into eyebolts screwed into the sides. The eyebolts were a last-minute inspiration before I left the United States. Anticipating that I might have more stuff than capacity, I had drilled holes around the perimeter of the suitcase, then affixed small but sturdy eyebolts from my local hardware store.

On top of this ungainly pile I wrap a thin foil ground cover intended for the tent. Not only will this protect the load from rain, but its magnificent reflective capacity ensures that I will be highly visible to motorists—and most likely to orbiting NASA satellites.

I knew the wagon would be heavy, but I didn't know how heavy until just this moment. My guess is that I'm pulling close to seventy-five pounds, not including the bike. On this dreary Friday morning, I begin to wonder how the hell I will get to Lapland and beyond with all this crap.

There is only one way to find out. I snap the wagon yoke into my bike's bronze trailer hitch, hop onto the bike, and officially begin my epic adventure with a slow coast down Sandviksgatan.

My second thought on this formless morning is that this is nuts, followed quickly by an admonishment that would become the Expedition mantra: *The only way I can do this is to take it one day at a time.* I banish the thought of Lapland and the Barents Sea, and think only of the day's destination: Marieberg, some 50 miles to the west.

Thanks to the design of the wagon and the miracle of wheels, the bulky load that I dragged down the hostel stairs is manageable when towed by the bike, though it is a bit ungainly on turns. Initially, it feels like the bicycle version of a semitrailer. I find the path to the first causeway, feeling only a slight tugging of the load on uphill grades. By the time I pass Nokia's research center and reach Espoo about three miles from the hostel, I am in a pleasant cadence. I entertain the thought that this might be doable after all.

By eleven in the morning, I have reached Stensvik, the final bit of suburb before the main road west, Highway 51, crosses the last causeway into, as far as I'm concerned, *terra incognita*. I congratulate myself for making splendid time and having the foresight to scout the route. Not one to let a celebratory moment pass, I stop at a gas station-restaurant and treat myself to coffee and a donut, the latter of which would soon become the official Expedition comfort food. When traveling solo, small pleasures are important.

I reconnect with National Bike Route 1, which leads to a quiet path paralleling the seething buzz of traffic on Highway 51. In a grove of birch trees with a splendid view of Espoo Bay, I come upon a modernistic steel arch monument before the path empties onto a secondary road that crosses the Saunalahden Strait. This channel marks the official end of metropolitan Helsinki from the Porkkala Peninsula, but in September 1944 it also marked the beginning of what would become de facto Soviet territory for the next twelve years.

As part of the 1944 armistice between Finland and the Soviet Union ending the Continuation War, the Russians were granted a fifty-year "lease" of the Porkkala Peninsula for a naval base—an area of some 610 square miles. Less than a month after signing the armistice, 7,200 Finns and 8,000 farm animals were evacuated and relocated from this rich farmland and replaced by 30,000 Soviet military personnel and civilians. The main railroad line between Helsinki and Turku was rerouted, but later the Soviets allowed Finnish trains to operate through Porkkala, providing they used Russian locomotives and that the shades on the passenger cars were kept shut and the doors locked. Finns dubbed the passage the "Porkkala Tunnel."

As the years passed and the 1950s heralded the age of nuclear bombs, the costs of maintaining the base outstripped the defensive benefits that seemed necessary after World War II. In his memoirs, Soviet leader Nikita Khrushchev grouses about the enormous cost of maintaining the base and concludes that it made much more sense to negotiate a new treaty with the Finns that included dismantling the base as a goodwill gesture. So in January 1956, Porkkala was returned to Finland. After eleven years of darkness, the shades of the passenger trains were raised.

For me, crossing into the Porkkala marks a different transition. My magical time on dedicated paths comes to a jarring end as National Bike Route 1 empties unceremoniously onto the entrance to Highway 51, a busy two-lane road disgorging an alarming number of trucks, buses, campers, and cars from Helsinki. They all seem to be roaring into the countryside on this late Friday morning at 70 miles per hour. *Are these the latecomers to the national vacation period?*

I wait patiently for an opening to merge onto the highway, but the traffic is relentless. A motorist next to me also waits, but soon gives up. He turns around and retreats across the bridge. I don't have that option so I continue my vigil, mentally calculating how quickly I can defy the laws of physics and marshal enough momentum from a standing position with all my gear to cross the road before being obliterated. The answer is: I don't know and now probably isn't a good time to conduct experiments.

So I wait, stalled by monster traffic. At last, I see a narrow break forming down in the parade of traffic. I pump into action. It seems like I am in a slow-motion movie, gaining traction foot by foot as I cross the crown of the road and scuttle to the far side as a truck the size of Godzilla bears down on me. But I have done it! I have crossed the lair of the epic's first metaphorical dragon, ferociously guarding the entrance to the countryside.

I turn west and am shocked by the narrowness of the shoulder. Buffeted by the wind whipped up by the nonstop parade of trucks and buses, I pedal for dear life until I finally reach a quiet side road with a sign pointing out Route 1 away from the mayhem.

Tranquility is restored. The road enters a land of rolling hills and stands of white-barked birch interspersed with pine forests. I pass through the villages of Masala and Jolkby, where old stone Lutheran churches grace the town centers that are ringed by modern stores, gas stations, and modest homes. Farther west I pedal through spruce forests mingled with spacious wood-framed homes. Almost all are painted the uniform red-brown with white trim. Like pennants for a medieval jousting tournament, banners of white with blue stripes—mimicking the national flag—fly from peaked roofs or front yard flagpoles. Small outbuildings are puzzling at first, but then I realize these must be the ubiquitous saunas, standard in virtually all Finnish homes. One homeowner has whimsically fenced his yard with narrow round logs that are painted to resemble different colored pencils. Around a bend, I startle a mottled-brown groundhog-like animal that scurries into the undergrowth. I am relieved that there are few cars; I have the country lanes to myself. The day remains overcast, with a slight wind from the north and east. But these are trifles because I am finally under way and all, for the moment, is glorious. The traffic monsters of midmorning have been quickly forgotten.

The road leads unexpectedly down a narrow forested path, but I have confidence that National Bike Route 1, whose little brown signs I watch for with great anticipation, will not lead me astray. I slope down an embankment and onto a wooden causeway that might have been built by elves. Built-in benches line the crossing, which spans a sluggish river, its banks overgrown with alder, oak, and elm. A fishing boat is moored downstream. The place, which has a Huck Finn feel, is deserted.

A causeway on National Bike Route 1

In this sylvan paradise I stop to eat the journey's first lunch of salami, a hard-boiled egg, cheese, bread, and orange juice. As I munch contentedly I think the just-concluded morning (except for the Highway 51 bit) is one of the best country rides I have ever taken. I have covered nearly 30 miles and have hardly broken a sweat. *Are epics usually this effortless?*

After lunch, I pass cultivated fields vibrant with yellow and purple blooms, while other farms sprout wheat and barley. The roadside is a bright collage of white, pink, and blue lupine and red yarrow. I am still making good time when I reach the village of Degerby and stop at a small wooden building with a sign announcing that I have arrived at the Igor

Museum. It's not on my itinerary, but I decide I have time to give the place a look. I park the bike next to an old Soviet military jeep with its headlights poked out.

The tiny room is filled with bits and pieces left behind by the post-World War II Soviet occupiers, which, given Finland's current prosperity, seems more than several life times ago. According to the log book, I am the only visitor today.

"An American came by about two years ago," says Sonya, an eighteen-year-old college-bound student who is minding the museum today. Degerby was the epicenter of the relocations in 1940, when the Russians gave the Finns only nine days to get out. Sonya tells me her grandparents were among the refugees who were resettled throughout the country on property requisitioned by the government. The church here was turned into a cinema and bunkers were built. German prisoners of war were shipped in to tend the farms and construct barracks. Five thousand Soviet troops were in Degerby.

Back on the road, the country lanes alternate between dirt and pavement. Past Inkoo, I encounter more gravel roads that twist into the thickly wooded hills. So far I have been managing the hills well. Now my legs begin to tire. As I enter the woods, the friendly looking houses are replaced by a long fence. Nailed to the top railing is a series of photos of a vicious German shepherd, with teeth bared. The beast looks like it belongs on one of those "Most Wanted" posters that decorate the walls of U.S. post offices. In the distance, I hear barking—lots of barking. I press on, thinking I am getting close to Wim's house. When I round a bend, however, the road abruptly ends, barred by thick forest and posted signs that I initially read as "boiled soup." *Why would they boil their soup here?* But the glossary section of my guidebook translates *kielletty* as "prohibit," which I interpret as "no trespassing," and not *keitetty keitto*, which is boiling soup. Perhaps, I am beginning to realize, it was a mistake to eschew an English-Finnish dictionary. I make a mental note to buy one before I make more transposition errors that could result in unpleasant consequences. I study my map, wondering where I've gone wrong. A couple of joggers, whom I had passed earlier, stop to help. We all conclude I must have taken a wrong turn after Inkoo.

I turn back, retracing my route, adding five miles of unnecessary hill work to my day. By the time I reach the Inkoo Church where I made my wrong turn, I am tired and hungry, the image of soup, boiling or otherwise, having been planted in my mind. I pause briefly at the offending intersection, searching for the little brown National Bike Route sign, but I do not see one. I make another mental note to write to whomever is in charge of the route's signage to suggest that they make sure unmarked intersections are indeed marked.

I wind through more farms hacked from the forest and make another brief detour that dead-ends before finding the King's Road. At 5:30 p.m. I spot wooden shoes hanging from a mailbox. I pull off the main road and wearily coast into Wim's driveway.

I quickly learn that Wim is much more than a simple farmer tending to his wheat, beans, and hay, which appear to grow effortlessly in this climate. Born and raised in the Netherlands, where he studied horticulture (with a parallel interest in the folk arts), Wim moved to Finland as a young man to continue his studies. He liked the country, stayed and married, and bought land at Marieberg. The house is homemade, with an inside composting toilet.

"I need to feed the horse," Wim says, taking me around to his barn. The horse seems quite pleased to see us and tucks into his pail of oats with relish. The barn houses an ancient Ford pickup truck, a vintage World War II Dutch-made one-speed bicycle, and a horse-drawn carriage. Tomorrow, Wim says, he will hitch up the carriage and take it to town to give rides to tourists.

I am not the first cross-country cyclist to stop at Wim's house. He tells me that many years ago a man on a recumbent cycle stopped by for the night. He, too, was on his way to Lapland.

Like many of the inhabitants of this country, particularly those who have traveled, Wim is multilingual. He speaks five languages, though be concedes that after all these years he still struggles with Finnish. We wander through a garden to an open-air fire pit where his wife is entertaining friends, all busy preparing the evening sauna.

After a light meal of cheese, bread, and tea, he invites me to take a ride in the pickup to the old ironworks factory at Fagervik, a few miles down the King's Road. We poke around the remains, which are tucked among the hills and cloaked in alder, ash, and oak trees. The factory's old forge and red-brick waterwheel house were used to produce iron during the days when Sweden, and then Russia, ruled Finland. Though it's difficult to imagine such an industrial enterprise in this now-tranquil setting, Fagervik, built in 1646, is a reminder that the land here has a lengthy human pedigree. It was important enough to warrant a visit by Sweden's King Gustavus III in 1775. A few years after Sweden ceded Finland to Russia, Czar Alexander I also spent the night here. Production continued until 1902. Above the ironworks stands a small eighteenth-century wooden church, now being prepared for a wedding; the surrounding bungalows that once housed workers have been restored. Across the street looms an old three-story manor house, said to be haunted.

When we return, Wim drives me to the house where Vivica and her husband, Hans, live. While we wait for Vivica to come home from Helsinki, Hans, along with Wim, shows me his massive barn. As my eyes grow accustomed to the dim light inside it, I see that I have walked into a virtual museum of transportation artifacts, dating back to czarist times. The barn is stuffed with old wooden sledges and a fleet of antique wooden buggies with worn black leather upholstery (Wim is in the process of restoring the upholstery). The buggies look as if they had just carried the king and his couriers down the road. Hans wheels out an elegant, black push scooter, one of the first manufactured in Finland. I wonder if all the neighboring farms harbor such treasures.

When Vivica arrives, we gather in the kitchen. I ask about the origins of Marieberg, the name of the original farm estate, and am told it was the property of a Swedish nobleman who settled here because he "did something bad." The "bad" thing has been lost to history, though we all speculate it must have had something to do with a woman.

Wim Van Der Kooij shows one of the old buggies he's restoring.

Our conversation turns to the various animals that roam these parts. Neither Hans nor Vivica can figure out what the groundhog-like animal I spotted earlier in the day is. Vivica says the forests brim with deer, which she refers to as "bambis." I am also curious about the road signs I passed, depicting a moose.

"What is this moose?" asks Vivica.

I describe the sign. Hans says what I saw is a picture of an elk, but I insist it is a moose. Hans solves the mystery by looking it up in a dictionary. It turns out that the words "elk" and "moose" describe the same animal in Finnish. We agree to call the animal on the sign a moose-elk.

Given my hosts' professions as doctors, I ask about the national health care system in Finland. Hans, who is an obstetrician, shares his time between two clinics in nearby towns. These clinics, along with others in Finland's 440 municipalities, provide primary medical service to residents. Specialized care is provided by regional hospitals. Medical care is free for children. Adults get free preventive and maternal care, but are charged a fee for doctor visits and hospital stays. By American standards, the fees are ridiculously cheap. For example, the maximum hospital charge per day is $40, which includes doctor care, meals, and medication.

Someone, of course, has to pay for this system, and that someone is the Finnish taxpayer. I do not know the specifics of the Finnish tax system, but the health care that is described to me seems far superior to what I am paying for back home: a bare-bones catastrophe policy with an annual cost that would buy me two months of full care in a Finnish hospital, no questions asked. Because out-of-pocket costs are negligible and preventive care is emphasized, Finland's overall health care costs are about half that of the United States.[20] Finland's current health care system has elevated the country from the ruins of World War II to ranking among the healthiest in all major health care categories, including infant mortality, where it is number one. One issue that the Finns have not been able to subdue is alcoholism, which may have something to do with the long and dark winters that counterpoint the long, light-filled summers like I am now enjoying.

By eleven we are all exhausted. Vivica shows me to the upstairs guestroom, where her children, now grown, once romped. As I slide under the covers, rain taps on the windows. I drift off to a fitful sleep, hopeful that the storm will pass by morning.

Lightning

RAIN FALLS THROUGHOUT THE NIGHT, but I am snug inside the big farmhouse. In the morning, Hans prints out the weather report for me, using the word "unsettled" to describe conditions expected for the next few days.

Despite the forecast, the clouds break and I am savoring the 21-mile ride to Ekenäs, a resort town at the tip of the Hanko Peninsula. Within an hour of heading out that morning, I reach the old ironworks at Fagervik, which Wim and I visited yesterday. As I stop and take a brief rest, a car pulls up behind me. The driver gets out. It is Hans. He's holding a pair of reading glasses. Mine. I had left them at Marieberg, and by divine providence my hosts had found them before I got too far along. Without the glasses, I would have had no hope of reading my map or guidebook. I thank him profusely, while feeling a bit of embarrassment for a serious lapse of Expedition attention to detail.

I have no more mishaps on this short day of riding. En route, I photograph a sign pointing to the village of "Snappertuna"—a Swedish name that I find irresistible—and visit the Raseborg Castle, a massive stone fortress that dates back to the fourteenth century.

In Ekenäs, I wind through a residential district on the way to the Ornmas Campground, which is perched on the waterfront of a fjord that stretches to the Gulf of Finland. The place is packed with holiday-goers. I bike through rows of campers, giant tents, and trailers that occupy almost every square inch of available real estate. Luckily, I'm able to shoehorn into a tent site next to a few other cyclists. My neighbors are a quiet German couple and two teenage Finnish girls dressed in army fatigues. The girls are armed with a boom box that threatens to make my night a long and wakeful one. After pitching the tent and unhitching the wagon, I pedal into town to celebrate the Expedition's "first night without friends." I find a pleasant café with an outdoor patio and select a table under the awning. After ordering dinner and a beer, I lean back and watch a couple of black swans swim gracefully in the bay. A persistent buzz, like angry bees, emanates from farther up the bay where jet boats race.

During these idyllic moments I do not notice the towering cumulus clouds that are seething with energy directly overhead. With alarming speed, the pastoral scene turns gray, as if some diabolical movie director has yelled, "Turn on the storm!" Thunder growls. At first there are a few hailstones, which I initially think are white marbles or ice cubes tossed by a hidden prankster across the street. Then all hell breaks loose. Violent gusts threaten to vacuum up nearby umbrellas sheltering other diners, while those sitting in unprotected areas get bombarded by the oversized hail balls. Waiters desperately grab umbrellas and hang on; it seems as if they might be sucked into the clouds at any moment. The sea, calm a few minutes ago, appears to be boiling as the hailstones pelt the water.

I watch this mayhem from the relative safety of the awning, as hail bounces all over the place. A man at the next table—with less protection—peels off from his party, grabs his beer, and asks if he can join me under my small but stable shelter.

He says he is a farmer who lives nearby, and is worried about his hay crop. "The wet will be very bad for the hay if I don't get it cut," he tells me.

I ask him if this is normal weather for the area.

"I live here my entire life. I maybe have seen storms like this once," he tells me.

When I return to the campground later than night, I find that the tempest has partially collapsed my tent. My clothes sack sits in a pool of water. The copy of *The Economist*, which I read piecemeal each night, is a pulpy mess. It now weighs about ten times its original weight.

It could have been worse. At least my sleeping bag is not wet, and the granola and other goods are still dry. From now on, the Expedition will definitely need to pay more attention to securing the tent and keeping gear in plastic bags.

Shortly after I crawl into my sleeping bag, a car approaches, and from the proximity of the oncoming crunch of tires, I think it might roll right over me. I pop my head out of the tent in time to see a family of four—a mother, father, and two little girls—emerging from their station wagon. They unfold an enormous tent a few yards from mine. I retreat into my cocoon, serenaded by the clanging of tent stakes, the slamming of car doors, the zipping of zippers, and the curt commands of an exhausted dad trying to organize his restless band into a workforce. As if on cue from the other side, my teenage neighbors, who have been giggling away the evening, unleash their boom box rock music. *There will be no second night in Ekenäs.*

Up early the next morning, packed and ready to roll by 6:30, I encounter the two men I had seen staggering around last night, each clutching a beer bottle. They are still staggering around, still dressed in the same jogging suits, and still clutching beer bottles.

"Good morning!" yells one of the men to me. He does a double take when he sees the bicycle and wagon. "Where are you going?"

"Lapland."

"Lapland," says the man, considering the destination. "Lapland is a long way." He gives me the thumbs-up sign and wishes me luck. "Would you like a beer?"

"It's a bit early for me," I say, waving and then pushing off to begin the day's ride.

I am 80 miles from Turku, where I plan to spend two nights and figure out how to get to the Åland Islands. But 80 miles violates the Expedition's 50-miles-a-day rule. When I planned the trip, I had concluded that 50 miles should be the average distance I would cover in a day and allow for a full day of rest every third or fourth day. This seemed reasonable and would allow me to conserve strength for the long distances I would need to cover once I reached Lapland. Fortunately, the bicycle map shows a campground located on a fjord about 50 miles from Ekenäs.

The National Bike Route signs lead me away from the busy highway onto country lanes, many of which are not paved and wind through hilly farm country. At times it seems like the loopy bike route is twice the distance of the main road. I get wise to this near the village of Ylonkylä, where the bike route and Highway 183 momentarily merge. Ylonkylä, where I had planned to have lunch, is only a mile down the road, so I am perplexed when the bike route diverts me to a narrow dirt lane splitting off to the north. I dutifully follow, winding past turkey and horse farms, through patches of forest, and up and down wearisome hills. Several junctions are not signed so I have to guess the right direction. By the time I am dumped back onto Highway 183, I discover I have completed a gigantic loop, gaining precious little linear ground while tiring myself out—and being taken past my lunch stop. I vow to stick to the main highway the rest of the day. It's too late to backtrack to Ylonkylä. I press on.

By noon, the clouds begin to thicken. I am worried about being pulverized by hail again. So when I reach the town of Kemio, I dart into a restaurant for lunch and hope the storm blows away while I eat.

w/w   w/w   w/w

The stillness is eerie as I step out of the restaurant and prepare for the afternoon ride. Off toward the west, the sky has turned a foreboding hue of dark gray. Thunder rumbles in the distance. Quickly, I saddle up and ride out of Kemio. According to the map, I only have to bike 25 miles on Highway 161 then cross a bridge spanning a narrow fjord to reach the turnoff to the promised campground. It's a reasonable distance. I mentally prepare myself to carry out the afternoon's assignment.

The thunder rumbles closer. I stop, zip up my parka and slip on my blue rain pants as a precaution, although by now I hope to outrun the seemingly slow-moving storm.

I am not so lucky. As I ascend a hill, the heavens open, like a shower turned on full blast. Rain ricochets off the pavement. Thunder growls.

Unlike virtually all other hills I have climbed today, this one is barren except for some hay stacks; there's not a tree in sight. I am the tallest object. Lightning flashes as I swish downhill, my vision blurred from the rain slamming into my eyes. I wonder how the motorists are coping, and I hope they see my little blue bike hugging the thin shoulder. The rain is relentless. Ahead I see a wall of gray. The Expedition is in trouble. I keep moving.

As I ascend another hill, I spot a tiny roadside fruit stand. I cross the road and drive under its awning. Apparently its proprietors have hastily evacuated, leaving the cashbox and a calculator displaying an unfinished transaction. In the back are boxes of strawberries, though the front counter is bare. The structure is so small that the only place to stand and keep dry is behind the counter.

A car splashes into the turnout. A woman jumps out and runs to the stand. She wants to buy fruit. There is not much I can do because the only Finnish words I can remember are "boiled soup," "excuse me," "good morning," and "yes." After weeks of study I can still only count to one, which will make taking large orders of fruit rather challenging. Besides, I have never sold fruit in my life; I don't know what it costs. I don't even eat that much fruit, though I should. Perhaps this is God's way of enforcing my mother's admonition to do so: marooning me in a fruit stand while hurling scary thunderbolts and causing a downpour of Biblical proportions. Why couldn't this have been a bakery?

I shrug and tell her in English that I'm just staying dry and have no idea where the farmer disappeared to.

"Sorry, I don't speak Finnish," I say.

She glances at the bike and appears to grasp that I don't have the slightest clue about fruit or the Finnish language. She smiles, jumps in her car, and drives off. Then I remember I'm in the Swedish-speaking part of Finland. *Oh well, I don't speak Swedish either.*

The downpour continues. Rain funnels off the eaves of the tiny stand in faucet-like quantities. *Will it rain forever?* I wonder. *Will I spend the rest of my life at this lonely spot, amid a grove of trees, pretending to sell fruit to befuddled passersby?*

Thankfully, no more customers arrive. Then, thirty minutes later the downpour abates. But soon after I continue my ride, the rain pounces again. I dodge cloudbursts by hiding in bus shelters, then pedal a few miles before the next one hits. What sustains me is the knowledge that the campground is near. By 4 p.m. I reach the cantilever bridge crossing the fjord. I am so very ready to call it quits for the day.

On the other side of the bridge, I look for a sign indicating a campground. But I see nothing. This is not good. I pull off the road and yank out my map. There, clearly marked, is the red campground symbol. I examine a roadside sign denoting major attractions in the area. A campground is not among the attractions. I am screwed.

As I straddle the bike at the pullout, rain dripping off my helmet, I quickly conclude I do not have the energy to explore side roads to confirm what the absence of the sign is telling me. I am 24 miles south of the nearest town (Paimio) that might have a cheap hotel.

The disappointment of not finishing my day here is bad for Expedition morale. I am wet. I am tired. I am grumpy. But I clearly cannot stay here on this muddy split in the road next to a nameless fjord in the middle of nowhere.

The Expedition presses on as the first vestiges of despair gain a toehold in my subconscious. The next two-and-a-half hours are a soggy blur as I cling to the side of the busy highway and slowly grind out miles. At mid-evening, I wearily crest a hill that seems to stretch forever lured by a sign for the Hotel Valtatie 1. I am still a few miles from Paimio, but I figure this will do just fine. As I pedal up to the lobby door, the place looks so deserted that I wonder if it's closed.

Mercifully, it is not. The friendly clerk, eager to practice his English, assigns me a choice room. In minutes, I am unlocking the door and shedding wet clothes just as the heavens open again with another deluge.

Later, in the deserted restaurant, I am assured by the same man who checked me in that it, too, is open. He appears to be the only employee. There is no menu.

"Just tell me what you want."

"What do you have?"

"We have many things, but cow and salmon are good."

The salmon *is* good. I eat happily away, my immediate needs satisfied, watching the news on a television suspended from the ceiling. More *unsettled* weather is expected the next few days. Inmates in Finland's two prisons request a lockdown after the murder of a prisoner. Drugs are thought to be responsible. Trouble in paradise? An African American basketball player, a former Portland Trailblazer, has become a star on a Helsinki team—but most amazing to me is his ability to respond to his interviewer in Finnish.

That night I drift off into a deep sleep knowing that thanks to the 66 miles I covered today, I only need to ride 21 more to reach Turku tomorrow.

Rescued by Little Nuns

IN CONTRAST TO YESTERDAY'S *Sturm und Drang*, the ride into Turku is delightful once the sun breaks free from the dawn's shroud. Not only am I happy about being warm and dry again, but the prospect of my first two-day layover adds to my buoyant spirits.

Ten miles outside of the city, I find myself on a dedicated bike path. I stop for lunch at a roadside park, where a passerby asks where I am going.

"Turku today; Lapland eventually," I tell him, while gnawing on my usual fare of cheese and salami.

"Lapland is 1,000 kilometers," he says, then gives me the thumbs-up sign (they seem to do that a lot here) and continues on his way.

Soon I near the day's destination; however, the sign pointing toward a narrow driveway to the Bridgettine Convent on Ursininkatu near downtown Turku is unobtrusive even by Finnish standards. Perhaps the Catholics, a thin minority in Finland, prefer a low profile now that they are awash in a sea of Lutherans.

It wasn't always that way. Bishop Henry, an Englishman, introduced Finland to Catholicism in the twelfth century. His portfolio included some serious miracle making—raising the dead, curing the sick, and restoring sight to the blind—all of which helped elevate him to saint-hood after he was murdered by a disgruntled parishioner. However, historians are perplexed by the scant record Saint Henry left behind. For example, no one seems to remember his last name. Thus, Henry's existence is still debated.

Another Catholic with fewer dazzling miracles to her name, but with more solid ecclesiastical credentials, is Saint Bridget of Sweden, the fourteenth-century founder of the Bridgettine order. Haunted by childhood visions of Christ, which intensified after she became a widow, Bridget devoted her life to charity and good works, ultimately undertaking a pilgrimage to the Holy Land. Eventually she settled in Rome, where her new order was sanctified by Pope Urban V; she was canonized in 1391. Besides continuing the good works of Saint Bridget, in modern times the order has found it worthwhile to operate guesthouses adjacent to their convents.

I usually do not stay overnight in convents, though I confess a small trickle of papal blood runs in my veins. My mother is a nominal Catholic, though after fifty years of marriage to my father she now seems more Jewish than he. Given my feeble attempt in Helsinki to track down the elusive great-grandmother on my father's Jewish side, it is only fair to give equal time to my other lineage. Truth be told, the biggest reason for picking the convent came from my handy Lonely Planet guidebook, which said the guesthouse is a decent and relatively cheap place to stay, providing you are quiet and do not violate the curfew.

I am admitted by a diminutive nun wearing a black and gray habit. With skin the color of coffee, this sister can't possibly be Finnish. I guess that she is of Indian, or maybe Filipino, descent. As I register, she reminds me about the need to keep a tranquil and quiet environment. Liturgical music and the faint hypnotic tone of chants waft in from the sanctuary. I follow the tiny sister to the elevator, which lets us out at a second floor hallway. The linoleum floor glistens with a seemingly virginal purity.

A crucifix hangs above the head of my narrow bed. But I also have a writing desk and my own bathroom. It appears as if the room has never known dust. The sister leaves me to unpack so she can return to the sanctuary.

Finding the room more than satisfactory, I retrace my steps along the hallway to the elevator. The steel door closes and the lift descends to the first floor, but the door does not reopen. I study the control panel. There are only three buttons, one for each floor. I paw the panel, looking for a hidden "open door" button. I find nothing. I pray for Saint Bridget to open the door. I chant "Open sesame" and even "Open says me" (which is how I thought the phrase went as a kid). The door does not budge. I wait for someone else to call for the elevator, but after a few minutes I worry that I might spend my entire summer in this steel cell. I have coached myself endlessly to prepare for the unexpected, but I really did not expect the unexpected to strike, *well*, so unexpectedly—in a convent elevator, for crying out loud.

My options are limited. In fact, I seem to have only one embarrassing choice in the form of a red emergency button. The Riding with Reindeer Expedition will need to be rescued by nuns.

The red button unleashes a shriek that I am sure not only disrupts whatever holy happenings are occurring in the sanctuary, but surely guarantees me a place in purgatory, if not worse. After a few unbearable moments, the elevator moans and the door swings open. Before me stands the sister, not exactly looming at about four-feet, eight-inches tall, but looking—to say the least—stern. Fortunately, she is not holding a rod; my butt is already sore from three days of riding. I wonder if my faux pas will result in excommunication from the premises.

"Yes," she says. "What is the problem?"

"How do you open the door?" I squeak.

"Just push."

"Oh."

Having thus been humbled, I thank her and meekly go outside to retrieve my gear. Fortunately I am not excommunicated, this being my first offense.

After securing my mud-splattered bike to a rail in the convent's courtyard, I stroll into the reception area, only to be greeted by another nun. Oddly, she is exactly the same height and stature as the first. Hands on her hips, she doesn't look happy. The hymnal music has stopped. The place is as quiet as a morgue.

"I'm going to bike to Lapland," I say cheerily.

This greeting does not have the desired effect—not even the "My! Lapland is far" comment that I have come to expect.

"You cannot park that thing here," she says, motioning to the bike leaning against a railing in the courtyard. "It is very unsafe."

I wonder just how unsafe it is, considering I am in the safest place in the safest country in the world. But judging from the scowl on her face, I can see that my folding bike is not eliciting the wonder and awe I have come to expect, but rather disapproval, as if this "thing" is an instrument of the devil himself. I walk the bike to the back parking lot, where I chain it ingloriously to a downspout. In the evening when I prepare to ride into the city center for dinner, I discover a flat rear tire. Things are not going well at the convent.

៷៷៷   ៷៷៷   ៷៷៷

Turku wears its age well. Founded in the thirteenth century by the Swedes, Turku, or Åbo as it is called in Swedish, flourished as the trade, cultural, and political center for Swedish Finland. The Russians, after defeating Sweden in the War of 1807, stripped Turku of its capital status, preferring Helsinki, which was closer to the motherland. During my rest day in Turku, I explore the city center, then cycle along the path paralleling the Aura River. The waterway bisects the city and is a navigable canal for the scores of tourist boats that serve as floating restaurants and pubs. The riverbank is lined by stately neoclassical buildings and hundred-year-old elm trees.

In the middle of a busy street adjacent to the river is a bronze statue of Turku's native son Paavo Nurmi, Finland's greatest Olympic athlete. Between 1920 and 1928, Nurmi won nine gold and three silver medals in track. During the 1924 games, Nurmi, who became known as the "Flying Finn," pulled off a physical feat that seems impossible even today by winning the 1,500 meters, resting for twenty-six minutes, then running and winning the 5,000 meters. When the statue was unveiled in the 1950s, Nurmi was dumbfounded with the classical Greek depiction of him in full stride. "But I don't run naked," he told reporters. In his later years, he admonished his countrymen to get their butts (naked or not) out of their cars. "Do not let the new means of transport kill your instinct for exercise!" he chastised.

A cobblestone street in Turku

My butt is reminded of my painful ride from Ekenäs three days ago as I leave the river and jounce along a cobblestone street leading to the magnificent towers of the seven-hundred-year-old Turku Cathedral. The crescendo of a fugue issues from a gigantic pipe organ booming its chords through the nave as I wander down the stone floors and attempt to decipher the chiseled names on the crypts. The most prominent is that of the sixteenth-century heartthrob Catherine Månsdotter,[21] who began life as the daughter of a jailer, and absent some bad luck, may have ended it as Queen of Sweden. Her union with Eric XIV might have gone down as a real-life Cinderella story, if not for her husband's descent into madness.

Prior to his marriage to Catherine, Eric had pursued matrimonial ties with an all-star cast of potential queens, starting with Elizabeth Tudor, later to become Elizabeth I of England, followed by Mary I of Scotland,

Renata of Lorraine, Anna of Saxony, and Christine of Hess. Perhaps they all detected slight character flaws in Eric. This unprecedented record of royal rejection may have contributed to Eric's growing mental instability (not to mention his waning confidence) and certainly did not help Sweden's ambitions of becoming a regional power through matrimonial alliances during the go-go days of the sixteenth century. The beautiful Månsdotter with her long, flowing blonde hair and winsome manner was the only member of Eric's court who could calm the king. She became Eric's consort, and in 1567 they married. Foreshadowing future events, the Lord Chamberlain stumbled and dropped her crown during the wedding ceremony. Scandalized by this marriage to a commoner, albeit a gorgeous one, and troubled by Eric's growing insanity, his family rebelled. Eric was imprisoned, and Catherine was exiled to Turku Castle, a mile downriver from where I now stood. After Eric died in 1577, Månsdotter was released and granted a manor in Kangasala, Finland. Though never a hit with the Swedish royal family, she was popular with the Finnish peasantry, who spared her house during a revolt in 1596–97.

Later I whisk down to the bay, passing tall, old sailing ships and spanking-new yachts. Where the river empties into Turku Bay, I reach the object of my day's search, the terminals of the Viking and Silja cruise lines. Both ship companies have daily sailings to the Åland Islands, my next destination. Docked at this moment are two of the biggest passenger ships I have ever seen. I count nine decks above the water line on the Viking boat as it disgorges hundreds of passengers and vehicles. I manage to grab a schedule in English, which tells me that the Viking Line's *Amorella* departs tomorrow morning at 8:30 for Mariehamn, the capital of Åland. I can't find a place to buy a ticket so I bike back into the city, locate the Viking ticket office, and book a passage. I am told to be at the car loading area by 8:00.

While wandering near the city center, I do a double take when I think I see a mariachi band playing in a pedestrian mall. Rain begins to fall as I wander over and ask one of the musicians where they are from.

"We are from Romania," he says.

"I thought you were Mexicans," I say, thinking the discovery of a Mexican mariachi band in Finland would be a striking ethnological find for my fledging Expedition.

The man consults with a portly guitar player as if to confirm that they are indeed Romanians, not Mexicans.

"You pay some money?"

"But you aren't playing."

The man considers this comment, turns, and consults again with his compatriot.

"It's raining," he says glumly.

I dig out a euro coin, thinking that a contribution to a Romanian band might ward off even more rain.

"I expect you to be playing if I come by later," I say.

◦◦◦   ◦◦◦   ◦◦◦

At 7:30 the next morning I have finished breakfast, packed the bike, and am ready to pay for my two nights at the convent. A sign at the reception desk tells me that the little nuns are in the sanctuary performing their morning prayers. Liturgical music, like a mystical fog, permeates the reception. I see a buzzer with another small sign noting that if the desk is unattended, the buzzer can be rung for assistance; however, I am not keen on disturbing the morning's prayer. After my prior offenses, I figure I am one step away from the Inquisition. On the other hand, I need to be at the dock in less than forty-five minutes, otherwise the *Amorella* will leave without me. One thing I've noticed about Finnish public transportation is that it leaves on time.

I press the buzzer button.

The irritating screech echoes down the hall, penetrating the inner sanctum of the convent. I wait uncomfortably for five minutes, shuffling around, glancing at Finnish newspapers scattered on a low table. No assistance is forthcoming. I press the button again. Nothing happens. Minutes tick away. I begin to calculate how fast I can ride down the canal to the Viking terminal. The answer: not very fast. I wham down on the buzzer a couple of more times, trying a few short bursts followed by a long one—a sort of SOS designed to startle one of the sisters from her religious trance. I briefly consider leaving money and a note on the counter, but am not sure what the room charge is. I have no small bills. Is tipping in a convent a sin? I'm sure shortchanging them is.

A few minutes after eight, one of the sisters silently arrives, takes my 84 euros for two nights and bids me adieu, without recrimination. I hop on the bike and pedal like a madman through damp streets to the bay. Amazingly, the jaws to the *Amorella's* car decks are still open and devouring automobiles. Within minutes, I have stowed the bike on the car deck and find myself wandering the decks of the immense ship. After the austerity of the convent, I am dazzled by the vessel's slot machines, several restaurants, a disco, and a duty-free liquor shop the size of a bowling alley. The Bridgettine nuns would not approve.

The Åland Islands

THE EXPEDITION IS HAPPILY ENSCONCED aboard the *Amorella* for the four-and-a-half-hour voyage that wends through a gauntlet of islands before reaching Mariehamn, the capital of Åland, which is both the name of the island we are approaching and the name of the entire cluster of islands that make up this semiautonomous region of Finland. I admit that part of my motive for coming here is the romantic image I harbor of Åland, inspired by the poetic look of its name, which conjures a magical Brigadoon-like land of eternal spring, singing villagers, and overall pleasantness.

I have officially designated Åland as the Expedition's true starting point because it is the most distant part of Finland from the Barents Sea, though not the southernmost spot on my route. Ekenäs, where I was bombarded by hailstones while trying to eat dinner, holds that distinction, though you wouldn't know it if you looked at a map. It has something to do with the curvature of the planet. The disheartening reality of my first epic week is that I have actually been adding distance to my trek to the Barents Sea. That nonsense will end at Mariehamn, where I will finally point the bike north.

My image of Åland is not entirely an illusion. My research indicates this is the best place in Finland to tour by bike. Interlaced with bike paths, the islands are connected by ferries and causeways. There is a plethora of pleasant campgrounds. It is flatter than the rest of Finland, which, if I recall, was supposed to be flat, too.

Åland is also where Giuseppi Acerbi, an intrepid Italian traveler, first touched Finnish soil during his heroic trip to the Arctic Ocean. Like me,

Acerbi's eventual goal was to reach the "North Sea," but the logistics of pulling that off in 1799 were a bit more complicated. Few Europeans, other than missionaries, had actually been to Lapland, and Finland itself was still a thinly populated province of Sweden. Remarkably, Acerbi arrived in Åland from Sweden via a horse-drawn sled across the frozen Baltic Sea in the frigid winter of 1798. He was impressed by the heartiness of the islanders, whom he called "ingenious, lively, and courteous." He wrote that their thatch-roofed homes were "very neat and convenient, kept in good repair, and well lighted." These attributes, Acerbi claims, allowed the islanders to live unusually long lives. He noted that one woman reportedly lived to be one hundred and twenty years old.

But even paradise had world politics to contend with. Halfway between Sweden and Finland, where it guarded the Gulf of Bothnia, Åland was a strategic prize for the great powers. The Russians were the last occupiers, constructing fortifications in the 1800s, but when Finland gained independence, islanders were not sure whether to hold out for independence themselves or become part of Sweden. Sovereignty was finally settled by the League of Nations, which decreed that the Swedish-speaking islanders form a self-governing, demilitarized province of Finland. These days Åland, which consists of six thousand islands— most are nothing but rocky nubs rising a few feet above the sea—is a prized summer vacation getaway for both Swedes and Finns, who find the island's strategic position on duty-free booze most appealing.

※※ ※※ ※※

The *Amorella* is enormous. Like the ship I saw the day before, I count nine decks, and in addition to the disco, restaurants, and slot machines I spotted earlier, I find a helicopter pad, a full-service sauna, and a shopping mall. Several decks are devoted to cabins for overnight passengers who will continue to Stockholm after the Mariehamn stop. Incessant announcements over the ship's loudspeaker remind passengers that an "up to 25 percent to 50 percent discount" can be had in the ship's liquor store. I spend most of my time dazed by the overstimulation of my surroundings in the "Jack Lives Here" karaoke bar. I'm not sure if Jack—which is probably a reference to the first name of the popular whisky brand—is home today, but after a few morning drinks, the Finns and Swedes are not shy about belting out melancholy folk songs. The singing continues nonstop all the way to Mariehamn, with the only interruptions coming from jarring loudspeaker announcements for the "Scotch whiskey sale—40 percent off for whiskey lovers!" The duty-free deals get better every mile we sail away from the Finnish coast.

By noon the *Amorella* is passing the low-lying islands of outer Åland. The clouds have parted and the sun has emerged again. Ponderous thunderheads still rise in the horizon, but they seem a distant threat. I make one more round on the deck, nearly colliding with a man dressed as a giant mouse. I wonder if his getup is designed to entertain children, or if it's an advertisement for something like Big Mouse Whiskey, "…available at a super discount at the duty-free store!"

I do not see Mariehamn harbor because I am busy reattaching my wagon in the enclosed car deck. When the last car rolls down the ramp, I follow, emerging into brilliant sunshine. I coast down the ramp and within seconds find myself on a path shaded by immense trees and lined with pleasant homes, all of which sport flower boxes sprouting pansies, begonias, lupines, and poppies. Even the pavement of the street is an attractive reddish brown. I find my way to the town center, then head to the bay, where I hope to find the Gröna Uddens Campground. With memories of the mob at the Ekenäs camp still fresh in my mind, I am not about to waste time. I want to stake out my parcel of land before the next ship arrives. After passing a miniature golf course and entering the spacious grounds of the camp, I am surprised to see vast areas of unoccupied open lawn interspersed with trees. Only a few tents dot the grounds. RVs and other motorized vehicles have been banished to another area. I pay my fee, pitch my tent, and contentedly sprawl out on the grassy slope.

My gaze wanders to a sandy beach brimming with families, children playing, and clusters of young bikini-clad sirens splashing in the Baltic.

My last thought before drifting off on a mini-nap ponders the heretical question of why I find it so important to bicycle to the Barents Sea. *Why not just stay here?* At the moment I cannot answer this question because I am drifting off to sleep on the sun-dappled lawn, a gentle breeze blowing away the recent memories of lightning bolts, torrential rain, and hail the size of jawbreakers hurtling from a mean sky. Have I found my Brigadoon?

When I awake, I see not sirens, but a large crow cawing annoyingly, his beak nudging my daypack, searching for my precious supply of gorp. I rise with a start. Our eyes meet momentarily. He makes another caw that sounds suspiciously like "Get up, you bum!" The crow flies off, and I remember that I promised to fly the Expedition pennant when I got to Åland.

My sister Maria had handmade a triangular pennant for me, featuring the white outline of a reindeer and the inscription "Åland—Arctic" on a blue background. The flag already has weathered its own travail. Several days after Maria shipped it to Seattle, I received a mysterious rumpled package along with a letter from the manager of the postal service's regional bulk-mail facility. He wrote that the original box had been obliterated by another that had held a vat of honey. The vat had leaked, which the manager took pains to inform me had not been packed in accordance with postal regulations. The pennant ended up coated in honey, so the Postal Service had it cleaned, repackaged, and sent on its way to me. This explained the sweet aroma that wafted from the package when I ripped it open back home.

Now unpacking a wooden dowel I had brought from home, I slide it into the sleeve of the flag and plant it in front of the tent. The Expedition, with a faint smell of honey sweetly lingering in the air, is now officially under way. It didn't occur to me until much later that the honey-infused pennant might make an excellent bear and wasp attractant. But those debacles lay many weeks ahead. Today, the fragrance merely adds to the celebratory air of the moment.

But I have lounged around enough. Before I am tempted by more bikini-clad sirens, I decide it is time to explore Åland. I ride back into town, through a pedestrian mall bustling with small shops, cafés, and an open-air market. Once clear of Mariehamn, I connect with a bike path that leads to the village of Gottby in the middle of Åland. The path merges onto a busy causeway, and for a few moments I have anxious flashbacks of a week ago when I left Helsinki. But soon I shunt onto a quiet country road that winds among farms and patches of forest.

Gottby is not exactly a metropolis, just a few houses and a fire station. An old wooden windmill sits idly in a nearby field, yellow with blooming rapeseed. At the town's crossroads stands an enormous midsummer night's pole elaborately draped with streamers and flower bouquets. Decorating the pole, which is usually left to stand year round in most Finnish communities, is a tradition to celebrate the onset of summer. Near the top of the pole, perhaps thirty feet off the ground, four wooden sailboats representing the directions of the compass turn slowly in the afternoon breeze.

\/\/\/   \/\/\/   \/\/\/

In the morning, I am packed and back on the road early. For the first time, the official Riding with Reindeer Expedition banner flutters from the dowel clamped awkwardly to the rear of the wagon. I ride north on a pleasant country road that winds lazily past little villages with bright yellow, wood-framed houses nestled among big shade trees and freshly mowed lawns. Beyond are farms with neatly cultivated fields and immaculate outbuildings. Bluebells, cow parsnip, and yarrow are all in bloom beside the road. For a half-mile, I keep pace, though at a safe distance, behind an ancient pickup truck with Model A tires hauling a load of beehives. Thankfully the bees remain in the hives and leave the wildflowers next to me—as well as my pennant—alone.

The road continues past fields with hay stacked around long poles that resemble toothpicks stuck into a pile of shredded wheat. It then skirts Lumpara Bay, with portions of its shimmering waters darkened by the shadows of swiftly moving clouds. The breeze at my back makes pedaling almost effortless. From the opposite direction, I pass other cross-country cyclists laden with panniers, sleeping bags, and tents. Exchanging "ehs" and "hellos," we are all smiles on this glorious morning.

This overall pleasantness of Åland, the essence of which Acerbi reported back in 1798, is one of the hard-to-explain reasons why I have chosen to embark on this journey. One purpose, I think—and one tends to do a lot of thinking on these trips—is to experience moments of pure bliss like this. The feeling is not easy to describe because you have to be here, right now, in this moment to understand why days of sodden misery are worth a few golden moments of pure joy—moments I will remember fondly forever. These moments are intensified when traveling alone, just as the moments of despair and isolation are also amplified. I revel in the good moment now, hoping to ward off the moments of despair that are inevitable on such a journey.

The Expedition's objective for the day is to continue north to the village of Godby, then turn west and cross a bridge to the island of Sund. There I plan to explore the remains of the old Russian fortress called Bomarsund, which may contain the last hope of confirming the origins of my mysterious great-grandmother. It is a tenuous, almost hopelessly thin thread, but I cling to it.

I sail past Godby and make my turn, but then the road does something I do not expect. I rapidly shift into my lowest gear. How has a hill manifested itself in the Åland Islands, touted as one of the flattest places in Finland? This is no small hill. Soon, I am soaked in perspiration, struggling to haul my load up this mountain that appeared from nowhere. I bitterly remember the last thing I read about the Ålands in my Lonely Planet guidebook: "Cycling is a great way to tour these flat, rural islands." The golden moments of morning bliss are gone. I grunt on.

I reach the summit, which is dominated by an observation tower. A sign informs me that I have ascended the highest hill in the Åland archipelago. This was not in the plan, but as long as I'm here I pay $2 to ascend the steps to the top of the tower. The view is stunning. Westward I see the causeway I'll cross to reach my destination, Sund. In all other directions, I spy forested islands and water dotted with sailing boats. Way off in the Gulf of Bothnia, I spot a giant "duty-free" passenger ship steaming toward Mariehamn.

After crossing onto Sund, I round a bend and see the massive stone walls of a fourteenth-century castle. This is Kastelholms. Its brooding presence amid the fairy tale-like setting I've been pedaling through is a reminder that not all was peaches and cream in the land of Sund. Here, in 1571, Eric XIV—the same insane husband of the gorgeous Catherine Månsdotter, whose crypt the Expedition encountered in Turku—spent three months imprisoned in a "small, darkish room" as part of a multi-year tour of Swedish dungeons arranged by his half-brother John, who had ascended to the throne.

While clambering up and down the castle fortifications, I learn that Eric's imprisonment wasn't the only dark mark in Åland history. In 1666, the region was aflame in a full-fledged witch hunt. The incident began when a beggar woman, Karin Persdotter, was accused of stealing rye. Although Persdotter said the rye had been stolen by others, she was flattered by all the attention and let it slip that the devil had visited her three times, bestowing her with the power to cure disease but also to wreak havoc with the local fishing industry. Local authorities did not find these stories charming. She used her confession to take revenge on everyone who had treated her badly. This eventually led to six more island women being accused of witchcraft. They, along with Persdotter, were burned at the stake. Their trials were not exactly models of impartial jurisprudence. The chief witch hunter, Bryniel Kjellinius, vicar of the Sund parish, would often lapse into long discourses citing noted ecclesiastical works in German or Latin, languages that none of the accused, nor anyone else in the court, understood.[22]

By the time I emerge from the castle, the sun has disappeared. The once scuttling clouds have fused into a dense cloak of gray. I now know enough about Finland's unsettled summer weather not to linger, even though I am momentarily distracted by what appears to be a reenactment of either a medieval jousting tournament or a public hanging in a field next to the castle. Horseback riders dressed in medieval garb and gripping lances are skewering a disturbingly lifelike dummy, hanging from a scaffold by a rope around its neck.

Within an hour I reach the crumbling stone fortifications of Bomarsund. Adjacent is a campground, along with the requisite min-iature golf course that I've started to notice is the typical accessory to Finnish campgrounds. It is only midafternoon. I still have plenty of energy, but with the clouds thickening and the wind increasing, I think it best to pitch camp while it's still dry. The acres of lawn that comprise the Puttes Campground are almost deserted except for a few stray motorized campers and one or two tents. I am amazed at how quickly I have left the vacationing hordes behind.

Before I wander off to explore the area, the Expedition needs to make some vital decisions. In the last twenty-four hours, I have hatched a vague plan to circumnavigate the islands, which would mean using a bike ferry to get to Lumpo Island in the south, then island-hop through the southern archipelago back to the mainland at Galtby, southeast of Turku. From there I would begin anew my long trek north to the Arctic. There is only one problem with this plan.

"The bike ferry doesn't operate anymore," says the woman in charge of the campground. "You must call the man, and maybe he will come with his boat and take you to Lumpo."

I am not sure who "the man" is, but I take the scrap of paper with the phone number the attendant has scribbled on it.

I bike past the ruined fort to where the road ends at a ferry land-ing serviced by a small car barge that connects with neighboring Värdö Island. But there is no sign of *any* type of boat service, let alone a bike ferry, to Lumpo. As I ponder the situation, the heavens open up with a vengeance. I backtrack through the downpour and find a secondary road that leads to another ferry crossing, but it looks like it hasn't been used since the last witch trial. A handwritten sign nailed to a post confirms that the only service to Lumpo is by a "BAT Ferry." I assume the acronym is Swedish for bike ferry or perhaps I have discovered a way to the secret cave of Batman and Robin. The same phone number the attendant gave me is scrawled on the bottom of the note. I'll call later.

I start back to camp but am distracted by a sign pointing down a dirt road that says it leads to the old Bomarsund Cemetery. I start down the road, wondering if by chance any of my great-grandmother's family's remains lay at the end. The Russians who came here after 1809 to garrison the fort were a mixed lot: Russian Orthodox, Jewish, and Muslim. I know that I am grasping at straws, but when I see the Star of David on the sign, indicating a Jewish cemetery, I am filled with hope. Perhaps my great-grandmother was the daughter of a soldier who manned the fort and later moved to Helsinki. *It's worth a shot to check it out*, I think.

I follow the dirt road for about a mile through dense forest before I come to a clearing and then continue on a trail leading to some decaying gravestones overgrown with grass and shrubs. After propping the bike against a tree and investigating a few of the graves—they are Russian Orthodox—the downpour resumes. I huddle under a tree, watching rivulets of muddy water course down the red-soiled road. I move on, and for the next hour I dodge cloudbursts, bike down muddy roads, and hike through sodden underbrush. I cannot find the Jewish graves. The rain is relentless. With the rain threatening to turn the road into a quagmire, I pedal slowly back to the main highway, then retreat into my tent.

I tried, Masha, but I cannot find any trace of you. I do not know what else to do. Briefly, I am overcome by a feeling of helplessness, then frustration because I can usually solve mysteries. But I also know that I tried my best: pedaling to this isolated island's rain-drenched forest in hopes of discovering something about my ancestors. *In the end, it really doesn't matter,* I tell myself. *I exist, my father exists, my grandmother existed, and therefore Masha must have existed.* I now absorb that logic as an article of faith and silently declare an end to my search. Bomarsund will keep its secret.

With the cell phone I carry for just such situations, I call the number for the bicycle ferry, but there's no answer. Salvos of rain slam into the tent. The wind rips through the trees. During a pause in the storm, I escape my tent prison to explore what remains of the fortifications, a symbol of the Russian Empire's power in the region. With Åland and Finland firmly under control after 1809, the Russians began constructing these massive stone walls. Soon the area bustled with not only soldiers but also merchants, craftsmen, and bureaucrats. Forty-five years later, the fortress was still only a quarter complete when twenty-five British and French ships sailed up the narrow passage separating Sund from Värdö and pulverized it.[23] After two days, the Russians had had enough. They surrendered. The fortress was largely demolished, thus beginning Åland's era as a demilitarized zone.

I have had enough, too, of getting drenched while wandering among the ruins. I take refuge in a pleasant café near the miniature golf course. I linger for hours over a bacon cheeseburger and Karjala beer before riding back through the rain to my soggy camp.

ᴡᴡ   ᴡᴡ   ᴡᴡ

In the morning, I awake to the wailing of a gaggle of boisterous gulls that are bickering outside the tent. The screaming birds seem fixated on pecking through the rain fly. I take this as my cue to get up. I shoo the birds away, but am disheartened by the unrelenting grayness of the morning. At least the wind has died down. Although I am not normally prone to superstition, I have taken the absence of the bike ferry and my unanswered call as an omen. I decide to abandon the idea of trying to get to Lumpo, then circumnavigating the islands. The Expedition, I conclude, must continue forward. I'm not sure to where, but there will be no retreat to Mariehamn. If I am interpreting the Swedish ferry schedule correctly, it appears I could continue hopping between islands via the northern archipelago, perhaps even reaching the mainland by late afternoon.

Under brooding skies, I quickly pack and head down the same road I scouted yesterday. At the landing, I wait with a car and a few other cyclists as a small barge churns its way toward us. Here, I discover another pleasant surprise to biking in the Ålands: the ferries are free for bike riders. Good news for the Expedition budget. I roll the bike on board, and we make the crossing in five minutes.

There is little traffic on Värdö, which is mostly flat with scattered farms throughout. No one stirs as I roll through the quaint village of Vargata, the only settlement on the island. On the far side of town, I fall in behind a lumbering tractor hauling a shed with a wooden boat protruding from it. Passing this contraption takes some effort because for the first time, I encounter stiff headwinds. On a low ridge, giant turbine-style windmills churn in the breeze.

I arrive at the ferry landing at Hummelvik on the east end of Värdö with forty-five minutes to spare. There I am joined by other cyclists. Among them is a Finnish family out for a week-long tour. The father is pulling an enormous wagon, while the wife rides a bike laden with panniers. The two young children have small panniers, but of course their parents are bearing most of the load.

The *Alfägeln* will sail the 30 miles to the Brändö region, part of the Åland northern archipelago, with several stops along the way. As it approaches us, the ship doesn't look like much, but when it docks I see that it sports two decks and a café. I cannot make out the directions issued to the bike riders by the ferry crew, but I take my cue from the family of four and follow them onto the boat. *I hope they are going to Brändö.* As the ship pulls away and churns into the Gulf of Bothnia, a dark squall obliterates the shore with a torrential downpour.

For the next two hours, the boat crosses open water to the islands of Enklinge, Kumlinge, and Lappo. After Lappo, the clouds part and the sun emerges. Passengers, who had been huddling in the small café, filter onto the open deck like sleepy bears emerging from their winter dens. By the time we reach Torsholma, the first island in the Brändö municipality, the day has turned brilliant.

Brändö consists of more than a thousand islands, but has a population of only 561. The main road connects the villages of Torsholma, Björnholma, and Längö via a series of causeways and bridges. Halfway across the 15-mile length of Brändö, I pull off the road, climb a small hill where a picnic table is conveniently perched on the summit, and enjoy my cheese, salami, and crackers. The vegetation indicates that Brändö gets less rain than the other islands. The soil is rockier. Pines are replaced by ash and elm with a liberal sprinkling of juniper bushes. Near the edges of ponds grow rushes and cattails. My afternoon ride, pushed by a tailwind, skirts bays where the hoops of fish farms float and eider ducks swim in silent convoys.

Cyclists board the MS Viggens.

By midafternoon I reach the landing at Längö where the MS *Viggens*, its nose open, is ready to load cars and bikes. The *Viggens* takes me away from the Åland archipelago to Osnäs, a large island close to the southwestern Finnish coast. One more barge ride across a strait lands me in Kustavi, the most substantial town I've seen since Mariehamn. Kustavi is also on an island, but it is linked to mainland Finland by a bridge.

A helpful young woman at the town information center tells me the campground indicated on my map no longer exists, further damaging the credibility of the map's little tent symbols. However, she tells me a new campground has opened three miles to the south, along a country road.

I follow her directions and find Loma Palvelut, which is a big grassy field with a log house containing a bathroom and cooking facilities. I have most of the acres of grass to myself, though for the sake of variety I pitch my tent near a pond, which is presided over by a large, white goose that honks out instructions as I set up camp. I like the goose's attention to detail and briefly consider recruiting her for the trip.

I use the afternoon sunshine to dry my clothes and carefully lay out the soggy pages of my day notebook (used for quick notations and observations) and passport, which were packed in the front carrier for easy access. In general, the wagon has kept my extra clothes, provisions, journal, and maps dry. Sprawled on the sun-splashed grass, I think this is the perfect end to a day that began with quarrelsome gulls and threatening skies. I congratulate the Expedition team for a job well done; we've covered 75 miles by sea and 32 by land—all by correctly reading the Swedish ferry schedule and connecting seamlessly with four ferries. I thank the goose for not being a quarrelsome seagull. Not a bad day at all.

There is just one problem with this brilliantly executed day. My first plan had called for me to circle the Åland Islands in exactly the opposite direction. I was supposed to land at Galtby, located on a peninsula east of Turku. I consult the map and see that I am now at least 100 miles off course, west of Turku in another part of Finland that I hadn't planned to cycle through and is barely described in my guidebook. I am off my lonely planet and into the unknown.

Off the Planet

THE THRILL OF SNAGGING ALL THOSE FERRIES and making my way through the entire northern Åland archipelago in one day has faded in the bright light of early morning, its brassiness accented by the incessant honking of the resident goose. There is no escaping the fact that I am roughly 100 miles from where I had planned to be. I call an emergency Expedition team meeting to discuss how we intend to get back on course.

Perhaps you are wondering who exactly is on this team besides the narrator? If you have not suspected this already, I have taken the liberty of personifying certain key inanimate objects that have accompanied me so far on my epic. Truly, a human companion would have been preferable, but friends and acquaintances politely declined or failed to volunteer when the trip was in its planning phase. "Are you nuts?" "Why are you doing this?" and "Where is Finland?" were the common responses to my call for others to share in my adventure.

My failure to recruit a sidekick runs contrary to epic lore. Huck Finn had Tom. Lewis had Clark, as well as a boatful of men and, later, a beautiful Indian maiden. Don Quixote had Sancho Panza. The late British travel writer Eric Newby had his wife, Wanda, who threatened to leave him numerous times during a dubious epic down the Ganges River in the 1960s, chronicled in his travelogue *Slowly Down the Ganges*.

Lacking another human being, my situation is more like Tom Hanks's character in *Castaway*, where Hanks, the lone survivor of a plane crash, winds up on a deserted island. Going mad from loneliness, he draws a smile (in his own blood) on a Wilson volleyball and adopts it as his constant companion "Wilson." My "Wilsons" are the bike, known as "Friday," and the wagon, known as "Wagon"—both full-fledged members of the Riding with Reindeer Expedition. Due to their inability to speak, they serve as sounding boards during conclaves such as this or on long stretches where I encounter few real people. Hey, I had to do something to keep from going bonkers.

"Here's the situation," I explain to the team, map spread on the grass. "We are here, near Kustavi. To get to the Ox Road, we need to go back to Turku."

The Ox Road is another one of Finland's historic roads that has been transformed into a national bike route. Starting in Turku, the road passes through the countryside of south-central Finland and ends in Hämeenlinna, about a two-day ride, presumably longer if towed by an ox. The problem now is that it will take me an entire extra day just to get back to Turku.

I can tell that Friday is not anxious to return to the convent, the scene of the unpleasantness with the nuns and the mysterious flat tire. The wagon just sits there like a big lump. It will go where I lead. The goose, who has invited herself to this confab, has decided to eat the map for breakfast.

"Hey!" I yell, shooing it away. This elicits more honks and a raised wing, but the goose sees that I mean business and retreats behind the wagon to munch on grass.

"As I was saying," I continue, pointing to a big blue spot in the map. "We can head northeast toward this giant lake, Pyhäjärvi. I think it's about 60 miles from here. According to the map, there are two campgrounds on the eastern shore. I say if the weather remains good when we get to the town of Pyhe, where the road splits—one heading south to Turku, the other north to Pyhäjärvi—then we go for the lake. If it's crummy, we ride to Turku and regroup. Are we okay on this?"

Friday is in. The wagon is off in its own little wagon world. The goose waddles off toward a camper trailer where a family has just laid out breakfast on a folding table.

"Great, let's get going."

The morning is brilliant, with mottled sun slanting in between the pines and alders. At Kustavi, I turn onto Highway 192 and begin making my way through the last series of islands, all connected by bridges, before reaching mainland Finland. Heading in the opposite direction are other cyclists, some waving, others with their noses to the handlebars, pumping hard, sleeping bags and tents strapped to the back racks of their bikes. Shortly after I pass the bridge connecting with Mussalo Island, an old man wearing bright pink shorts and churning on a one-speed overtakes me. Seeing the banner he looks again, then turns and shows me a big toothless grin. He gives me the thumbs-up, and roars something that I can only interpret as "You go guy!" The banner says it all: I am finally pointed toward the Arctic.

Once I reach the mainland, the forest thins, the hills end, and I roll onto a broad plain of tilled fields brimming with peas, barley, wheat, and hay. The traffic is heavier, too. I cling to the narrow shoulder, not daring to take my eyes off the road for more than a second at a time.

But I am in good spirits and making steady progress. The weather is holding. Unsettled conditions do not appear imminent. When I reach Pyhe, I do not hesitate. I turn north on Road 1951, a quiet country lane that snakes its way among farms and dairies. By noon, I have already booked 30 miles and find myself sprawled on the lawn of the Mynämäki fire station trying to make the best of my usual lunch fare, which was once novel in its simplicity and routine, but has now become mundane. I consult the Lonely Planet, but this is useless. Neither Mynämäki, nor any other place I will pedal through in the next couple of days, is in the book. I am off the planet, in a region called Ostrobothnia.

Under way again, I somehow manage to miss a turn and wind up at a crossroads. My compass points north, but the sign tells me the road I think I should take leads to Turku, which is south, and the opposite direction I want. I retreat to Mynämäki, stop in a residential area, and study the map, careful this time not to set it on fire with the magnifying glass. Across the street, a door slams and a man in sweatpants runs out of his house toward me. He doesn't speak a word of English, but through sign language and my extremely limited Finnish he manages to convey that I should continue to backtrack to the *kirko* (church), then turn right. This, he tells me, will get me on the road to Yläne, a few miles from the southern tip of Lake Pyhäjärvi. I thank my helper and follow his instructions, noting from the map's detail that I should pass a canal and then a village called Raimela. Both landmarks appear, confirming that I am on Road 2020, heading north into a thinly populated region. Yläne is 37 miles away.

The farms diminish in size, the clearings now sharing equal time with the forest. There is no traffic. A tailwind pushes me happily along. Near a roadside pullout, a red fox darts from the brush and sprints across the road to a clump of shrubs. Quietly, I pedal over to investigate. The fox probably is used to cars whizzing past. He has no idea that I am lingering nearby. I find him sitting among some weeds. He appears to smile as I snap pictures. Foxes are not that uncommon in rural Finland, where they are unwelcome guests at henhouses. Another bane of the Finnish farmer is the lynx, whose territory is expanding from the isolated forests of Karelia to more-populated areas of central and southern Finland.

I rest on top of a sunny knob overlooking a small clearing with a red barn, painted the familiar reddish brown with white trim. From my grass bed among the red columbine and purple fireweed, I continue to puzzle over the bizarre readings of my compass. In the last few miles, I watched the compass intently and saw it whirl crazily, the needle spinning in the exact opposite direction from where it had pointed a few moments earlier. I desperately need the compass because my inner sense of direction is still discombobulated. I cannot yet fully adjust to the fact that here the sun rises in the northeast, makes a near circle around the sky, then settles in the northwest, not far from where it rose. And that only applies when the sun shines. In the flat light of a cloudy day, I am clueless about directions. Though the maps are useful, I need a second navigational device to confirm that I am cycling in the correct direction.

Before leaving Turku I had sent an urgent e-mail to a friend in Seattle asking if he thought the problem was due to the discrepancy between magnetic and true north, a correction that geographers refer to as "the declination." Since I was so far north already, was the discrepancy playing havoc with the instrument? He had soundly disproved my theory.

Suddenly I have a eureka moment as I stuff the map back into its clear plastic sleeve mounted atop the front carrier. I keep the compass in the sleeve too, so I can see it while riding. The carrier snaps onto the top of the front handlebar bag with the assistance of magnetized buttons. The compass, coincidently, is usually positioned above one of the buttons. *Is the magnetic field from the button causing the compass to gyrate crazily?* I speculate. I pull the compass out of the sleeve, walk a few steps, and take a bearing. The needle points north by northeast, exactly where it should. It holds steady. I walk back to the carrier and hold it above the magnetized button. The needle flips to a southern direction. Problem solved.

By five in the evening, I pass the old stone church at Yläne, turn onto Highway 204, and head north to the Loma-Säkylä Holiday Camp, perched on the southeast shore of Pyhäjärvi. Holiday camps are distinctly European-flavored resorts designed mostly for family vacationers who are traveling with camper vans, recreational vehicles, and trailers. The camps might include cabins or even a small hotel. In Finland, they include a miniature golf course, play area for children, trampoline, ping-pong table, sauna, a café, and usually a few tent sites.

With the lake shimmering in the afternoon light and a faint breeze rustling the pines, Loma Säkylä looks like it has potential to be a fine place to spend my evening. The trouble is, I still have lots of energy. I've cycled a little over 60 miles, but I feel like I can grab another 10 to shorten tomorrow's triumphant 65-mile ride to Tampere, Finland's third-largest city and my next major layover.

But amid my feelings of friskiness, I detect a faint whisper of caution. In the back of my mind I recall the advice of Fred Matheny, author of the *Complete Book of Road Bike Training* and one of the gods of cross-country cycling. I had been lucky to meet Matheny during a week of organized cross-country bike training in the desert south of Tucson the previous winter. Matheny's advice was aimed specifically at those of us over fifty.

"Do not overreach," he told me. "When you reach your goal, stop and rest even if you feel like continuing. Over a long haul, you will need to conserve your strength."

Now five months later, I remember the sage's advice. I also remember vowing to stick to my 50-miles-a-day limit and rest every third or fourth day. But that was then and this is now.

This afternoon the sun shines. My muscles and ego are yearning for more. The map tells me another campground lies at the north end of the lake past the town of Säkylä. I've already blown 10 miles past my 50-mile limit. I feel good. I feel strong. I feel like Superman. What's another 13 miles?

I shoot out of Loma-Säkylä and merge back onto the main road. As I pedal a few miles through forest, the shimmering waters of the endless lake on my left, a nagging doubt enters what had been a clear mind. *What if the map has led me astray again? What if there is no campground?* I try to silence the doubts that have suddenly awoken in my consciousness. *Nonsense,* retorts the part of me that egged me on in the first place. *Look at that lake! Who wouldn't build another campground on such a beautiful body of water?*

A little after six, I reach Säkylä, a pleasant village that in a parallel universe could easily pass for a modern American town next to a lake with a lot of recreational potential. But as I turn off the main highway and venture into its center, I am a little concerned that I have not seen the usual sign indicating a campground. In my short time in Finland, I have come to rely on these signs as the gold standard. When the Finnish Highway Department says something is down the road, it most certainly is. As I roll into town, I hope to see such a sign. *Or, is this the one place where the sign makers committed an oversight?* One thing I am certain of: the combustion of energy that propelled me this extra 13 miles has consumed itself. I am ready to rest.

I cycle down the road, then stop and study every millimeter of the map. The campground should be here. Did I pass it? I don't see a sign—only forest and homes hugging the shore. I pedal back and forth along the road, but there is no sign, no campground, no nothing.

Back in town, I wheel up to three sullen teenagers sitting on a park bench, looking as if they are up to no good; that is, if being up to no good is even possible in Finland. It's Saturday night, and it appears there is not a lot for teenagers to do in Säkylä. They sport black T-shirts with various Gothic inscriptions that in another era would have gotten them burned at the stake. When they see me heading their direction, they stop talking.

"Eh," I say, deploying most of my Finnish in one grunt. I then ask if anyone speaks English.

Judging from the lack of response, my conclusion is no, that somehow the Säkylä school system has failed these three. On the other hand, when was the last time a swarthy guy on a folding bike rolled up on Saturday night and said hello? They stare at me as if I have just landed from Mars. By now I am having a linguistic panic attack because even though I have studied the word for "campground" and can now count to two on a good day, I seem to have forgotten everything except the words for "soup" and "guts," which are not particularly useful here.

"Camping?" I say to the biggest boy, then make an inverted "V" with my hands and point down the road to the north. For the record, the Finnish word for campground—*leirintäaluetta*—bears no resemblance to its English equivalent. I later realize that if they understood me at all, they thought I was asking where the nearest comb (*kampa*) was or possibly hairdresser (*kampamo*).

"This strange man wants a comb," I imagine the larger boy telling the girl next to him.

"No," she says. "I think he says he needs to get to a hairdresser."

I smile and point up the road, again saying the word "camp."

They smile and nod their heads yes.

"*Kittos*," I say, as I cycle off. I pass a hairdresser's salon, closed, then ride out of town along a pleasant forested path. There is no campground. By now I have lingered long enough. I am too tired to ride back to the holiday camp. The map, whose credibility regarding places to stay is now at an all-time low, indicates there is a hotel a few miles ahead. I have no choice but to press on.

When I pull up to a beautiful old farmstead converted into a fancy inn, I can see that this might not work. In front of the main building, an old two-story, wood-framed structure, young men in tuxedos and women in formal dresses are posing for pictures. Another woman, in a bridal gown, whisks by with a photographer in tow. More guests arrive in sleek cars—a fair number of Mercedes and Saabs. Strangely, no one seems to notice or pay any attention to me as I lean the bike against a bush, stumble up to the front door, and slink into the lobby where guests mill about, drinking from champagne flutes and nibbling from platters of hors d'oeuvres served by a waitress in a black dress and white apron. I am sorely tempted to grab what appears to be goose pâté on a cracker and make a dash for it. I have not eaten since noon.

But I resist this temptation. Instead, I wander to the reception table, feeling very out of place in my cycling shorts and bright orange cycling jersey depicting little green cacti sprinkled around advertisements for the *Pac Tour Training Camp*. More guests arrive, and I continue to be amazed that no one, except perhaps the woman that looks like someone's troublesome aunt, has looked in my direction and screamed. But this doesn't happen, as I shift nervously about, searching among the pile of brochures on the reception table for a rate card.

While snooping around, I nearly collide with a tipsy man bearing a striking resemblance to the Italian actor Marcello Mastroianni. He smiles at me, shakes my hand, tells me in English that he loves my outfit, then moves on to greet someone else. I feel like I have somehow become entangled in some weird Fellini film, improbably set in Finland.

As much as I would enjoy a wedding, particularly a wedding feast, it is apparent that the place is booked. I wend my way back through the crowd, out the door, and to my bike. As I pull away, I notice the man who had shook my hand waving good-bye.

Wearily, I bike up a hill, over railroad tracks, and toward a building that looks like it might be an inn or hostel. Fortunately, the sign is translated into English. The building is a mental hospital.

I bike on, unsure of when this day will end. I wobble into the town of Eura, where a festival is being held in the parking lot of a shopping center. Music wafts from a series of tents.

By now I am famished and out of ideas about where I might spend the night. Across the street from the festival tents sits a lonely Grilli stand—a Finnish food kiosk— where a plump, smiling woman is dishing out some kind of food into a paper napkin for a lone customer. The man turns to watch me pull up on the bike. He greets me as if I am a regular. I think he tells me either that the food is good or the local hairdresser is closed for the evening. The menu is posted on a board. I have no idea what she's selling so I point to *ligburgeri* and a Coke™. The woman nods, then asks me a series of questions, all of which I nod yes to. I hope the questions have to do with what I want on my *ligburgeri* and not whether I just escaped from the local mental hospital.

A pita filled with meat, a *ligburgeri* turns out to be quite tasty. I recommend it with grilled onions.

Having exhausted the area's single hotel option, I turn a skeptical eye to the map. On the west side of the lake, about five miles from where I lap up the remainder of my *ligburgeri*, the map shows the symbol of a tent: my last hope, a place called Kiperin Leirintä. I heave myself onto the bike, ride down a hill, then turn onto Highway 43, which parallels the lake heading south.

Twenty minutes later I see a sign pointing to a road that heads down to the lake. As I approach, I see that the words Kiperin Leirintä have been blanked out, though I can still see them under the fresh green paint. Is this some sort of trick? Are the campgrounds being systematically wiped out as I approach? I turn down the road anyway. Where else am I going to go? I coast down a steep hill, thinking I will never make it back up given my state of exhaustion. It is nearly nine o'clock when I pull into the abandoned parking lot of a ghost campground.

I have been riding nearly thirteen hours. I have overreached and am paying big time for my mistake. Enough, already. I get off the bike to investigate, thinking I can just pitch my tent here. I wander around a boarded-up wooden building that once, not long ago, was a restaurant. The menu board still offers beer and *ligburgeri*, among other items. Plastic chairs are stacked in a corner and most of the kitchen equipment is still in place. It is as if a neutron bomb was dropped on the place, wiping out the people but leaving the fixtures.

Near the entrance to what was once the reception area sits an old couple, a kind of Finnish version of Ma and Pa Kettle. We exchange "ehs" and then I motion to the campground, asking in English what happened. The couple looks at me and my bike with a degree of thoughtfulness, if not pity. A hundred feet away, a group of boys who were recently swimming in the lake are silhouetted against the late afternoon sun, which is now dipping dangerously to the northwest. It is a perfect place to linger and contemplate the nature of all things.

Unfortunately, the pastoral beauty is not registering high on my consciousness at the moment. My legs feel like cement blocks, my butt is on fire, and my back aches. The only question that lingers momentarily in my mind is what catastrophe has befallen the campgrounds of Pyhäjärvi.

The old man and woman do not speak English, but they surely know what I seek. I have traveled long enough and in enough places to know that sometimes you don't need a translation.

"Do you think I can camp here?"

"No."

I wander around the grounds, looking for a nook or cranny out of sight of the old couple who are perhaps the caretakers. I search for a place where I can pitch my tent, sight unseen. But I find nothing that works. And it's clear that the two old folks aren't going to leave anytime soon.

I have only one option left. On the access road from the main highway, I passed through a large tract of forest. That will be my home. It is time to invoke the Finnish doctrine of "Everyman's Right." To an

American who risks getting shot if he trespasses on private land, this common law dating back to medieval times is truly remarkable. The modern version allows anyone to camp on private forest property providing that you act responsibly, set up a reasonable distance away from the owner's house—as in, out of sight—and do not light a fire.

I painfully make my way up the road and then turn right onto a dirt road that winds through the forest. I bike a few hundred feet, then decide to follow a faint path through the woods. But the wagon quickly gets stuck among rocks and holes covered by a carpet of moss on the forest floor. I drag the bike back to the road, looking for another way to disappear. I soon find another rough path, one that perhaps serves as a snowmobile trail in the winter, and push the bike and wagon over a bluff deeper into the forest. I come to the rusting metal skeleton of an old truck resting beside a granite boulder and a few old beer cans. For a moment, I wonder if this is a local drinking hideaway for Eura's youth, this being Saturday night. On the other hand, I am so far away from anything, there are probably more convenient hideouts closer to town.

I search the area for a flat place to unroll the tent when I notice that the troublesome bushes I've been pushing the bike through are festooned with huckleberries. In the golden light slanting in through the pines, I see an endless berry paradise. *Dessert!* I fall to my hands and knees. Like a hungry bear, I greedily pluck the succulent fruit and stuff them into my mouth. I cannot believe my luck. The berries are perfectly ripe, the juice bursting with flavor. If only I had some ice cream or a Belgian waffle. I decide that "Everyman's Right" is the greatest law ever created!

The euphoria from my discovery is short-lived. A few minutes after pouncing on my first berry, I detect a subtle hum. At first I think it's the distant buzz of traffic, but as I single-mindedly harvest berries, the hum grows louder. I look up and am horrified to see that I am slowly being enveloped in a dense cloud of mosquitoes. My rustling of the bushes seems to have aroused a billion of them from a long slumber. Before I can mount a plausible defense they dive-bomb into my eyes, attack my ears, and cling to my jersey. I swat and windmill. I jump up and race back to the bike. In a panic, I hastily unfold the tent and pitch it before I become one big festering bite. I frantically search for my mosquito hat, but can't find it, and dive into the tent. In my haste to close the mosquito fly, I jam the zipper. The buggers buzz in for a fresh attack. I duct tape myself into the tent and spend the next twenty minutes ridding its interior of the pests.

The last rays of the sun fade through the woods, and with the dying light the buzz ebbs. Before diving into the tent, I had noted from the odometer that I had logged 83.6 miles today, a personal record while carrying a load. Believe me, it's a record I did not want to set.

I wiggle into my sleeping bag, my body caked in sweat and dead mosquito parts. This is not a pleasant experience—in fact, it's the polar opposite of that effervescent giddiness I felt in Åland. What could have possessed me to leave my comfortable house in Seattle, equipped with not one, but two, bathrooms with showers, for this misery? The aches from overused muscles only now fully manifest themselves. My calves seize with cramps. Too tired to eat, I down a couple of aspirin and vow to check into a hotel tomorrow, no matter the cost, and rest properly.

As darkness settles over the forest, I am startled by a shriek from either the world's largest owl or a pterodactyl. I listen carefully, wondering if the thing is heading my way, but silence ensues. I promise my battered and stressed fifty-two-year-old body that I shall never overreach again.

The author camps in a forest near Lake Pyhäjärvi in Ostrobothnia.

A Miserable Day

IN THE GLOOM OF NIGHT, I find myself crammed inside my small tent with a woman of unknown origins and two large dogs. In the dream, I never see the woman's face, only her outline; the only other sense I have of her is the feel of her back. The dogs, both mixed breeds with seemingly a lot of Labrador retriever and maybe some Irish setter, press against me. I feel claustrophobic and struggle to move them off me but can't seem to make headway. I need fresh air, but I cannot get the tent's rainfly open; it's sealed tightly with the duct tape I used to keep out the mosquitoes. The mystery woman and I discuss the need to get out of the tent before dawn, to make an early start and leave this place.

In the next sequence, dawn arrives and I am sitting on the big rock outside the tent. Puttering up the nearby path is a tiny car. A man in a ranger outfit steps out and approaches. In one hand he holds a pad, looking like a meter maid ready to write a citation.

"You don't have a permit," he tells me.

My heart sinks and anxiety grips my stomach. I tell him about the disappearing campgrounds, the wedding at the hotel, and the attack of the mosquitoes.

"What about Everyman's Right?" I blurt out.

"I'm sorry," he says. "This is a special forest."

He begins to write a citation. I am mortified. I have broken the law, probably the first criminal act recorded in Finland this year. I have disgraced the Expedition, sullied the epic, and now face certain deportation.

I awake with a start, relieved that the dream dogs are not piled on top of me, though less pleased that my mystical tent mate has vaporized. I stretch my legs and can tell from their stiffness that I have not yet come close to paying the price for allowing my ego to persuade me to bike a few more miles yesterday. I fumble with the little pouch that holds my watch. It's six a.m.

Then I hear the sound, the unmistakable patter on the rainfly. *No, it can't be. It was perfectly clear when I tucked in last night. Could those be pine needles falling on the tent, masquerading as raindrops?* In the filtered light of the tent's interior, I cannot tell if it's sunny or cloudy outside. The patter intensifies. I rip off the duct tape and stick my head outside. The golden hues of the forest that shimmered so magically last evening have been replaced by a somber gray. It's the kind of day where you want to roll over, go back to sleep, and forget about it. I roll over, but I cannot sleep and I cannot forget about it. I have the feeling, just like in the dream, that I've got to get out of here.

I pull on clammy nylon cycling tights and socks that are so foul they should just be burned rather than worn again. Various muscle groups in my legs cramp, and for a few tortured moments I am a withering pretzel of pain. When the spasms cease, I will myself to finish getting dressed. Every move seems to require special encouragement and a promise that better times lie just ahead. I feel filthy. I smell the foulness of myself. It is not a good smell. I tell my body to bear with me for just this one bad morning. I promise some vague god that I will take perfect care of myself from here on out, if he (or she) would please let me off the hook this one time. I gobble down a cinnamon roll. I forgo my cup of coffee, promising myself a double dose of caffeine when I get to the first open gas station.

Thirty minutes after emerging from the tent, I have rolled up the soggy mess and stowed it away. I push the bike over rocks and through bushes to the dirt road, then up the hill to the main highway. On this Sunday morning with a cloying mist obscuring the tops of the surrounding spruce forest, I am the only object creeping along the highway. It is as if something has swallowed up all the cars and anyone else foolish enough to be moving along this course.

Believe it or not, there is a plan to my retreat. Before retiring last night, I had studied the map and discovered that in my quest to find a place to camp I had veered at least 20 miles off course. I calculated that I could shave about five miles off that mistake by carefully following a series of country roads for the first half of today's ride before merging onto the main highway to Tampere this afternoon.

When I pass through Eura this morning, not a soul is stirring. Nothing is open, not even a gas station. Coffee will have to wait. The mist seems to close in. I grimly retrace the last few miles of my path of yesterday, then turn east on Road 2111 to Köyliö, the first major navigational event of my newly complicated route. I find that Road 2111 stretches through a corridor of unbroken forest in a line so straight it appears to be a tunnel without end.

By now I know I am going to have trouble today. My legs remain stiff, and the aches and pains that usually arise much later in the day are already manifesting. The bounce and zest that I began other days with is not materializing. It is at least 75 miles, perhaps longer, to Tampere, the next reasonable place to layover. I don't know how I will make it, but I grind on through the relentless forest nevertheless. Even though the road is flat, I have to pump away as if I am going uphill, the thick air itself parting reluctantly.

Köyliö is like Eura, shut down and enveloped by a cloak of mist. I stop, drink some water, then continue. My muscles sting from the lactic acid buildup. I begin to dread rest stops, since the pain associated with starting again is almost unbearable.

I cross a causeway over Köyliönjärvi, another huge lake, winding my way around an island dominated by an elegant nineteenth-century Lutheran Church with a classic steeple. On this Sunday midmorning only a few cars are in the parking lot. There are a lot of churches in Finland, but oddly, few parishioners. I pedal up small hills that now seem Himalayan, knowing that when I reach each top I can expect to see a cell phone tower, then enjoy a short coast downhill and momentary relief. The hills abate. I cycle down a single-lane road lined with tall poplars, dairies, and hay fields. A solitary farmer in his baler waves as he tries to mitigate the damage from the onslaught of moisture.

By 11:30 I reach a road that parallels Highway 12 to Tampere. In the distance I see the outline of the sizeable city of Huittinen. Somehow, through sheer willpower I have managed to click off 30 miles. The most cheering moment of all comes when I see the towering sign of a gas station. This isn't just any gas station, but a behemoth super-sized fueling center with a big restaurant that looms out of the miserable mist like El Dorado. Normally, I am not a person who gets excited about gas stations, and back home I will only eat at one as a last resort. I don't know if it's the circumstances I find myself in or if there really is something special about these Finnish megaplex filling stations—and I'm not talking about a fast-food minimarket like many American gas stations have. I'm talking about a place where you can order not only a simple hot dog, but also a chicken dinner with all the trimmings or a plate of reindeer parmesan. Plus, the bathrooms are wonderfully clean.

I wobble over to the station, park the bike, and walk in. Dazzled by the pictures of seemingly every kind of hamburger in existence, I hastily consult the language section at the back of the Lonely Planet guidebook and reacquaint myself with the word for cheeseburger. This is not the place for a linguistic foul-up. The pictures of perfect burgers have stimulated sharp hunger pangs that were suppressed by Expedition orders to cover as much ground as possible in the morning and worry about eating later. During the morning, I took a few sips of water and nibbled at a granola bar, meaning I had consumed only a few hundred calories while burning a few thousand to pedal the crew forward and keep warm. A few days of this negative math, and I will melt away to nothing.

I order a *juustohampuilainen*—a cheeseburger.

The kindly woman taking my order looks perplexed. I repeat the magic Finnish word like a wizard incanting a spell, but my tongue cannot get a firm grip on the last couple of syllables. The last part of my verbiage sounds like I'm ordering a trampoline. Desperate, I point to the picture.

"Oh, you mean you want a cheeseburger," she says matter-of-factly.

I am awash in relief. Apparently, I am back on the planet. She speaks better English than I do. I savor my high-calorie, high-fat repast and linger in the warm interior for as long as possible, knowing that I still have almost 50 miles to cover.

When I saddle up and head back out, the post-cheeseburger renewal that I hoped would carry me for the rest of the afternoon just isn't there. If anything, my legs seem more lethargic. Each crank on the pedals is an ordeal. I limp into Huittinen, where I notice a strange sight. The town's telephone booths are stuffed with giant, life-sized statues of portly men, all of whom bear the likeness of Winston Churchill. Is this the town's way of celebrating the death of the modern pay phone? Are they honoring Churchill? In Turku, I recalled seeing a brochure warning tourists that the country's last pay phone had been disconnected last year. The national phone company had concluded that pay phones were obsolete because virtually every Finn now had a cell phone. I pass the defunct booths and continue on my way.

Huittinen does sport hotels and for a moment I think about decamping here. But it is also in the middle of nowhere, an agricultural hub known for its food processing and the birthplace of Risto Ryti, the former Finnish president who had the misfortune of presiding over the Continuation War. But much of the day still remains. I quickly decide I have, or *should* have, enough energy to power my way closer to, if not all the way to, the much more interesting city of Tampere.

Somewhere on one of the endless little hills between Huittinen and Vammala, the next city about 20 miles away, I conclude that I cannot make it to Tampere. My legs feel like they weigh one hundred pounds each. Mist continues to shroud the land, giving the impression that the sun will never again shine in Finland.

My exhaustion takes many forms. I daydream, then find myself straying haphazardly into the middle of the road. Fortunately, on these side roads there is little traffic, but the last 25 miles to Tampere will be on the narrow shoulder of a busy highway, where such carelessness could put a premature end to the epic. Instead of keeping an even pace by shifting gears to maintain the same pedal rate, I apathetically pedal a few revolutions, then stop and coast for as long as possible. On hills, I no longer have the strength to sprint in high gear while descending to build momentum to climb the next rise. I barely notice my surroundings—with the broad Kokemuen River lazily winding through verdant farmland, past villages of wood houses and church steeples— which on a sunny day with a restored body would have struck me as exceedingly pleasant.

I have enough clarity, however, to spot a bus shelter, where I pull over and take out the map. It appears that Vammala, a picturesque resort town straddling two lakes, has a campground and several hotels. Upon closer examination, I notice on the map a thin black line stretching from Pori, a major city on the Gulf of Bothnia, passing through Vammala, then continuing to Tampere. This is part of the Finnish railroad system. Further scrutiny of the microscopic symbols reveals a train station in Vammala.

Rolling into Vammala with the last of my strength at about 3:30 p.m., I make one last amendment to my emergency plan. I ride past the campground and several promising hotels. My new goal is to get to the train station. It's worth a try to see if there are any passenger trains to Tampere, even on Sunday afternoon. If not, I'll stay here.

The train station, a wooden relic from another era, is closed, but posted on the door a schedule tells me that a passenger train to Tampere is due in 30 minutes. I confirm this wonderful surprise with a solitary passenger waiting on the platform.

The next thing I know I am hoisting the bike and the wagon up to a conductor who stashes it in the baggage car. I have no ticket, but that's not a problem. The conductor is happy to take my seven euros (about $10) and print one from the computerized dispenser wrapped like a belt around his waist.

The train is crowded, but I find a seat and flop my miserable body down. To this humble Expedition team leader, who has been slogging along at unbelievably slow speeds—sluggish enough to observe the pattern of the asphalt, noting each rock and weed in the road—the electric train seems to travel at a mind-boggling speed. Trees, farms, and entire towns flash by at warp speed.

By 4:30, the train eases into the bustling Tampere station. I am the last one off my car, reluctant to leave the comfortable seat and warmth of the carriage. I am immediately greeted by a smiling, college-aged woman.

"Welcome to Tampere. Can I help you?"

I wasn't prepared for a personal welcome. Did the conductor phone ahead and alert the station that a rather bedraggled American with a ridiculously small bike and a suitcase on wheels just got on the train and would need all the help he could get in Tampere?

I stand rather stupidly for a second, but then manage a nod.

"Follow me!" she chirps.

I follow, walking the bike and trailer, not having the slightest idea where this angel of mercy is taking me.

She leads me to a freight elevator that conveniently drops to the street, directly below the platform. This saves me the trouble of uncoupling the wagon and making a couple of trips down the stairs. As I roll my bike out of the elevator and toward the busy streets of Tampere, my angel remains behind to aid some other epic-seeker who might find salvation through the magical appearance of a Finnish passenger train.

A couple of hours later, I sit in a restaurant with faux Tiffany lamps, located in the Tampere Hostel, where I have checked into a single room for two nights. I have showered and exchanged my fetid clothes for clean ones. I am a new man. I contentedly sip beer and listen to the murmur of restaurant conversation. I feel an incredible lightness and detachment, as if I am acting in a play with multiple scenes that range from despair to quiet contemplation. My brain can barely get its synapses around the events of the day. Twenty-four hours ago, I was huddling in a clammy sleeping bag slathered in sweat, dirt, and mosquito carnage. A few hours ago, I seemed to be on my last legs, muscles screaming in pain, wobbling through a misty landscape that had no end. Then, I am rescued by a train that, at least in my mind, seemed to glide out of nowhere and whisk me to my destination—my own version of the Hogwarts Express.

And now here I am: bathed, wearing a clean shirt and pants, and savoring every morsel of the salmon medallions I ordered. There is a lesson here, and in my tired state I try my best to parse it out. Is it redemption? Is it that no matter how poor the conditions seem at the time, if you keep moving—even at a snail's pace—you will reach your goal? Does this only work on bike trips in Finland, or are there universal applications? Am I lucky? I had no idea a train line went through Vammala, let alone one with passenger service. What are the odds of snagging a passenger train on Sunday afternoon? Europeans, with their excellent train service, might not think this particularly out of the ordinary, but for an American used to Amtrak's limited schedule, this event in itself is nothing short of a miracle.

Back in my second-floor room, I continue to digest the events and circumstances that brought me to this pleasant little hostel on a tree-shaded street. Outside, the mist has parted and shafts of sunlight radiate with an ethereal quality off the red-brick building across the street. My muscles still ache, but now the pain seems more a souvenir of a memorable day than the product of a miserable journey. I arrive at no conclusions, though a vague theory starts to formulate in that part of my brain that is still open for business. I think it has something to do with the nature of epics and their unpredictable "thrown to the winds" nature. You cannot plan for what might happen. You cannot predict the outcome with any accuracy. Some of your experiences might be good, some unpleasant. Somehow, though, in the final accounting of these things, it all balances out. You just need to hang in there and go with the flow. Or at the very least, just survive to journey another day.

With the Expedition barely two weeks old, I know I will have more opportunities to test my little theory. But I hope that after today, the bad stuff has played out its hand for awhile.

Lenin Slept Here

TAMPERE HAS A DIFFERENT FEEL from the old-world charm of Turku or the cosmopolitan trendiness of Helsinki. Straddling two giant lakes, Näsijärvi to the north and Pyhäjärvi to the south, Tampere is to Finland what Manchester was to England during the heyday of the Industrial Revolution: a manufacturing center.

The massive red-brick buildings and towering smokestacks of the Finlayson textile factory straddle the Tammerkoski rapids that connect the two lakes. In the nineteenth century, the turbulent water powered the looms and mills, and in 1882 it provided the energy for electrical current that lit the first light bulb in Scandinavia. Today, the hulking textile factories, fully refurbished, are as much a symbol of Finland's transformation into an ultramodern, twenty-first-century nation as they are of its industrial past. The workshops are long gone, replaced by a ten-screen cinema, microbrewery, shopping mall, and chic restaurant that again make this a center for commerce.

In the morning, I cycle across a sleek pedestrian suspension bridge that crosses the Tammerkoski downstream from where the rapids smooth out into a river. It leads to an open-air market of food stands and farmer's stalls, most of which are selling fresh berries. A few blocks away, downtown is dominated by an expansive cobblestone square with an ornate city hall anchoring one end and the city theater at the other. Surrounding streets bustle with shoppers and workers, giving Finland's third-largest city the feel of a human beehive. With all this capitalist hustle and bustle, it's hard to believe that Tampere was once the stronghold of Finland's communist movement. After all, Lenin slept here.

As I walk through the displays of the small Lenin Museum, housed in what was the Workers Hall not far from the Tampere Hostel, it becomes abundantly clear that Vladimir Ilyich Lenin slept many places in Finland before making his triumphant return to Petrograd (now St. Petersburg) in October 1917. His Tampere roots date from December 1905, when Lenin and his wife, Nadezhda K. Krupskaya, stayed at a guesthouse a few blocks from the railroad station. They were here to participate in the first congress of the Russian Social Democrat Labor Party, which would later evolve into the Bolshevik Party. Another partygoer of significance, Joseph Stalin, would later play a rather noteworthy role in Russian and Finnish history later.

After the congress, Lenin used Finland as a giant hideout from the czarist police. He lived in Vasa and Vyborg,[24] slummed at several Helsinki residences, including that of the city's police inspector, and slept in a hollowed out haystack in the Karelian Isthmus. In 1907, as he was pursued by czarist police, he jumped from a passenger train at Piikkio, a village near Turku I had biked through a week ago. From his hideouts, Lenin wrote some of his more noteworthy manifestos. In *On the Czar's Policy Toward Finland,* he urged the Finns to join the Bolshevik movement as a means to secure independence. *State and Revolution,* one of his most important tomes, predicts (as it turns out, incorrectly) the eventual dictatorship of the proletariat.

As I read the correspondence between Lenin and his Finnish hosts and supporters, I can't help but conclude that the eventual father of the Russian Revolution was grateful for the refuge he received in Finland and came to genuinely like its people. There is also little question that Lenin believed that once the Bolsheviks established the world's first socialist government in Russia, Finland would quickly follow.

In November 1917, the Bolsheviks stormed the Winter Palace in Petrograd, overthrowing the weak provisional government. Lenin, as party secretary, became the leader of the world's first socialist state. On December 31, Lenin granted Finland its independence.

For the next few months, Lenin's prediction that Finland's Bolsheviks would soon establish a sister communist state looked good. Tampere became the capital of Red Finland. But Lenin did not count on heavy resistance from anti-Bolshevik forces that received arms and reinforcements from Russia's implacable foe, Germany. Nor did he anticipate the galvanizing effect that one Gustaf Mannerheim would have on the government forces.

As the fate of the young nation hung in the balance, Lenin received letters from his Finnish comrades pleading for arms and supplies. One haunting photo in the Lenin Museum shows men in civilian clothes hunched behind barricades with rifles pointed at an unseen enemy in Tampere's central square. Supplies from the Soviet Union, itself involved in a horrendous civil war, never arrived. Mannerheim quickly organized the White Army and within months crushed the Reds.[25]

Two other items in the museum catch my attention. The most interesting is a copy of a letter Lenin dictated to his wife. Known as "Lenin's Testament," and composed while he was recovering from a severe stroke suffered in December 1922, Lenin strongly suggests that Stalin be expelled from the office of the General Secretary and moved to a lesser position. Stalin was a wild card, and Lenin showed a growing distrust of him and his increasing power. As we now know, Lenin's advice went unheeded and Finland suffered for it seventeen years later in the winter of 1939 when Stalin ordered his massive armies to attack.

The second is a photograph of Lenin taken in September 1922, perhaps the last photo of him alive. He is sitting with his sister, Maria Ulyanova, in Gorky. Lenin, his face gaunt, his body frail and shrunken, still sports his famous goatee and peaked worker's cap. He looks much older than his fifty-two years. He died sixteen months later.

Given my adventures of the past week, I wonder if a night in a haystack is in my near future. But what really courses through my mind as I leave the museum has almost nothing to do with Lenin, but everything to do with the vagaries of age. Lenin's severe stroke was no doubt encouraged by the stresses of administering the world's largest country, which at that time was in chaos, while also attempting to manage the bitter rivalry between his heirs apparent, Stalin and Leon Trotsky. While I am not in any danger of administering a large country, in chaos or otherwise, I had of late become acutely aware of how stress can play havoc with one's life.

There were moments after quitting my job as CFO of the Seattle Public Library when I wondered whether I had done the right thing. But now, after embarking on this journey, I realize once and for all that I absolutely made the right decision. Even on days here in Finland when the rain is relentless, the mists eternal, and my mind and body are exhausted, I think of the alternative and my spirits lift momentarily. I wouldn't for a moment trade places with my former life.

Look at me now: I pedal through the streets of a vibrant city I didn't even know existed until recently. And today, as the sun shines, my body joyously sheds the pain incurred from the past two days of hard riding. My days are long and full. And for better or for worse, these days are all mine to fill as I see fit. I celebrate my freedom. I celebrate the conquest of my fear so that I could come this far. I celebrate that I look a lot better than Lenin did at the ripe young age of fifty-two.

I pedal past the railroad station, then turn north, entering into a large wooded park where National Bike Route 9, the trail I plan to take tomorrow, shoots off on hard-packed dirt toward the east. I rest near a signpost.

And then I am ambushed. My old nemesis—fear—in its most sinister form, anxiety, launches a surprise attack. The fanny pack that I use on my day excursions for carrying my camera and passport is missing. It is not around my waist. I search my daypack, but it is not in there either. Could the belt have stealthily unfastened itself while I was consulting a map or when I was giddy with my morning celebratory introspection? *You fool! Never let your guard down, not even for a moment!* My inner father is yelling at me, and I yell back that now is not the time to cast blame. We need to find the pack and deal with recrimination later, if ever.

I carefully retrace my route back to the Lenin Museum, cycling slowly, my eyes glued to the pavement, looking for the little pack. As I search, I hope some fine Finnish citizen finds it, sees the passport, and turns it over to the police. If I had been in any other country, I would have concluded it was lost forever, but the Finns' relentless honesty gives me hope. On the other hand, I accept that I might end up taking the train back to Helsinki and groveling for a temporary replacement passport at the U.S. Embassy.

One other possibility keeps me from lurching into wholesale panic: maybe I left it in the hostel room. I search my memory, but most of my daily movements are now so automatic that I cannot picture the routine. After biking to the museum and finding nothing, I retrace my route back to the hostel. I promise the gods (yet again) that I will be good forever if I can just regain my pack. I will be extra kind to animals, with the exception of mosquitoes. I will call my mother more often. I will change water into wine, heal the sick, and try my best to have clean thoughts. I will do just about anything to make that pack appear in my hostel room.

When I open the door, I immediately see the pack lying on the bed, waiting for me to strap it around my waist. I breathe a sigh of relief. The anxiety quickly evaporates, and I am once again amazed at how the human mind always seems to dwell on the worst outcomes. Then I remember my profuse promises. I will try to be better, starting tomorrow. Really I will.

∿∿ ∿∿ ∿∿

In the afternoon, I ride randomly through the city, exploring nooks and crannies. I watch people. Interspersed among the sea of white faces on the crowded sidewalks is a smattering of African and Arabic-looking men, as well as Muslim women wearing head scarves. Maneuvering through the sidewalk crowds is tricky. For the first time I see outward signs of Finland's alcohol problem as I swerve to avoid the unpredictable stagger of drunks—usually decaying, time-worn men.

Earlier in the day, I had passed a "Tex-Mex" restaurant—the last thing you would expect to see in Finland. It sounded good, so now I stop there and order a couple of tacos. They aren't bad, but given my recent diet almost anything besides a hard-boiled egg, a chunk of cheese, and a cracker seems positively delicious. After dinner, I cross the street to a Happy Penguin kiosk, where I buy an ice cream cone. On the breast of one of the happy penguin signs, someone has scrawled "Fuck the police."

For the first time on the trip, I hear sirens. Across the street, I see a building wall filled with graffiti. The inscriptions are in Finnish, but judging from the liberal use of red paint I wonder if Tampere's leftist past lives on. Near the city center, a lone city employee in white overalls laboriously paints over the day's scrawl on the panel of a bus shelter.

Evening descends, bathing the city in golden light that makes it radiate like a beautiful flower slowly opening to the long-awaited sun. I can't seem to tear myself away from my wanderings. Tampere is irresistible. When I get to the hostel, I cannot bear to go inside even though it's getting late. I ride to Näsinpuisto, a park that straddles a forested ridge interlaced with manicured gardens and paths. To the north shimmers Näsijärvi, where commercial passenger boats link a score of cities as far as one hundred miles away through a labyrinth of freshwater lakes tied together by canals and rivers. Screams of joyous terror drift from the roller coaster of a nearby amusement park. I push the bike along the ridge as the sun slowly retreats to the northwest. Lovers and clusters of friends are scattered, quietly necking, talking, smoking, or sipping from amber bottles of Karjala beer. The now familiar gaggle of teenagers in their black dress, studded belts and chains, Mohawk haircuts of various hues, and tattoos and body piercings galore are prominent near the ridge, like a colony of seabirds perched on a rock. The sweet scent of lilac lingers like the perfume of a beautiful woman.

Meet the Press

COASTING DOWN A SIDEWALK near the Tampere Library on a sun-kissed morning, I hit a bump, then hear a pop and feel a sudden lightening of my load. *This cannot be good.* I turn to see the wagon freelancing down the path behind me. The yoke that hooks the wagon to the bike's back frame is scraping along the pavement. As luck would have it, the runaway contraption comes to a rest intact against a nearby tree. I have dodged another potential disaster. The wagon could have easily veered onto the street and smashed into a bus or run over the mayor of Tampere.

A hasty inspection reveals that all parts are present and accounted for. I apparently had not snapped the wagon securely onto the trailer hitch, an inexcusable error and one that I'm sure the wagon will not let me forget.

"Yes, yes, I know. Pay attention to details," I mutter, as I snap on the hitch with extra force. My trouble is there are so many details to keep track of, perhaps too many for one epic-bound human.

The tree-lined streets near the hostel are quiet in the early morning as I retrace yesterday's passport-panic route that started with the search for National Bike Route 9. The Expedition is once again under way after two days of rest in Tampere. Despite the early morning mishap with the wagon, I am in good spirits as I head down Hämeenkatu and swoop through the underpass tagged with graffiti where the railroad bisects the city. Once I'm on Itsenäisyydenkatu, on the city's east side, rush-hour traffic begins to thicken.

Crossing a busy thoroughfare, I hear another troubling snap, like the crack of a dry branch. This time when I glance back, I see that the dowel and the Riding with Reindeer banner are lying in the middle of the four-lane street. Only a jagged stump remains where the dowel once attached to the wagon. This, too, is not good.

My impulse is to dart back into the street to retrieve the proud symbol of the Expedition, now ingloriously prostrate on the pavement. But as I'm about to make my dash, the light turns red. I check oncoming traffic. A phalanx of trucks and cars manned by sleep-deprived Finns, who no doubt were frolicking in the midsummer night's sun last night, rev up their engines like they are at the start of a NASCAR race. The automotive might of Tampere is about to obliterate the Expedition's symbol of hope.

As I cringe on the curb, a near-miracle occurs. In a display of precision driving that I did not think possible from morning commuters, the trucks deftly steer around or over the flag, as do the cars. The fallen banner seems to have its own force field of protection as the vehicles nimbly avoid running over it. I say "near-miracle" because just as the last car steers cleanly over the flag, a lone cyclist, the last oncoming vehicle before the light changes, drives his wheels right over the banner's white leaping reindeer.

When the light in my direction turns green, I run into the street, grab the banner, and hastily return to my bike. I'm not sure what sort of material my sister used—Kevlar perhaps—but whatever it is, the flag holds up brilliantly, with nary a treadmark or even a hint of dirt. The dowel has sheared off at the base, another case of rather shoddy craftsmanship on my part. There is no time to improvise a repair, so I tuck the banner under the bungee cords that hold the duffel to the wagon, and the Expedition resumes its eastward push. I wonder what else might go wrong this morning.

The answer comes soon enough. I find the leafy Petsamo neighborhood, wheel past an indoor recreation center, and enter the fringes of the large park I had explored yesterday. Bike Route 9 is clearly signed, with markers pointing along a narrow dirt path through miles of birch interspersed with meadows blooming gold and purple. But my faith in Finland's bike signage system is again shaken when I reach the village of Rustholli, which is little more than a cabin and some outbuildings. It seems as if the sign makers ran out of signs here. I wander down an unsigned path, looking for some indication of where to turn. The main path shoots right into a small lake surrounded by homes. *Where do I go?* I consult the map and decide to circumnavigate the lake in an eastward direction. This provides the best chance of intersecting one of the main roads heading east. I carefully pick my way through a tangle of short paths, and then, miracle of miracles, I hit the main road. National Bike Route 9 magically reappears. At these times, I wonder if the Finns have created these little puzzles for me, just to keep me on my toes.

It is 110 miles to Jyväskylä, the next big city and layover. My plan is to split this distance into two days by following the circuitous Bike Route 9 that winds through the countryside past innumerable lakes. While this is a scenic route, the blue zigzag on the map promises that the distance will be greater than on the motorway, which shoots like an arrow to Jyväskylä. Today I opt for the scenic route.

By noon I am picking my way along dirt roads past fertile farms and crystal-blue lakes. Most of the farmhouses are—you guessed it—the seemingly national color of reddish-brown with white trim. Occasionally, I pass the homestead of some radical who dared paint his house yellow. At one point, the path turns off onto a rough-rutted wagon road that takes me straight across a farmer's hayfield. It seems as if no one has come this way since the time of the czars. While the countryside imbues me with a feeling of sleepy tranquility, the endless rolling hills take their toll on my legs. On dirt and gravel, I cannot gain momentum downhill, turning the uphills into a struggle to gain traction on the loose rocks even with the extra wide tires I purchased before I left for Finland. The small wheels probably make such stretches more difficult than if I had a standard-sized hybrid. By midafternoon, I am walking the bike up the hills.

Heading down the road less traveled between Tampere and Orivesi

I give a silent cheer when I finally turn onto the paved main road to Orivesi. Although it's still relatively early in the day and I've only covered 33 miles, the struggle on the roller coaster dirt roads has drained me. When I see a sign advertising the lakeside Säynäniemi campground, I impulsively turn and coast down to it. The camp is perched seductively on a peninsula surrounded on three sides by Lake Pappilanselka, which, like many others in this region, interconnects with other lakes, forming a vast navigable network. There are a few camper vans and trailers, but otherwise the place is uncrowded. The sunbathed outdoor café at the registration office seems to be calling my name.

"That girl over there would like to interview you," says the woman who takes my registration and hands me the tag to stick on my tent.

I turn and see a young, attractive woman with a pageboy haircut, standing nearby. A camera is slung smartly over her shoulder, and she grasps a reporter's notebook. Her no-nonsense outfit and chipper appearance remind me of Maria in *The Sound of Music.* The way she looks at me, I wonder if she's going to burst into song.

"Are you busy?" she asks. Her name is Kati Pääkkonen, and she says she represents the *Oriveden Sanomat.*

It's a little after two o'clock, and I'm done traveling for the day. I am in the middle of Finland, though I don't immediately know what day it is. As far as I can recall, I have no major appointments or tasks today other than pitching the tent, taking a shower, and lying around for the next sixteen hours.

"May I interview you for my newspaper?"

This little interaction has taken place in the span of about three seconds. Granting a press interview after winding in and out of country lanes all day was probably the last thing I had expected. As usual the Expedition, whose existence until now is totally unknown to the world except for a handful of passersby and friends who read my occasional blog posts, is caught unprepared. I have no press kit, press agent, or press anything. But the thought of being a media star in Finland is rather appealing. As it turns out, I may be a media star in the Orivesi area, but probably not until I'm long gone. The newspaper, she explains, is published every couple of days.

Clearly it has been a slow news day in Orivesi. Kati tells me she thought she would hang out at the campground and pray something interesting would turn up. When a swarthy guy, obviously not Finnish, riding a folding bike hauling a wagon pulled up, she knew her problem was solved.

Kati apologizes for her broken English, but I find it perfectly acceptable. She is from Kurikke, a small town near Vasa. Swedish is her first language. She now lives in Tampere, where she is studying journalism at the university. I suspect her current gig at the *Oriveden Sanomat* is a stepping stone to a bigger paper and an escape from assignments requiring her to hang out at obscure campgrounds waiting for oddballs to roll through.

After asking where I am from, where the ride started, where it will finish, why I have come to Finland, and what brings me to this lovely campground, she drops a bombshell, inadvertently touching a sensitive topic.

"Do you get lonely?"

The answer as of this day and time, sitting here at this pleasant picnic table with a Julie Andrews look-alike is, surprisingly, no. The stimulus of the ride, the picturesque scenery, the battle with the elements, and the constant decision making and route-finding has reduced my psychological existence to a simple moment-to-moment montage of experiences, most of which are new and interesting, some even pleasant. True, I have no sidekick, but it seems as if Finland, itself, has become my trustworthy companion. She slowly reveals herself each day. Sometimes she is bright and cheerful, sometimes pensive and moody. She is never dull. But most importantly, she has made me forget about the stresses of the nine-to-five routine I have forsaken: life in the office, where tension built and fomented like a daily afternoon thunderstorm, much worse than the literal ones I've encountered here. The old routine has been replaced by simple, solvable problems like Where am I going to camp tonight? What am I going to eat? Should I rest here or there?

In the past, this uncertainty might have provoked anxiety, but during the trip I seem to have weaned myself off this annoying habit. Things work out; that's what I am learning. They work out whether I worry about them or not. So I have stopped worrying because it takes too much energy and is no fun anyway. By now I have gleaned enough battle experience to know that even on the worst days I will find a place to sleep, even if it means camping in the forest amongst a swarm of mosquitoes. As long as I move forward, even by walking, I will be okay.

I am not sure I convey the full meaning of my answer, but Kati seems to be grasping much of what I say. She asks how I have fared so far with the Finnish language.

I tell her I study new words every night and have learned much more beyond "boiling soup." On a good day, when all my synapses fire at top efficiency, I can even count to two.

"Say something in Finnish?" she requests.

Reporter Kati Pääkkonen of the Oriveden Sanomat
with author at the Säynäniemi campground.

My mind is suddenly blank, loose letters and extra vowels with umlauts float randomly through my brain, desperately looking to form a word other than *kittos* (thank you) and *eh* (hello). I really want to show this attractive woman my amazing capacity to speak Finnish. Instead, I show my amazing capacity to say "boiling soup," which does not impress her, because even this morsel I manage to garble, judging from her puzzled expression.

The interview concludes quickly thereafter. I want to keep talking, but Kati needs to snap a few photos of me and interview other campers to round out her story.[26] Despite my pronouncements about not being lonely, these last precious moments remind me what a pleasure it is to converse in more than one-word sentences.

As we part, I mockingly plead with Kati to promise it will not rain tomorrow.

"I'm sorry," she says, "but the weather forecast is not good. A big storm is coming."

The words "big" and "storm" set next to each other is exactly what I do not want to hear. Is there an unwritten Finnish law that prevents me from enjoying more than twenty-four hours of good weather? By the time I pitch the tent, enjoy a beer at the café, and return to my camp, sure enough, clouds have moved in from the south. The rain falls as I tuck into my sleeping bag later that night.

An hour after I turn off the headlamp and put away *The Race to Timbuktu,* I awake with a start. Something in addition to me is in my sleeping bag. A bug of unknown origins is crawling up my leg. In the second it takes my nervous system to flash the intruder warning to my brain, the creature halts. It takes a bite. I reach into the bag and swat the thing off while scrambling about, looking frantically for the headlamp. Then I begin a crease-to-crease search. The light momentarily glints off a pair of bulbous eyes attached to metallic skin. I am face to face with Robo Fly. The beast appears to be smiling.

Meanwhile, a horde of little mosquitoes, more deft than their clumsy cousins that I easily eradicated before I went to bed, are buzzing around the light, dive-bombing into my eyes, attacking undefended bare patches of skin. They have entered through the opening in the rain fly that the broken zipper refuses to close. It is an all-out night commando raid with air support. But first I must deal with the leg chomper. I find my weapon of choice, my tattered *The Economist* magazine. I roll it up and begin flaying away. The fly from hell seems unfazed by the pounding. For an instant, I consider reading aloud some of the articles on the insane run-away inflation in Zimbabwe, thinking that might kill it; but no, only brute force will work. After more vigorous whacking, I manage to stun the beast, then toss it out of the tent.

Dealing with the mosquitoes is more challenging. Each one is hunted with the headlamp and downed by a well-coordinated hand clap, not an easy feat when groggy. By midnight, I have tracked down the last of the little terrorists, and I seal up the mosquito fly with more duct tape. Outside, rain pelts the tent, adding further proof that there is no such thing as a dull moment on this trip.

15

The Gods Are Angry

AS MY RIGHT EYE BLINKS INTO FOCUS, evidence of last night's battle is plainly visible. Splotches of blood stain the tent walls, marking where I cornered and mashed my tiny attackers. This gives me a moment of satisfaction until I realize that the blood is mine, not theirs. My attention is quickly diverted to another problem that has manifested during the wake-up process. While my legs, arms, and other critical parts appear present and in working order, I am having a problem with my left eye. Like a malfunctioning garage door, the lid remains stubbornly closed, even with multiple attempts to open it. I rub it, thinking that perhaps the buildup of the night's detritus might require a little extra action. But the lid stays tightly shut.

Worried, I pull on pants and a shirt and walk briskly to the restroom, where there is a mirror and more light. Peering into the mirror with my good eye, I see that the closed one is swollen, like someone has decked me in a barroom brawl. I pry the lid open with my fingers and am relieved when I see that the eye is not red or otherwise wounded. I can also see with it. That's the good news. But as soon as I withdraw my fingers, the lid slams shut. My eyelid muscles appear to have been dismantled.

Mimicking a Cyclops is not part of the trip plan, though I am aware of the giant's role in classical epic lore. A more critical concern is that I need both eyes to help me navigate my way through *this* epic. I've had enough trouble even with both eyes in good working order. I consider making an eyepatch; perhaps the swashbuckling pirate look might improve my appearance. Because the eye itself looks fine, I suspect the lid was disabled by last night's attackers, whose strategic bites have caused the swelling. The bastards knew exactly what they were doing. Taking out my eyes was no doubt part of their diabolical plan to stop the Expedition dead in its tracks.

My suspicion of Finland's night creatures is not entirely unfounded. Shortly before the trip's departure, I had read in the international edition of the *Helsingin Sanomat* that a tear-sucking moth (*calyptra thalictri*) had been recently observed in southeast Finland. The creature's mode of attack is to land on the eyes of elk or livestock and suck the tears from the eyelid. Was I a human victim of the vampire moth?

I do not have time to contemplate the loss of tears or my eye. The Expedition must carry on. Heeding Kati's storm warning, I pack up and load the bike, guided by my one working eye. Under skies with scuttling clouds, I lurch onto the main road to Orivesi.

With more than 80 miles to cover to reach Jyväskylä, I had decided to skip the rest of the picturesque scenery of National Bike Route 9 and opt for the direct route provided by the motorway. Shortly after reaching Orivesi, I turn off the road that Bike Route 9 follows onto the larger Motorway E63, wiggling my way onto the tiny shoulder. Cars, buses, and trucks whoosh by at 70 miles per hour, creating a wake that sucks me along, momentarily boosting my speed. I try to blot out the highway noise and think pleasant thoughts. But these quickly dissolve into vengeful images of obliterating the first moth I encounter.

The road slices through rolling hills of wheat, barley, and hay. As I gain speed descending a hillock, the bike gives a violent lurch toward the rushing traffic. I jerk the handlebars, desperate to steady the shuddering bike and keep it on the shoulder. In the same instant, I hear a sound like a power saw cutting through cement. I put a death squeeze on the brake levers. When I slow enough, I glance back to see what has happened. The wagon's left axle is scraping the pavement. Sparks fly. The left tire is gone.

Stopping the bike, I lean it against a guardrail and inspect the axle as traffic roars by. Almost half the diameter of the axle stub, the part that holds the tire, has been filed down by the pavement. The tiny hole from which a cotter pin secures the tire is intact, though barely. The pin itself is gone, probably shattered by the tremendous stress caused by the journey's jarring from dirt and gravel roads. But where is the tire?

I scan the highway shoulder, searching for the tire. Not seeing it, I scan the opposite shoulder, wondering if it could have rolled across the roadway without being obliterated. I hike back up the grade I have just descended. A helpless feeling of catastrophe begins to cloud my thoughts.

I do not have a spare. I never thought I would have a problem with this pair of tires, let alone anticipate that one would fly off and vanish into thin air. Without the tire, I have no way to haul my mound of gear. I will be stuck here on the side of a hill a long way from Jyväskylä.

The tire is not on the shoulder, not in the road, not anywhere. I deliberate. I could drag the wagon and nonessential gear to a grove of trees, leave it there, bike to the nearest town—a place called Längelmäki—and scrounge around for a replacement.

Keep looking, I tell myself. I hop over the embankment railing and begin a traverse, searching clumps of weeds and shrubs. Far down the slope, I see a black shape partially hidden under a bush. I skitter down the pitch, my hopes rising. *Yes!* I pry the tire from its napping spot. Remarkably, it's in pristine condition after its little solo adventure.

The crisis is far from over, however. As I hike back up the embankment, I pray that the axle stub has not been deformed to the point where the wheel will not fit back on. I tell the gods I will be *extra extra* good if they rescue me this time, even though I already have a debt to pay from the little passport incident of two days ago and my encounter with lightning the day before I reached Turku.

The tire hesitates, but with the slap of my palm it snaps on snugly and turns freely. Carefully, I walk the bike and wagon up the road about fifty yards to an intersection with a dirt road. I find a flat place away from the traffic and set to work. The Expedition carries spare parts, including an extra set of cotter pins, an array of crescent and Allen wrenches, and a Leatherman with a set of pliers—which is what I need now to squeeze the new cotter pin into place. In twenty minutes I reinstall the tire, tighten other parts of the wagon, and lubricate the bike. One more mishap on the left axle and the Expedition is cooked. For now, though, I have dodged disaster yet again. I am beginning to feel like that famous cat, the one with nine lives. But how many do I have left?

*Hasty repairs are made after the tire flew off the rear axle
of the wagon on the road to Jyväskylä.*

There is one piece of good news emerging from this near-catastrophe: my left eyelid has begun functioning again. The enemy's potion has worn off.

The Expedition resumes, somewhat shaken, but still rolling forward. I am now leery of the little protuberances in the pavement along the shoulder. These little annoyances serve as a warning to motorists who stray too close to the road's edge. But on a bike, they are the equivalent of a monstrous Magic Fingers ride without the soothing aftereffects. I was coasting down along these undulations when "the accident" occurred, and I'm thinking that the extra stress is what caused the cotter pin to break. Now I find myself attempting to avoid the little bumps, but this leaves only about six inches of usable shoulder for my rig.

By midmorning I regain my pace. The weather remains good with only scattered clouds. A tailwind, as if the gods were offering compensation for my morning's mishap, pushes me forward, allowing me to sustain a 15-miles-per-hour pace. *Whoever described Finland as flat has never biked on this road,* I grouse. I methodically cycle up each hill, then pedal like hell on the downside to gain momentum for the next rise. Each summit seems higher than the last, but with the tailwind I maintain the strong pace. I rest only briefly for lunch and water. I keep my nose to the road, careful to avoid rough pavement. This means, unfortunately, that I do not allow myself to observe much else. When I do look up I see the same rolling farm country—hilltops crowned with spruce and valleys spotted with lakes.

By the time I pull into a Neste gas station at Korpilahti at around 5:30, for a Coke and bathroom break, I am only 17 miles from Jyväskylä. Even with my lame eye and wandering wagon wheel, I already have logged 62 miles and still have the pep to go the last segment. I realize that I have once again broken my 50 miles a day limit, but I really have no choice.

Overhead the clouds have thickened and coalesced, but of course I think I can avoid the storm. When I emerge from the store it seems as if someone has used time-lapse photography to speed up the movement of the clouds. The day has darkened considerably. The puffball cumulous clouds of the early afternoon are now foaming white towers with menacing dark gray underbellies. I have seen this before: unsettled weather. I pull on my rain pants and parka. The race is on.

I don't know when I got it in my mind that I could outrace a storm cell on a folding bike, lugging a suitcase, but that is my plan. As the road twists into a pleasant valley of pasture and horse farms, I pedal as fast as possible, but somehow the harder I push, the slower I seem to go.

Traffic lightens, then disappears. For a moment a strange calm, broken only by the subtle beat of my pedaling, descends over the valley. The sweet fragrance of freshly mown hay fills the air. I glance across the road and see a white stallion watching me. He rears, throws his head back and stamps the ground, neighing wildly as if frantically trying to warn me about something. The sky turns yellow. The clouds darken. Dogs bark. Ahead looms a forested hill and, of course, a cell phone tower. I think that this has to be the last hill before the descent into Jyväskylä, a city that now has taken on mythical proportions in my mind as a safe haven from storms, flying tires, and vampire moths.

The clouds get darker as if some undefined evil is overtaking Earth. I push hard as I begin my ascent. I do not dare look back.

The first flash is to my left, striking near a barn. Another flash fills the sky. There is no time to investigate. I focus all of my energy on pedaling. *I've got to get out of here.* In the nanoseconds that follow the first flash of lightning, I brace myself for what will come next. There is a crack, like someone breaking a giant egg, and then I am nearly blown off my bike by a monstrous concussion. A few large raindrops splatter. Seconds later, super-sized drops belt out of the sky. I am instantly drenched. I now know that I cannot outrun a thunderstorm; I am foolish to even try.

Traffic has resumed, and now it seems the road is filled with glowering logging trucks—enormous trees layered on their beds, sticking out of the rear ends like massive Lincoln Logs. Bits of bark and branch fly in my face, already sopping with the backsplash of passing vehicles. Lightning continues to flash, sheets of it raking the sky. Thunder roars from everywhere. I glance around to see if there is a barn or some other shelter that I can hide out in, but the only possibility is a pipe-like culvert. I decide to maintain my course and continue to pedal toward the hilltop. To my left, through billowing clouds and a dark veil of rain, I see blue sky. The road twists in that direction. If I can get over the mountain, I figure I will be safe. I press on, my speed dwindling to five, then four miles per hour. My mind races back to old high school science lessons on lightning and the principles of conduction. An image of Benjamin Franklin flying his kite in a storm forms in my addled mind. I am now that kite, and my hope is that the trees and cell tower are much better rods for absorbing the few million extra volts that the gods are zinging from the heavens.

At last I reach the top. When I crest, I do not see the magical spires of Jyväskylä—only more hills, more forests, and more storms. The blue sky gets no closer. The storm cell is keeping perfect pace with me. I race downhill, the storm following me like Pig-Pen's dust cloud. I can't shake it. It seems as if Thor himself has taken charge, personally hurling the bolts and slamming cymbals in an all-out attempt to keep me from reaching the enchanted city.

I am beginning to take this personally. In the distance, I hear the wail of sirens; not the mystical seductive voices of mythological beings, but the kind that are attached to emergency vehicles. *Fires?* I guess. *People hit by lightning?* I grind on, wiping water away from the front of my odometer so I can check my progress. It is time to implement my emergency plan.

Back at the Neste gas station, I had noticed on the map the tiniest of roads, a slender sliver of a line jutting off from the motorway and rejoining the spurned National Bike Route 9 at a junction marked by a Lutheran Church. I've got to get off this highway and onto the diminutive road before I am either electrocuted or side-swiped by one of the trucks whose drivers probably cannot even see me in this downpour.

At a sign for a church I turn, not bothering to look at the map. The narrow, deserted road cuts through the forest, leaving the mayhem of the busy highway behind. Ahead I see a gleaming white cross on a bell tower. When I reach the church, the sun breaks out in a blaze of yellow. Steam wafts from the wet black pavement, and from me. The storm cell, impatient with my slug-like pace, moves on.

I find Bike Route 9, apologize for forsaking it, and wobble down its quiet pavement at a slow pace. I know the path will take me on a circuitous, but less hectic route. It adds more miles to my day, but at this point I don't care—though I have a feeling Thor isn't finished with me yet.

The second storm cell hits about twenty minutes later. This time I am ready for it, having entered Jyväskylä's hilly suburbs, which are sprinkled liberally with bus shelters. I huddle in a shelter with a few evening commuters, then continue when the rain stops. Thor pounces yet again, but

I am too quick, finding another shelter. I crest a hill. In the distance, I see the hilltop spire of the red campanile, a bell tower designed by the renowned Finnish architect Alvar Aalto, who thought Jyväskylä's hills reminded him of Tuscany.

Tuscany is not what I have in mind as I hide in a tunnel waiting out the latest squall. Outside, Thor unleashes his grand finale in a thunderous downpour. When all is finally clear, I creep out and cycle along the shore. Jyväskylä rises from the bank in a series of hills—more evidence that Finland is not flat. I ascend the city streets, find the university's summer hotel, and totter up to the reception desk. The clerk cheerfully tells me they have a single room with a kitchen. Perfect. Unfortunately, it's on the third floor. Not so perfect.

"Is there an elevator?" I gasp, noting that I have a bike and a lot of wet luggage.

"No, I'm sorry. But the stairs will give you good exercise."

I stare at her in disbelief, my sense of humor momentarily escaping me. But I grab it back just in time.

"Oh yes, I can use some exercise today," I reply as I accept my key.

Land of Lakes

YESTERDAY IN MY BEDRAGGLED STATE, the picturesque surroundings had not really registered in a brain suffering from a bad case of over-stimulation. Jyväskylä's charms begin to emerge as I shop for groceries in the downtown pedestrian mall and buy oil for Friday's chain at a neighborhood bicycle shop. Later, I retrace my route of entry, exploring the park-like waterfront bordering Lake Jyväsjärvi.

Small by Finnish standards, the lake connects by canal to the massive lake Päijänne. From Päijänne you can row a boat through most of central Finland. Most of the country's 188,000 lakes are concentrated in this region, and many are interconnected by canals, rivers, and locks. The lakes, formed by retreating glaciers, are shallow. Only three are deeper than three hundred feet, which means the lake waters warm quickly in the summer and freeze just as fast in the winter, providing impromptu roads for snowmobiles. They brim with trout, perch, pike, whitefish, and a species of freshwater seal called the Saimaa.

Jyväskylä sits primly on the western edge of this vast water world. A slender suspension bridge arcs across the lake to suburbs on the opposite shore. The city itself is perched on a series of hills that climb away from the lake and are topped by the forested paths and the red-brick buildings of the University of Jyväskylä. With a population of 84,000, the city appears to have fewer immigrants than Tampere. But there is some diversity. Amid my wanderings I encounter a gaggle of Gypsy women. Their distinctive multilayered black dresses and colorful petticoats billow in the breeze as they load groceries into a car.

You cannot wander long in this city without meeting the ghost of Finland's most famous architect and Jyväskylä's favorite son, Alvar Aalto. His designs seem to meld into the forest, woods, and lakeshores, while emphasizing the practical aspects of what a building should do. "The fact that the countryside of central Finland is hard to spoil is no excuse for complacency," Aalto once wrote. "Given its tremendous potential, any disfigurement of this beautiful scenery is all the more offensive to the discerning eye."[27]

Being rather practical-minded myself, I find this approach appealing, though I admit I am not particularly wowed when I pedal by buildings Aalto designed for the university. And perhaps that is what Aalto was all about. He wasn't a "Wow" type of architect, at least not with a capital "w." The brick university buildings do not call attention to themselves—there are no flourishes, no soaring atriums or fancy porticos—nothing to mark the signature of the creator. They do fit into the surroundings, however, and may not have even caused a second glance if I had not known that Aalto was the architect. In short, they looked like utilitarian university buildings.

Born in Kuortane in the Ostrobothnia region in 1898, Aalto moved with his family to Jyväskylä eight years later. He spent his formative years here, first doodling in school, then drawing cartoons, and later, creating family portraits. He served as an apprentice to an established Jyväskylä architect, Toivo Salervo, who gave his young charge this advice after a summer internship: "Alvar, you don't have the makings of an architect, but you show great promise as a journalist!"

Fortunately for the world of architecture, and perhaps for journalism as well, Aalto stuck to his passion. He studied architecture in Helsinki, but his career path was disrupted by the Finnish Civil War. He fought on the side of Gustaf Mannerheim, but the horrors of the bloody war and its aftermath of summary executions left an indelible impression on the sensitive Aalto, who did his best to distract himself from this reality through his sense of humor and by wooing women.

Aalto's career blossomed as he gained commissions throughout Finland, then internationally. After World War II, Aalto was invited to teach at the Massachusetts Institute of Technology, but he cut his tenure short because he found American life too superficial. He married twice. His first wife, Aino, died in 1949. In the 1950s, he designed and built a villa modeled after a Roman atrium house, on the nearby island of Muuratsalo, where he and his second wife, Elsa, spent most summers from 1952 until his death in 1976. Despite his international reputation, Aalto remained partial to central Finland, taking on commissions to design buildings at the University of Jyväskylä and the museum of central Finland. He was particularly proud of the clock tower that stands on the hill above the city.

What I find impressive, besides the sheer volume of his work, is its diversity. He designed churches, city halls, libraries, bridges, houses, a mill, a workers hall, a dormitory at MIT, and one of Helsinki's most enduring buildings—the sleek, white Finlandia Hall.[28]

∿∿∿ ∿∿∿ ∿∿∿

My brief excursion into architecture ends. I am back to the business of serious pedaling after resting for a day. The fury of the gods appears to have spent itself for now as I make my way along the bike path that skirts the northern shore of Jyväsjärvi. The Expedition is resupplied. My legs are rested. The banner is fluttering again, as I used the shortened dowel to make a new flag pole. The wagon has been reassembled, the axle realigned, and other parts checked for excessive wear. Everything looks good. Both eyes and attached lids work. Clothes are washed, though getting them clean is a challenge because of the bike chain grease that continually stains my only pair of pants. Best of all, my ravenous appetite has been sated by the generously portioned meals cooked in my spacious student room kitchen. Behind me, high on the hill overlooking the town, is Aalto's clock tower. The sun peeks out from broken clouds, though the forest still glistens with wet. It still doesn't look like Tuscany.

The path is a conglomerate of National Bike Routes 4, 9, 13, and 23, all of which have fused together at this point before branching off in various directions. I chose Route 23, and certainly do not want to head on Route 4, which goes directly south. After scrutinizing the map last night, I concluded that the Expedition's next leg will take three days of steady cycling to reach Kuopio, my next layover, 150 miles northeast of Jyväskylä. Today, I plan a modest 45 miles, a reasonable distance to ease back into day-to-day cycling after my day of rest. I do not expect the terrain to provide any overt challenges, though I need to pay attention to navigation if I want to adhere to the schedule. The route I have chosen is relatively straight, along a highway that is colored blue on my map, a color which so far has meant roads that are lightly traveled (as opposed to the high-speed, orange-colored motorways).

Not more than an hour into the day, as I enjoy a good pace along a dedicated path through a spruce forest, my internal radar senses that something is wrong. I am on alert for a major intersection where Bike Routes 9, 13, and 23 split off from Route 4. The first six miles of the path were well signed, but now the signs have vanished and my compass indicates that I am heading due south. Then, the bike path abruptly ends, devolving into a rocky pitted track. The cute little farmhouses that I have been enjoying views of disappear and are replaced by shabby, run-down cabins littered with pieces of broken-down farm equipment. A dog the size of a small bear gallops out from behind some garbage bins, his snarling charge checked only by a thin chicken-wire fence. Suddenly motivated, I struggle to gain speed, but the wagon wheels can't make much time between the ostrich-egg-sized rocks littering the path. I drag the bike back onto the main road. After careful scrutiny of all landmarks and new bearings taken with the now-functioning compass, I conclude that I somehow missed a key turnoff.

Backtracking uphill for three miles does not put me in a good mood. I reach an unmarked path that dips under the road and peters out at an enormous service station featuring not only gas, but also three restaurants and a store. On the far side is a highway, which heads east. I conclude this is the correct route. I merge onto the busy road, which is filled (no surprise) with frenzied Friday traffic as every able-bodied Finn with a camper, fishing pole, and boat seems to be hightailing it to the lakes; so much for the lightly traveled blue highways. The exodus from Jyväskylä, itself perched on a beautiful lake with connecting lakes in all directions, is rather puzzling. Perhaps the water is truly bluer on the other side.

A causeway takes me across Lake Leppävesi, which confirms that I am on the correct route. I make another note to the mental letter I am composing to the Finnish National Bike Route Committee regarding the placement of signs.

The correct route (Bike Route 23), however, is not the idyllic ride I had imagined. The traffic is insufferable. Once again my attention is fixed on the narrow shoulder. Every few seconds I steal a glance at my rearview mirror to see what's coming. Mostly, I listen to the sounds of approaching vehicles. By now I can identify the growls that distinguish a car, camper, truck, or bus.

Shortly after leaving the causeway, I look up long enough to see another solo cyclist slowly making his way along the opposite side of the road. This is the first comrade I've spotted since the day after leaving Åland. The plastic bags shielding the sleeping bag strapped to his rear rack billow from the wind created by the traffic. His clothes are bedraggled. A tangle of cords and shreds of unidentifiable material trail his bike like party streamers. He's not wearing a helmet. We wave and shout "hello" across the roar of traffic, but there is no chance to stop and have a chat. Crossing the highway would be suicide. In a few seconds the apparition passes, leaving me to wonder who he was and where he had been.

Bike Route 23 finally leads me away from the mayhem of the main highway, through the town of Lievestuore and onto a quiet country road that snakes up and down forested hills. I eat lunch in a deserted schoolyard at the village of Niemisjärvi, enjoying the remains of a potato salad before delving into my regular ration of cheese, salami, hard-boiled egg, bread, and a banana. This menu, by the way, is not the product of a scientific analysis of the best, most efficiently digestible food required to replace burned calories. Rather, it is the result of what I could grab in local grocery stores and what might reasonably survive intact for a few days in my front carrier.

After lunch, more hills follow, and for inexplicable reasons the path again deteriorates into a muddy, potholed lane. I seek paved relief on the main road, but my nerves become quickly frayed. At Hankasalmen, Bike Route 23 mercifully veers off again onto a frontage road for a few miles.

My plan calls for me to leave Bike Route 23 and continue on the blue highway to a campground near Lake Naarajärvi. But my plan is not working out the way I had envisioned. At Riställa, I turn south, sticking to Bike Route 23, which will lead me in a long circuitous detour over country roads, some unpaved, but will eventually circle back to my destination. Again I'm trading miles for solitude.

The first quarter of a mile is uphill, but once I crest, I glide along for miles on a deserted road flanked by a swath of goldenrod and the white blossoms of angelica and yarrow. A tailwind materializes. The road seems perpetually tilted downward, allowing me to maintain a consistent speed. This is how I had (naïvely, it turns out) imagined the trip when I pored over maps in Seattle.

After nearly 10 miles of heading south, Bike Route 23 turns east again, slicing across the swath of ancient moraines that bisect central Finland in a north-south direction. For me this means more up and down. Before long, Bike Route 23 turns into a trail of hard-packed earth riddled with potholes full of muddy water. Fresh signs of logging abound. I pass enormous clear-cuts where all the unprofitable debris has been swept into immense piles. Other areas appear to have been selectively logged because the remaining trees are perfectly spaced. Immense rolls of shredded wheat-like hay are piled next to old log cabins with perfectly mortised corners. The hills get steeper. In the interest of saving my legs, I start walking the bike up the grades. *There is plenty of time*, I tell myself. No need to rush, no need to tax my muscles more than necessary. At least I'm still moving forward.

When Bike Route 23 finally intersects with Highway 447, I turn north again, completing the last leg of my detour. As my odometer turns to 60 miles for the day, I see a sign for the Lomatrio Campground, which, miracles of miracles, is on the map and is the place I was planning to stop for the night. The campground sits on the reedy shores of Naarajärvi. It's deserted, except for a few small recreational vehicles. The sun finally breaks free of the pesky clouds, as I roll out my tent and equipment. A couple of ducks waddle by as if on important business, while a magpie perches on a log and watches the proceedings. In the distance, a fisherman putters his boat along the far shore, fishing lines trolling behind.

The national bike routes have won me over again. Perhaps the slow road is the best way, after all.

Lake Naarajärvi

In the morning, the stillness of a sunny day is almost too perfect to smudge with travel. I dawdle by the shore, do yoga stretches and chant a mantra, anything to hold the moment and encourage more like it. Reluctantly, I finally break camp, load the bike, and ride to the gas station/store/restaurant/campground office where the woman who checked me in yesterday cheerfully asks how I slept. "Very well," I reply, and it's true. When I explain that I'm heading to Lapland, she provides the response I've grown accustomed to, even though Lapland gets a little closer each day.

"It's a long way," she says, waving vaguely in a northerly direction.

I have heard this reply so many times, it now feels like something all Finns must have learned by rote. Sometimes it's combined with a vague reference to another bike rider who years ago had announced he was heading to the mysterious land in the north. A week ago in a Tampere Internet café, the manager thought he remembered me from another time.

"I remember two years ago there was a man like you with such a bike. He said he was going to Lapland. You know, Lapland is a long way," he sighed, as if he too was contemplating the journey. As I showed him the bike tethered to a signpost, I wondered if his reference was to the same man who persuaded the young woman from Wim's Helsinki dance group to accompany him. Or was it the man with the recumbent cycle who had stopped at Marieberg?

Traveling to Lapland aboard a bike *is* a long way, particularly when the rider starts his trip heading in the exact *opposite* direction, then slanting up in a *leisurely* northeast direction. By car or train, the distance from Helsinki to Rovaniemi, the capital of Finnish Lapland, is 450 miles. My circuitous route will easily triple that distance.

I still cannot tear myself away from the pleasantness of Lomatrio, so I prolong my stay by buying a cup of coffee and a donut, thus establishing my first rest break after biking about 500 feet. Today I can justify my sloth-like pace because I plan to cover only 36 miles. This should get me to another lakeside camp at Leppävirta.

At last I'm under way, sticking to my new pal, Bike Route 23, which leads me into some of the steepest hills I have yet encountered. But unlike the previous week, I am not alone; rather, I encounter a small parade of various characters. I pass a column of road-racing cyclists who no doubt find the hills a perfect training venue. Another man rolls by me with long poles nicking the pavement, powering a pair of cross-country skis fitted with rollers. On a downhill coast, I flush a large bird with a white-ringed fantail from its hiding spot. I think it might be a capercaillie, the largest member of the grouse family. Just past the village of Jäppilä on an arduous grade, I fall in behind an old woman on a one-speed with white berry buckets swinging from her handlebars. Near the crest, I pass her, glancing behind to wave and say "eh." She looks at me with a blank expression and then continues to grind uphill as if I were an apparition.

I've had several of these encounters in the past few days, almost always with older Finns who are walking by the roadside. They *peer* at me. I'm sure they are curious. How many times does a guy on a little bicycle towing a makeshift suitcase on wheels with an "Åland-Arctic" banner fluttering in the wind and wearing a bright orange cycling shirt adorned with cactus come bombing down their peaceful country road? But their expression shows no sign of amazement, curiosity, or recognition that anything unusual is occurring; no wave or return "eh"—only a hardened stare. The reaction is almost the opposite with younger folks, who enthusiastically wave. If they speak a little English, they invariably want to ask me questions.

By midafternoon I reach my destination, Leppävirta, which for centuries has benefited from its location between two massive lakes— Kallavesi to the north and Unnukka to the south. For the second consecutive night, I strike gold with a lakefront view, this time from a terraced campsite overlooking Unnukka.

After setting up camp, I ride into town looking for a restaurant, but I decide the best place to eat is a gas station, where I celebrate my mishap-free day with a pork fillet in béarnaise sauce. From my table, I get a bird's-eye view of the comings and goings of the local citizenry. Many gas station complexes (as well as supermarkets) sport slot machines, giving them a Reno-like feel. The slots across from me are fully engaged. Beer sales are clearly fantastic as a succession of men—usually wearing camouflage or cargo pants, T-shirts with English slogans, and baseball caps—buy enormous quantities of the stuff; nothing less than a 12-pack leaves the store.

Back at the camp, activity abounds. I see several men and boys, stark naked, make a dash from the sauna cabin down a dock and dive into the lake. Below my perch on the next terrace, younger children bounce with joy on a squeaky trampoline. A few yards away, the hollow bonk of Ping-Pong balls mixes with the thunk of darts slamming into a target. In the bushes behind me, a towheaded preschooler hides and blasts me with make-believe bullets from his toy gun. I guess the guy in the bright orange shirt makes an excellent target.

In the morning, my diminutive stalker is awaiting me as I stumble out of my tent to the welcome sight of the sun. I quickly pack, then head to a buffet breakfast at the campground café. The buffet, an unusual feature in the classic epic quest, offers an unlimited opportunity to fill up on eggs, oatmeal, and rolls for a few euros.

I leave before I am barred from buffets throughout Finland. But as I trek north, now on Bike Route 5, up the spine of the hilly, forested peninsula between lake Kallavesi and another lake, Suvasvesi, I become concerned with a new sensation.

During the night, my throat started feeling sore. At first, I thought this might be dryness, but by midmorning my throat glands are definitely swollen. Like most people, I dread the telltale signs of a cold. Rarely do I catch one in the summer. Three months earlier, I had one that started with a sore throat, was followed by fever, and then turned into a horrendous cough that evolved into a viral infection of my lungs. The malady sapped my strength for days; I did nothing but lie around the house feeling miserable. The illness finally broke after my doctor prescribed a steroid inhaler. Fears of another lung virus are percolating through my mind as I set a slow but steady pace for the good-sized city of Kuopio. If necessary, I will stay there until the malady passes.

I stop to rest near one of the many small lakes that dot the region. As I nibble on gorp, I'm startled by a splash in the water. Instinctively, I look around, wondering if someone has tossed a rock into the lake. But the place is devoid of humans. Another splash sends out ripples in concentric rings. I watch the water. A trout the size of my water bottle leaps up to snatch a mosquito, triggering a memory of the taste of fried trout and bacon.

At noon, with the sun warming the air, I find a little bus shelter in the middle of a forest. It's time for rest and lunch, but I'm still thinking of the trout and mosquito, which shifts to solving the problem of fixing the broken zipper on the tent's mosquito net. The nightly routine of killing bugs and then hearing the irritating buzz near my ear later, followed by frantic slapping and thrashing in the dark is wearing me down. A couple of days ago, I had received an e-mail from friends in Seattle who asked if they could send supplies to me to coincide with my arrival in Rovaniemi, still some weeks away. Yes, I had enthusiastically replied. I'd asked for some magazines, packets of dehydrated food, ointment for my sore bum, and other assorted items. After I had dashed off the e-mail, I remembered the problem with the mosquito netting. I should have asked for clothespins, which would have provided a low-tech solution to opening and closing the mosquito net—better than duct tape, anyway.

As I absent-mindedly shell my hard-boiled egg, white fragments falling to the ground, I notice a familiar-looking object half-buried in the dirt. I pry it out with my fingers and soon I am holding up a clothespin. An interesting coincidence or divine intervention? I get down on my hands and knees and paw the ground. In a minute, I unearth four functional wooden clothes pins, the kind my mother had used to clip clothes onto our outside drying line at home.

An hour later as I labor up a hill, I am overtaken by two young Finnish cyclists out for a day ride. One, who introduces himself as Malka, strikes up a conversation as we make our way to the ferry landing where we will take a boat across Kallavesi. I tell him I'd been cycling for three weeks and outside of Åland have encountered only one other cross-country cyclist.

"What gives?" I ask, commenting on the intricate, though somewhat enigmatic, national bike route system.

"Mostly foreigners use the trails," he says. "If a Finn wants to go to Lapland, he will drive."

At least he doesn't tell me Lapland is far away.

Proof that Finland is not flat

Malka is curious about why I would even come to Finland, framing the question in a way that reveals an unspoken assumption that anyone with free time would go somewhere more exciting or interesting. *Why come here when you could lie on a warm beach in Italy or Spain, or stumble upon ancient ruins in Greece or Turkey?* The Finns I have encountered in these out-of-the-way places always seem a bit apologetic about the offerings of their modest country, as if to say, "We're not quite sure what possessed you to come here, but thanks for coming and giving us a try."

To Malka, I reply that I heard Finland is a good place to bicycle because it is flat. "At least, I thought it was flat," I say. "But there are many hills."

"Oh no," he replies. "It is very flat."

He makes this last statement as we labor up a steep slope in low gear. I shift into my mountain gear. Sweat pours down my temples.

"Have you ever heard of a place called Kansas?" I ask between gasps.

Apparently he had not, because by now Malka is speeding to the crest and bidding me good luck. I am left to ponder the flatness of Finland on my own. I am beginning to feel like a modern-day Christopher Columbus, but instead of claiming that the world is round rather than flat, I claim it is hilly.

A barge pulled by a cable drags me and a few cars across the startling blue waters of Kallavesi, another lake the size of a small sea. Malka and his friend are not on board. They apparently caught an earlier boat. On the other side, I treat myself and my throat to an ice cream before launching into the final 12 miles to Kuopio, a city of 91,000, and according to Lonely Planet, one of Finland's most likeable towns. Kuopio has a good campground, but I decide to skip it for more luxurious accommodations more appropriate for my convalescence. As the day has progressed, my throat has turned raw. It hurts to swallow. I need a bed. The guidebook recommends an inexpensive hotel that is part of the city's train station. I am advised to inquire at the station café.

The woman at the counter does not speak English, but her son, who is summoned, does. He checks me in, then his mother leads me around the back of the station, up the stairs, and along a hallway with immaculate hardwood floors that harkens to a time when train travelers stayed in these rooms while awaiting the next day's connection onward. The hotel, at least this wing, seems largely empty now. She leaves me with the keys to my room and the railroad station's back door.

My room is equally immaculate and surprisingly quiet; I don't hear the comings and goings of the trains. Finnish passenger trains are electric, and freight trains do not use these tracks. After hauling my gear up the stairs, I crack open the window, flop onto the bed, and promptly fall asleep.

Smoke Sauna

MY THROAT IS SWOLLEN. My sinuses are haywire. I have a cough. The good news, if there is any in this situation, is that I do not have a fever. I've also caught up on sleep, a situation helped when I dozed off last night with the television tuned to a progression of fishing and wild-life programs. One channel showed photographs of various mammals found in Finland's wilds, subtitled with their Finnish and English names. I learned *susi* (wolf), *karhu* (bear), and *poro* (reindeer). These important additions to my vocabulary may prove useful in about a week when I cycle through their habitats in remote sections of eastern Finland.

Another channel showed two men sitting silently in a boat in the middle of one of Finland's many lakes. Once in awhile they caught a fish. When this happened the narrator, like the voice of God, would interrupt the silence to announce something to the effect of, "They have caught a fish." I am not sure of this, but given the slow cadence of the program and a lack of other conversation, I believe this was a reasonable guess. At some point in this action-packed show, I fell asleep.

I confine my activities to checking e-mail at the library, visiting the city museum and an art gallery, and taking short rides. Like most Finnish cities of modest size, Kuopio has a large open square bordered by two department stores, a nineteenth-century city hall, and another historic building that houses the indoor market. In the afternoon, the central square fills with shoppers strolling among the stalls, where every-thing from fresh berries to T-shirts are sold. At one end of the square, a band sets up to play a concert. Posters announce the opening of the latest

Harry Potter movie, which oddly translate the name of the boy wizard into *Hoksopoli.*

The modern buildings near the city center and surrounding streets mask the fact that Kuopio was founded in 1653. The shores of the navigable Kallavesi and the thick forests that surrounded the town were attractive to early settlers. But the new town failed to fulfill its destiny as a trading center, and its charter was revoked in 1669. Almost one hundred years later, Sweden's King Gustavus III granted a second charter. This time the town took root, resulting in a detailed municipal plan consisting of a sensible grid of streets and smaller lanes designed to control fires—always a threat to the town's many wood buildings. This plan is still largely in effect today; the lanes, exactly 23.3 feet wide, provide ideal bike and pedestrian paths and are separated from the heavily traveled main streets (exactly 78.7 feet wide). Kuopio was bombed heavily by the Russians during the Winter War, but many of the ornate wooden buildings with painted trim and primly carved window frames with porticos survived.

If I want my Expedition to survive, I need a remedy to control my cough. I find an *apteckki* (pharmacy) and walk in among the bustle of white-smocked druggists scurrying here and there clutching pill vials or deciphering prescriptions. The over-abundance of pharmacists isn't the only clue that this drugstore is different from what I'm used to. For starters, unlike American drug stores, the *apteckki* takes a novel approach and sells *only* drugs and a handful of other personal hygiene items like toothpaste. There are no jugs of wine, selections of toilet bowl cleaners, or packs of flashlight batteries. The other difference is rooted in Finland's national health care system: Since everyone has insurance, most medicines are prescribed, which means there are relatively few over-the-counter remedies on display.

Armed with a slip of paper on which I had carefully spelled out the Finnish equivalent of "throat lozenge" with the aid of my dictionary, I waylay a scurrying white smock, who points me to the only brand available, something called a Codetab.

"These will help," she tells me, "but you should really take a sauna. The smoke sauna is the best thing for you."

This sounds like good advice. Fortunately, I am in the right city at almost the right time. Kuopio boasts the world's largest public smoke sauna at a place called Jätkänkämppä, about three miles south of the city center. Although most Finnish homes are now equipped with electric saunas, true connoisseurs will swear that the smoke sauna, which is heated by a wood fire, is the ultimate sauna experience. I am a bit wary about the "smoke" part, but I am willing to give it a try. The bigger problem is that the sauna is not open today; I have to wait until tomorrow.

"Then you must stay another day," says the pharmacist, whose tone gives this statement a command-like quality.

That settles it. I bike back to the hotel and pay for a third night. I'm in no condition to ride tomorrow anyway.

With time to kill in the afternoon, I set out for Puijo Hill. At one thousand feet, it is one of the highest points in the region and the training ground for Finland's ski jumpers. In the winter, the hill hosts the Nordic Ski Jumping World Cup.

After dragging the bike up a trail that meanders through another lovely spruce forest, I reach the top parking area, where I leave the bike. Most visitors come here to see the views from Puijo Tower, a Space Needle-like structure that shoots into the air another two hundred thirty feet and sports a revolving tower with a restaurant. But my primary interest is in the two giant towers looming out of the forest a bit farther down the hill. I make my way down a path, passing young men and boys dressed in ski suits and shouldering long, flat-edged jumping skis. In the background, I hear the *whoosh*, and then silence, as the jumpers launch off the giant tower ramp into space.

The sun is out. It is at least 70 degrees. Not a speck of snow is in sight. Yet, here in the middle of summer, the Finns, attired in ski suits, are skiing down the ramp and shooting into the sky like darts shot out of a blowgun, soaring through the air for seconds that seem eternal, with the forest and lakes framed nicely in the tips of their long skis. They land with a *plop* hundreds of feet below. Instead of snow, the tower ramps are fitted with artificial turf moistened by streaming water—a surface that apparently mimics snow. The final run-out is on grass.

Stationed on observation towers, coaches with timers, binoculars, and walkie-talkies provide a constant stream of advice, which I imagine goes something like this: "Petre, get your tips up!" "Marko, lean into it more!" The cement towers seem so tall that I get dizzy when I stand directly below one of them and look up. How people can actually hurl themselves off this structure, with their feet strapped onto two long, flat boards, is beyond my comprehension. Judging from the age of some of the skiers that trudge up the slope, it's clear that many start young.

I join the coaches on the stand and watch. An electronic scoreboard shows the speed of the skiers as they fly down the ramp. Some of the lads gain speeds close to 60 miles per hour. Not surprisingly, the Finns are among the best ski jumpers in the world, though Puijo Hill won its initial fame in 1915 when it became the country's first toboggan run. The course was so treacherous that one turn became known as the "curve of death" following a fatal accident. It was dismantled in 1931 after authorities thought the run might claim more victims.

ᴠᴠᴠ   ᴠᴠᴠ   ᴠᴠᴠ

Not quite sure what to expect at the smoke sauna, other than perhaps a lot of smoke and heat, I toss my swim trunks into my pack and pedal my way through central Kuopio toward Jätkänkämppä the next day. Until this minute, my stay in Kuopio has been marked by sunshine, but as the afternoon progresses, big troublesome clouds begin to appear on the horizon. Given my luck with the weather, I am not the least bit surprised that the storm cells form a defensive line in the sky exactly in the direction I'm heading. Shortly after I leave downtown, the downpour begins. Dodging cloudbursts by ducking under trees, store awnings, and bus shelters, I slowly make my way to salvation, while hoping not to catch pneumonia.

When I reach Jätkänkämppä, I come to a clearing with two log cabins. One is a long, unassuming one-story structure with no windows and no smoke issuing from the chimney. No one is around, which seems rather odd for the world's largest smoke sauna—that and the lack of smoke. I open the door to the second log building, where I confront a scene seemingly out of a medieval banquet hall. A musician pumps away on an accordion at the front of a room full of tables packed with tourists who are loading up plates of food. I quickly excuse myself from this bacchanalian feast after a man who is dressed like Ivanhoe directs me to the other cabin.

After a more thorough survey of that cabin, I find an unobtrusive door and a ticket office window where a young man is lounging. Yes, he confirms, this is Jätkänkämppä. It just opened for the day, which is why few people are here. But more will come soon, he promises. I fork over my $14. He hands me two blue towels.

"I'm new to this," I say. "What do I do?"

"No problem," says the lad. "The first towel is to dry off after the beginning shower. The second is to wrap around your middle when you enter the sauna. You can use it to dry off after the sauna and your final shower."

The attendant explains that Jätkänkämppä is coed. Most public saunas in Finland are segregated. Here, women wear swimsuits, men use the towels. That sounds simple enough, though I had expected something a little more grandiose. I shrug and walk into a small room, perhaps ten feet by ten feet, with benches on the side and hooks on the wall for hanging clothes. I undress, wrap the towel around my middle, and yank open the door to the shower room.

After washing off, the next stop and presumably the last, is through a door that opens into the third room: the sauna itself. The trick, I observe, is to get into the sauna quickly; you do not want to linger and leave the door open, which would allow precious heat to escape. In Finland, this might be considered a capital crime.

Dripping wet, with the towel once again strategically positioned around my middle, I open the third door and step inside, making sure the door closes behind me.

I am engulfed in a black void. Then, a blast of heat, enough to poach me alive, hits. For a few seconds, I stick close to the door in case I need to dash back to the shower room. My eyes slowly adjust, revealing a scene closer to Dante's Hell than a Roman bath. A narrow shaft of dull light from a lone window pierces the room, revealing shadowy figures hunched on three tiers of benches. The world's biggest smoke sauna is a square room, perhaps twenty feet by twenty feet, with wooden benches occupying three sides and a brick oven-like contraption that resembles a giant barbecue pit occupying the fourth. Strangely, there is no smoke. But there is heat. Oh man, there is heat.

I walk across the room, desperately trying not to pass out. I take my place on the lowest bench, where the heat is less intense. Once settled, I take stock of my situation. Mainly, I wonder how long I am going to survive before I need to retreat to the shower.

The sauna holds a mixed lot. There are families, fathers and sons, mothers and daughters. A large man with the girth of a walrus rises from the top tier and staggers to the source of the inferno. He grabs a long copper-plated ladle and dollops water from a bucket onto the red-hot coals. The coals hiss. Plumes of steam billow and fill the room. The chamber gets hotter.

A second door next to the one I emerged from leads to the women's shower room. As the heat slowly cooks my brain, I desperately remind myself to exit via the right-hand door to return to the men's shower. As I mentally repeat this mantra, an elderly man gets up and heads to the doors. He hesitates, then opens the door to the women's shower. A brief murmur rises from the assembly, but it's too late—the man has disappeared. A half-second later, he reappears and sheepishly scuttles into the men's shower room. I am determined not to make this mistake.

Time has no meaning in the dark chamber. Its passage is marked by rivulets of perspiration that drip off my body. I have no idea how long I sit. About half of the fifteen people in the sauna get up and leave before I decide to cool off in the shower. I rise slowly, making sure the towel stays around my middle. I walk to the doors, repeating silently "right door," "right door," "go through the right door."

I am normally a chicken when it comes to taking a cold shower, but the cool water now sluicing down my limbs has never felt better. I reenter the sauna for another round. By the third round, I feel like a veteran. During the second shower, I had noticed most of my fellow sauna-goers disappearing out a side door. This special door leads outside to a trail that ends at a long wooden pier, where my sauna mates leap into the frigid and rain-splattered waters of Kallavesi.

Back in the sauna, I tell myself I've got to do this. No one can bike halfway to Lapland, dodge storms, get sick, then find his way into the inner sanctum of the world's largest smoke sauna and not do as the Finns do: run down the dock and leap into the lake. I figure I am getting off easy because in the winter the Finns thrash around in the snow first, *then* they leap into the water through a hole cut in the ice.

After I have sweated an appropriate amount of time, I leave the sauna and fetch my swim trunks. As I walk to the outside door, I tell myself I cannot hesitate. If I hesitate, I might actually think about what I'm about to do, analyze the pros and cons, and debate my options. I cannot allow this to happen. Once outside, I must jump into the lake as quickly as possible. No thinking is allowed. If I think too much, I will chicken out.

I sprint through the forest barefooted, but I see trouble ahead. The wood planks of the dock are slick from the rain. I do not want to skid on the dock so I slow to a brisk, sure-footed walk, passing a couple of women who stand nearby, contemplating whether to jump or just turn around and go back inside.

"Don't think about it!" I shout at them, as I duck-foot past.

I reach the end of the dock feeling more like a condemned man than someone who has just had one of the world's greatest saunas. I steal a glance at the verdant scene: rain pinging on the calm surface, the dark forest hovering near the far banks.

I jump.

Somewhere in mid-jump, during the tiniest fraction of time when I am suspended in midair, a troubling thought bursts into my addled brain. It is a small, but important detail that was somehow lost in the halcyon moments leading up to my self-dare.

I can't swim.

Truth be told, I *can* swim, but it is not something I do well; in fact, I do it very poorly. I have a fear of deep, cold water. Maybe I went down on the *Titanic* in a previous life. For reasons unknown and despite hours of swimming lessons in my formative years, I never got the hang of breathing while swimming the freestyle. I know what to do. I just can't do it.

The seminal event of my swimming career came one summer at Boy Scout camp in the Sierra Nevada Mountains. Like Boy Scout camps everywhere, this one had a river flowing through it, the Stanislaus, if memory serves me correctly. To test our swimming skills, the scout leaders rigged up a course in one of the deep pools of the river. The scouts had to dive in, swim twenty-five yards to a buoy, then return. When I saw this, I was not fazed. At this stage in my life, I still enjoyed swimming, or what I thought was swimming. A little more coaching on technique, and I'm sure I would have been Olympic material.

But on that fateful sunny morning, the Stanislaus glistening invitingly, that was all about to change. My swimming experience until then had been limited to heated swimming pools. I had no idea what it was like to jump into a snow-fed river, no matter how inviting it looked. I did not know, nor did anyone tell me, that when the human body is subjected to extreme and sudden temperature changes, unexpected things can happen.

On command, I jumped into the river. The first few strokes were fine, but when I came up for my first breath, nothing happened. My lungs had ceased functioning. I couldn't breathe. I thought I was having a heart attack and would die right there at Boy Scout camp. I was horrified.

Somehow, I managed to reach the buoy, which I clung to for dear life, refusing the command of the scout leader to swim back. Gradually, my breathing returned to normal, but it was too late then. A lifetime of damage had occurred. I was ingloriously fished out of the river, then banned from swimming in it for the rest of the camp-out.

Later in life I did learn a decent backstroke, breaststroke, and butterfly, but I tire easily and for some reason could never coax my body to breathe properly. In any event, I hadn't been swimming in years.

In that fraction of a second after I jump into the Finnish lake, my brain is frantically processing several questions at once: *Do you remember how to swim or at least float for God's sake? Why did you pick now to test your skill level in this sport? Remember what happened at Boy Scout camp?*

I hit the lake and go down like a rock. I expect the icy water seizure of Boy Scout camp to reoccur, but this does not happen. The water is cool, not cold—refreshing, like jumping into a bottle of 7-Up. Instead of going into shock, my body seems to be energizing in a sensuous nerve-tingling way. I feel alive, wonderful.

I break the surface. The ladies applaud as if they knew all along about the Boy Scout camp and had been patiently waiting for this breakthrough moment. I suck the air, take a deep breath. My lungs work. Everything works! I swim, then hoist myself lightly out of the lake, feeling as if I had shed a burden I had carried subconsciously for the last forty years. I walk back to the sauna, the heat radiating from my skin, a lightness in my step.

I take a final round in the sauna, then return to the lake. This time I dive properly and swim, even frolic. When I emerge, my body feels like it has undergone a one-hundred-hour massage from a master. Every muscle fiber is relaxed; my congestion seemingly gone.

The young man who sold me my sauna ticket also sells beer. Clad only in my swimming trunks, I buy a pint and lounge on a bench in the rain, steam still rising from my arms, chest, and head. I marvel at the heat-absorbing capacity of the human body.

"The sauna is good, eh?" says the attendant. When he hears I'm from Seattle, he tells me has been to Kent, a suburb. The highlight, he tells me, was when he visited the Microsoft campus in nearby Redmond.

I picked a good time to visit Jätkänkämppä, because now it is crowded. I finish my beer. Light-headed, but feeling like a million dollars, I saunter back to the sauna cabin for my final shower and to dress. I yank open the door and find myself confronting an enormous woman with pendulous breasts. She looks at me only half surprised.

"Sorry!" I say, and hastily retreat into the men's shower room.

From the outside, Jätkänkämppä, reputedly the world's largest smoke sauna, did not look like much, but inside it was another story.

Another Miserable Day

THE MORNING BEGINS BENIGNLY without a hint of what will come. I awake at predawn, wiggle my head out of the sleeping bag, unfasten the clothespins that are successfully holding the mosquito net together, and peek outside. An endless procession of squawking bean geese flies across a swath of cloudless sky. Whiffs of fog hang above the ground and steam wafts from nearby stacks of freshly mown hay. *This is a good sign*, I think, as I snuggle back into my burrow to snatch a few more hours of sleep. I expect to reawake to a brilliant morning.

I reached Nurmes two days ago, an event marked by the one-thousandth mile of my trip. After two days of hard but steady cycling from Kuopio, I had taken an impromptu rest day here, giving me a chance to explore the town and digest the fact that I have actually made it to North Karelia, a region considered the soul of Finland. Historic Karelia stretches far into northwest Russia, a portion of which was part of Finland from 1918 to 1940, but was annexed by the Soviet Union following the Winter War. Briefly recaptured by Finland during the Continuation War, most of Karelia, save for this slender section, was lost for good after the 1944 armistice with the Soviets.

Culturally distinct from the rest of Finland, North Karelia is the haunt of Finland's folk heroes, who manifest themselves in the Finnish epic poem the *Kalevala*. Kuhmo, my destination later this day, is the center of all things related to the *Kalevala*. I am eager to get there so I can learn more about this other epic.

I noticed other subtle changes during my layover. The houses in Nurmes have ornately carved trim, but instead of the standard red and white color scheme I've grown accustomed to, the shutters and sills are painted with elaborate patterns, making liberal use of blue, red, white, and yellow. The fences here are distinct too, with long slender logs laid at a slant and stacked against a vertical post. Tall mounds of hay cling to poles that resemble giant toothpicks. On Nurmes's main street, an imposing stone Lutheran Church bears an inscription on its portico that notes the ascension of Russian Czar Alexander II in 1890 and Nicholas II in 1897. The inscriptions are a reminder to all that Nurmes is only 40 miles from the Russian border.

Nurmes Karelian design

While I sleep two extra hours, stealth clouds move in and cloak the shore of Pielinen, a gargantuan lake even by Finnish standards. I emerge from the tent and find the rainfly wet with dew, as is the wagon, the ground—everything. The bean geese have vanished. The family a few sites over is packing up with alarming haste. My guess is they want to start for home early before the hordes hit the road. The speed at which they fold chairs, dispatch garbage, and take down the awning connected to their recreational vehicle, however, gives the impression they are fleeing an invasion. *Are the Russians coming?* I decide to pack quickly, too.

Thirty minutes into my ride, I feel the first raindrops. Given the viciousness of storms I have already survived, a few drops are not alarming. I pedal on, slowly making my way north on Highway 75, which meanders through gently rolling hills thick with spruce. Only in the dells between hills does the forest relent to swamp and stagnant black pools, terrain I haven't seen before. I hope to reach Kuhmo in time to catch the final concert of its famed international chamber music festival. The possibility of hearing Sibelius played in his home country is my day's motivation.

The drops continue with increased frequency. I decide to press on, but feel no need to don rain gear. *Where is the thunder and lightning that has warned me of past tempests?* I ask myself. Without those dramatics, this couldn't possibly be a serious storm. The temperature is in the fifties—a bit cooler than normal. *I will tough it out. After all, I have survived worse.*

As I pedal, the forest and sky, already gray, seem to grow darker. The rain intensifies. I think about stopping and fishing out the rain pants, but decide it's too much of a hassle to disrupt my pace. A few minutes later, I feel a gentle push on my back from a welcome tailwind. Then, without warning, I hear a roar, as if a great beast suddenly exhaled into the forest, rustling a thousand boughs and branches in unison. Giant raindrops pelt from the sky. What was a faint breeze turns into a gust that pushes the bike forward at an alarming speed.

Hanging on for dear life, I whoosh down the road, the unseen tempest pushing me. I steal a glance backward and see a wall of blackness rushing toward me. Within seconds, I am inundated. The rain slams down like a shower nozzle turned on full blast. The road is awash, transforming into a river through which the bike tires cut a wake. Cresting a hill, I fly down the opposite side, raindrops smashing into my face and

forcing me to squint through half-closed eyelids. I can barely see the cars
that pass me by; no doubt the drivers can barely see me.

I am soaked. My head is wet, my nylon shorts and leggings dripping.
Water sloshes in my shoes. I keep riding, hoping to find a town or a shelter. I think about ditching the bike on the roadside and using the tent's
rain fly to make a shelter in the woods. But there is no place to stop. The
forest on either side of the road is thick, dark, and foreboding.

Instead, I cling to the hope that the monsoon will stop. I ride on for
miles, passing cars that have pulled off to the roadside, waiting it out.
I am now shivering, the first sign of hypothermia. I can't stop, though,
because the cycling itself is the only thing generating heat for my body.

In the distance I see an open-sided log shelter, a roadside rest area
opposite a lake. Shivering uncontrollably now, I pull the bike abreast of
the entrance, quickly unhitch the wagon, and park it under the roof. I
yank open the case. The stuff sack with my thermal underwear, sweatshirt, and head warmer is miraculously still dry. I wrench off my wet togs
and slip on the dry clothes and head warmer.

The shivering stops. I tear the new Primus stove out of the box.
Fortunately, I do not need a match. Within minutes, I am warming up
with a cup of coffee. I have survived yet another Finnish weather debacle,
though I am not sure how much more I can take.

The deluge continues for hours. I prepare to remain in my little log
shelter forever, if necessary. It is just a roof with a picnic table in the
middle, but it is good enough. A few yards away at the other end of the
turnout is an outhouse.

I lay my wet clothes on the picnic table. I eat lunch. I study the map.
I read. I pee in the privy. At times the rain eases, but then it continues
with renewed vigor. I will not be lured away from perhaps the only shelter between Nurmes and Kuhmo until I am certain the storm has passed.
Several cars ease up to the shelter, but when they see its occupant, the
drivers step on the gas.

At last, one car does stop. A thin man with a pockmarked face, who is
wearing a peacoat, gets out and stands before the shelter, as if awaiting an

invitation to enter. The other passenger, an enormous woman, remains in the car. The thin man and I greet each other. I motion for him to sit. He obliges. He lights a cigarette while I dig through my Finnish-English dictionary looking for something useful to say. He shows not the slightest interest in the odd-looking bike or his equally odd-looking shelter companion. He stares straight ahead at the lake across the road, puffing on his cigarette.

I find an appropriate Finnish word in my dictionary.

"Rain," I say.

"Eh," he says.

"Bad," I say.

"Eh," he says, snuffing out his cigarette.

He glances at me with a weary expression that seems to indicate I talk too much and that our conversation has exhausted him. He rises, trudges to his car, and drives away toward Nurmes.

The rain stops. To the south, the clouds appear lighter. Ahead is another 30 miles of soggy forest before I reach Kuhmo, but the promise of reaching the town is a good enough incentive to move.

I pedal as fast as I can, not wanting to be inundated with another downpour. But instead of more rain, the sky lightens. Patches of blue appear. My nylon cycling shorts dry, though my shoes remain wet. The road beelines for Kuhmo through a corridor of spruce and birch. Along the roadside, giant rust-colored toadstools poke their heads from the soggy soil.

The map shows I will go through the town of Mujejärvi. There, I hope to eat a snack, perhaps a pastry and coffee. I hold this pleasant vision and can almost taste the donut, but when I reach the crossroads that should have marked downtown Mujejärvi, I find nothing but a cell phone tower, a house, and a barking husky that wants a piece of me. Lauvuskylä, another alleged town farther up the road, features a mailbox, a woodpile, and more barking dogs. Wearily, I pedal on.

An hour later I spot something unusual—something that does not belong in the woods. The snout of a huge, rusting artillery cannon pokes through the trees. I am intrigued. I turn and follow a path toward it. I stumble upon a collection of decaying military hardware, antitank fortifications, and log-reinforced trenches. I have reached Jykänkoski, one of the first battlegrounds of the horrible Winter War.

Winter War defenses

It was at these hastily erected defensive positions that the badly outnumbered Finnish border guards prepared to take on the tens of thousands of Russian soldiers who were pouring across the border. My morning was bad, but it was nothing compared to the morning of November 30, 1939, when tiny Finland awoke to find itself under attack from its behemoth neighbor to the east.

Here in these quiet woods, Stalin's plan was to attack with the Soviet's Ninth Army, 54th Division, along two roads, capture Kuhmo, then proceed to Oulu on the Gulf of Bothnia.* This attack would be coordinated with a simultaneous thrust by two more divisions farther north at

---

* A division usually consists of between fifteen thousand and eighteen thousand soldiers.

Suomussalmi, a place I would reach in a couple of days. Soviet military planners were confident that the Kuhmo attack would divert Finnish reserves away from the much larger attacking force positioned farther to the north.

The Soviets miscalculated. Small detachments of Finnish border guards, nearly invisible in their white snow suits, moved silently through the trackless forest on cross-country skis and harassed the Soviet columns that were slowed by lumbering tanks, not to mention printing presses, band instruments, and truckloads of leaflets to distribute to the newly liberated lands. Winter—the element that had saved Russia from invaders in the past—now worked against her soldiers. When not fending off Finnish assaults, Russian tanks and supply vehicles stalled in the snow. Guns, equipment, and poorly clothed men froze in what would be the coldest winter in memory. By late December, Russian troops were strung out along miles of road, often cut off from each other by relentless Finnish ambushes. Farther north, the two Soviet divisions that were supposed to capture Suomussalmi were encircled and annihilated, allowing the Finns to send reinforcements to the Kuhmo front.

The Soviets never got past the spot where my bike rests against a monument describing what took place. By the time fighting stopped in March 1940, the corpses of ten thousand Soviet soldiers lay frozen in the forest. The Finns lost thirteen hundred and fifty—not a small number given the size of their army.

As I stroll among the monuments, old cannons, and mortars and peer inside trenches, it is difficult to believe that such fierce fighting once raged in these now peaceful woods. The only invaders I see now are cars with Russian license plates barreling down eastern Finland's impeccable roads, heading for a mall or a good fishing spot.

One trench system I follow leads to an improvised sauna. While the Russians shivered in snow holes or behind log barricades, not sure of when the next ambush would occur, the Finnish soldiers would retreat to their snug quarters and sweat in the wood-fired saunas.

The outskirts of Kuhmo appear suddenly out of the forest. I join the main bike path bordered by a berm bursting with violet, pink, and blue lupines. As if on cue, sunshine pours through a last layer of clouds, dissolving the remaining evidence of my miserable day. Twenty minutes later I push the bike up a short, steep hill surmounted by a wooden fortress with flags fluttering from stockade towers. This is the Kalevala Village, a sort of Finnish version of historical Williamsburg, Virginia. The faux village, with its staff dressed in traditional garb, displays various aspects of Karelian life; it is also the reception center for the campground I plan to stay at this evening.

As I park my bike, a crescendo of wolf howls fills the air. *What the hell!* I steady myself, thinking it impossible that I could be set upon by wolves here rather than in the long stretch of forest I have just biked through.

Later I learn that the creators of the village have wired the nearby woods and stockade with loudspeakers and loaded their sound system with some native sounds, adding another touch of authenticity to the Karelian wilderness experience. The sound quality, I must report, is excellent.

The wolf pack is still yelping when I reach the reception office.

"You are very wet," declares the woman at the window.

"I am having trouble hearing you," I shout. "The howling is very clever. I thought it was real, but can you turn it down?"

I appear to be the only visitor at the village. Perhaps it is a tradition to greet every bedraggled bicycle rider with wolf howls.

"Sorry," she says. The howling stops.

Behind her, two other employees peer intently at me.

"We watched you come up the path," said one in perfect English. "Your bike is very unusual."

I give a short history of my adventures. I cannot tell from their reaction whether they are impressed or think I am out of my mind. But they are kind enough to rent me a cabin for two nights.

"You are the first American visitor we have had for a long time," says the first woman. "In your honor, we will fly the American flag while you are here."

The cabin is situated with a few others in a grove of spruce on top of an adjacent hill. The place is largely deserted, though I catch snippets of Russian from two women sharing a bottle of wine on their porch several cabins away. Paths wind down to the shores of Lammasjärvi, a lake that stretches 45 miles to the south. A few fishing boats linger on the lake in the evening sun. My new quarters are stocked with two hot plates, a refrigerator, a table with chairs, and two single beds. This will do just fine, and all for $50 a night.

As I change into dry clothes and hang the wet ones to dry, I catch a glimpse of the stars and stripes waving alongside the Russian, Finnish, and German flags. I wonder how long the U.S. flag had been in storage.

Later, I call my friend Mindy, who was kind enough to take care of my house in Seattle while I undertook my epic trip.

"Are you having fun?" she asks.

I am not sure how to summarize my adventures during the past month. Given what I have been through recently, fun is not the word I have in mind.

"Let's just say I'm having an adventure," I say.

I miss the chamber music festival's last concert, but I treat myself to dinner. The fake village boasts an excellent real restaurant inside a replica of a Karelian meeting house. I celebrate my survival with salmon and beer. As I walk back to my cabin, I am serenaded by the howl of wolves.

Beware of the Gulo Gulo

Will I be eaten by a bear?

IT IS NOT A PREPOSTEROUS QUESTION, given my surroundings. For more than three weeks I have been slowly making my way northeast through the civilized girth of Finland. Kuhmo is the last city of any decent size before I wobble into the forests of North Karelia. Before I go farther, I think it might be a good idea during my layover to inquire about bears and other beasts.

My anxiety is not without justification. Finland's border with Russia is the last enclave of free-roaming brown bears in Europe. Sometimes called "European brown bears," the euphemism inspires an image of pretentious brown bears in berets, sipping espressos at a Helsinki sidewalk café while discussing Goethe. This bear sophisticate sounds nothing like its rustic cousin, the feared North American grizzly bear or *Ursus arctos horribilis*—the Latin providing amplified imagery. *Why worry?*

To learn more about this dashing Finnish bear, I find the equivalent of a ranger's station, the Petola Visitors Center, conveniently located about a half-mile northeast of my hilltop cabin.

It turns out that *horribilis* and the beret-wearing European brown bear of my imagination are one and the same. This is confirmed by a film showing a local bear feasting on a dead elk, not exactly café fare. Once ranging throughout northern Europe and Scandinavia, the bears were an object of terror in the Middle Ages. (The bear, though, is highly regarded in Finland. It is the country's national animal.) Encroaching civilization had wiped out most native populations, except in thinly populated eastern Finland and neighboring Russia.

The question of being eaten does not seem remotely ridiculous as I approach the young ranger at the counter. Her English, like that of most Finns under thirty, is impeccable. With a lilting accent, neither American nor English, her intonation only adds to her attractiveness.

"Oh yes," she enthuses, when I ask about the bruins. "Summer is a good time to see the bears."

She tells me that these large beasts are protein starved when they emerge from their dens in the spring. But the abundance of natural food—berries, roots, and small rodents—helps placate the bears' hunger. By late July, they have moved beyond salad and are hunting for fresher and meatier entrees like moose calves and, by extension, bike riders who wobble through the woods. With a chase speed of nearly 40 miles per hour, a bear could easily overtake me. I often dawdle along at a quarter of that speed—and that's when I'm pumping hard. I check the date function on my watch. It is July 29, definitely qualifying as late in the month.

"But am I in danger?"

She gives me a look that says, "You've got to be kidding."

"You will not be eaten," she assures me with mock sternness. "The bears are very shy. No one has been eaten in a long time. You will probably not see one unless you go deep into the forest and look like a sheep."

I confirm that I do not resemble and have never been a sheep. I am greatly relieved by this news. One of the many things I've noticed during my trip is that the Finns give you a straight answer—no sugarcoating. Bears were not going to be a problem—if they were, my attractive ranger would have said something like, "Yes, you will be eaten by a bear," and that would have been that. I thank her and turn to look at the exhibits inside the center.

"Wait!" she calls. I stop and return to the counter.

"You are riding a bicycle, yes? And camping?"

I nod.

"You didn't ask about wolves."

"Wolves?" Like Little Red Riding Hood, I had not begun to consider wolves until I encountered yesterday's fake howling. And that hardly counted.

"The wolves are a bigger problem than bears," she says, a hint of alarm in her voice. "They have attacked farmers' dogs and killed them."

The lilt in her accent falls neatly on the word *killed*, adding an emphasis that, intended or not, gets my attention. I recall a Helsinki newspaper article I had read before leaving on the trip that described an increase in the number of wolves sighted in eastern Finland. The rise was attributed to the return of wild forest reindeer, distinct for its oversized hooves and gigantic V-shaped antlers that grow narrowed to allow passage through dense woods. The animal was pushed out of Finland in the nineteenth century by settlers seeking to carve farms out of the forest. However, across the border, Karelian Russia remained untamed, a perfect habitat for the wild reindeer and its nemesis, the wolf. In the 1950s, thanks largely to Finland's desire to preserve the last vestiges of its wilderness on its eastern border, the wild forest reindeer slowly returned to these protected areas. The wolves followed. When not stalking reindeer, the wolves feasted on the less wolf-wise domesticated reindeer or made life miserable for Karelian farmers. In 2003, the region I was about to bike through reported that wolves had killed three hundred twenty domestic reindeer, thirty-one dogs, and one hundred thirty-five sheep.

The ranger explains that a bicycle might trigger the chase instinct inherent in the wolf pack; I begin having visions of a Jack London-like end to my trip.

"What weapons do you carry?" she asks me.

"Weapons?"

I had never considered such a question. Finland is one of the safest countries in the world. But then again, I had not thought about an encounter with wolves.

The ranger waits for me to answer. I think hard, but my arsenal consists of rubber bands, dirty underwear, and a pair of heavy-duty toenail clippers (you know, the big toe is always a problem). I can only hope to fend off an attack by putting out an eye with a well-aimed rubber band, asphyxiating the beast with my stinky briefs, then sliding in to give the wolf a bad pedicure. Clearly, the encounter would be potentially unpleasant for both parties.

"I might be able to find a stick," I say, rather lamely. My defense plan does not impress the ranger.

"You might want a rock, too," she asserts.

"Okay," I say, the color draining from my face. "Thanks for the advice." I turn to go, but take only a few steps when she calls to me again.

"Wait," she says. "If you insist on camping, I must tell you about one more creature. It is my duty."

By now, I am thinking about making a giant detour back toward friendly and less beast-infested western Finland. Meekly, I return to the counter.

"There is a creature in the deep forest that is very rare, but fierce. If you wander around at night, you might accidently encounter it."

Good God, I think, now what? And why does she think I will be wandering around in the deep forest at night? Then I remember. I am a fifty-two-year-old male. Certain functions must be performed in the wee hours—it's inevitable.

The ranger continues, "I do not know the English name, but in Finland we call it *gulo gulo.*"

"The what what?"

"Gulo gulo."

"You've got to be kidding. There's something out there called a gulo gulo?" I ask, pointing out the window toward the forest where all these creatures waited to pounce on me.

"Yes," confirms the woman, not the slightest hint in her voice that this is a joke or an attempt to scare the crap out of me. After all, she is Finnish: blunt and sincere.

"What does this thing look like?" I ask, feebly.

"It is furry, with a big snout and sharp teeth." The description conjures up a hairy, buck-toothed Sasquatch figure or the Jabberwocky in the famed Lewis Carroll children's rhyme—"Beware the Jabberwock, my son! The jaws that bite, the claws that catch." I want to know more, but the phone rings and my helper is soon engulfed in animated conversation. A gulo gulo sighting in sector three, perhaps? I wander away, nearly knocking over a stuffed lynx, apparently another local carnivore that dines well. I take out the stained notebook where I keep my grocery and to-do list. I write "gulo gulo?" next to "buy cheese and bananas."

At this moment, what I obviously need—besides a gun—is a better dictionary. I paw through my abridged phrase book, but find a scant six entries under "g." Only two represent living things: gynecologist and grapefruit. They could only help me if the attacking gulo gulo is, perhaps, a pregnant vegan.

I hang around until the ranger is finished with her phone call and thank her for the advice.

"Enjoy your visit in Kuhmo," she chirps, as I leave the building.

vvv   vvv   vvv

I ride back to town, my mind momentarily distracted from the gulo gulo by notices tacked to light poles advertising that the city that just finished hosting an international chamber music festival will welcome a monster truck demolition derby next week.

But the mayhem such an event might cause is nowhere in evidence on this quiet Sunday. As I ride slowly through the deserted streets past a supermarket and stores, the sun breaks out. The warmth seems to bring with it a certain joy, infusing me again with the energizing spirit that has managed to propel the Expedition this far.

I reach a park where families stroll on a path bordering a large neighboring lake and pose for pictures next to a life-size statue of a brown bear. Where is the big-nosed gulo gulo? For a moment, I feel a tinge of regret for wasting a decent day resting when I could be making a mad dash through the forest, perhaps putting some serious distance between me and the gulo gulos, wolves, and bears. But I fight this urge of over-ambition and let myself absorb the moment: the warmth of the sun, the green of the park grass, and the pleasant slap of waves on the shore. *What's your big hurry?* I think to myself.

There are two items left on the Expedition "to do" list for the day. I need more cash, and I need to find the Juminkeko—a combination museum, library, and archive that serves as the repository of the *Kalevala*, Finland's epic folk tale.

I stop at one of the two banks in town and try to draw euros from the automatic teller machine. The machine declares that it is out of money and spits out my card. I try the other bank across the street and receive the same result. Kuhmo is out of cash. I hope the 70 euros in my pocket will last until I make it to the next city.

I find the Juminkeko, a modernistic wood building, in the center of Kuhmo. I wander inside where I am greeted by a young woman. After I tell her I want to learn more about the *Kalevala*, she promptly leads me to a large auditorium where I have my pick of documentary films. Afterward, I wander into the small literary center, which holds a collection of *Kalevalas* in a variety of languages. After the movies, I am not sure my guide knows what to do with me. As I browse through the stacks and wander over to an art display, she sidles off, leaving me to rummage around on my own.

Prior to the nineteenth century, there was little identifiable Finnish culture, as the country had been controlled for so long by either the Swedes or the Russians. Swedish was the language of the government and the intelligentsia. Finnish was considered a strange dialect spoken by the rustics living in the forests. This changed in the early 1800s with the emergence of Finnish nationalism and its focus on the region's unique language and cultural roots. Finnish intellectuals sought a cultural tie that would link the Finnish people to a unique set of folk heroes and legends, much in the way that the Norwegians and Icelanders identified with the Viking sagas.

What they sought lay hidden deep in the forest among isolated Karelian villages in Finland and Russia, where generations of seers and storytellers had preserved a remarkable collection of epic poems and legends that were distinctly Finnish. Fearing that these oral stories would be lost to encroaching civilization, a young country doctor, Elias Lönnrot, arrived in Kuhmo in 1828. He made inquiries, hired guides, and ventured into the forest to find storytellers who could recite the poems.

He was not disappointed. For years, Lönnrot worked steadily to write down the verses, called runes. Between 1831 and 1835, Lönnrot meticulously transcribed the runic verses, one of which was more than four thousand lines long. He cobbled these together into the *Kalevala*— some twenty-three thousand lines and the first literature published in Finnish. After Lönnrot, others followed, arriving in Kuhmo to buy supplies and hire guides, then setting out into the forest to record the elusive oral runes. A second, enhanced, edition of the *Kalevala* was published in 1849. The poets were followed in the 1890s by painters and composers— Sibelius among them—who set their work to the themes and characters of the tales.

Big on rhyme and repetition, the runes had evolved into a form that could be memorized, though translations are challenging because of the many alliterations. The plot centers on the emergence of a central mythic hero, Väinämöinen, and a colorful supporting cast of other heroes and villains. The tale reads like a combination of the *Odyssey* and *Gulliver's Travels*. Väinämöinen is unusual among the folk hero pantheon for his remarkable ability to vanquish foes and extricate himself from jams by belting out a good tune. Indeed, singing is a major weapon for many of the heroes. He who sings best wins.

Many of Väinämöinen's adventures are focused on his thwarted attempts to find a wife. One seductress tempts him with a potential tryst by asking him to perform ridiculously impossible tasks, including building a boat from the splints of her girdle. When not sidetracked by dating frustrations, the hero focuses on his quest to make the *sampo*—the magic mill—a task that can only be done in the Far North. Why the *sampo* is so important is not particularly clear to the first-time reader, but given that this is a folk tale, one can assume that at best its possessor inherits magical powers, or at the very least, it is a real nice thing to have on the fireplace mantle.

For the actual forging, Väinämöinen recruits his friend Ilmarinen, the best blacksmith in the land, who wisely refuses this task. "Why go to the rainy and miserable northland?" he asks. But Väinämöinen sings the creation of a magic tree, which Ilmarinen unwisely climbs, and he is borne off by the wind to the north. There he meets Louhi, the resident sorceress and the mother of some very fetching daughters. Ilmarinen, who is also single, agrees to forge the *sampo* for Louhi in exchange for marriage to one of her daughters. Even though this seems like a good deal, it is not, and it serves as a warning to bachelors who come between a protective mother and her daughter. Unfortunately, Ilmarinen is smitten, and after much difficulty he forges the *sampo*. He even selects colors for it that he thinks will please his future wife, another mistake that ironically parallels the travails of many a modern couple's kitchen renovation. When he finishes, Ilmarinen asks the woman to be his wife. What follows is probably the longest rejection ever committed to verse.

Northland's fair and lovely daughter
Answers thus the metal-worker:
"Who will in the coming spring-time,
Who will in the second summer,
Guide the cuckoo's song and echo?
Who will listen to his calling,
Who will sing with him in autumn,
Should I go to distant regions,
Should this cheery maiden vanish
From the fields of Sariola,
From Pohyola's fens and forests,
Where the cuckoo sings and echoes?
Should I leave my father's dwelling,
Should my mother's berry vanish,
Should these mountains lose their cherry,
Then the cuckoo too would vanish,
All the birds would leave the forest,

Leave the summit of the mountain,
Leave my native fields and woodlands,
Never shall I, in my life-time,
Say farewell to maiden freedom...

Dejected, Ilmarinen returns home and tells his buddy Väinämöinen to forget about the *sampo*. Louhi locks up the magic mill at Stone Mountain (with nine locks), which appears to be the ancient equivalent of Fort Knox.

Undeterred by Illmarinen's warning to stay away from Louhi, Väinämöinen travels to the northland, called Pohjola (presumably Lapland), and asks to share the *sampo*, but Louhi refuses. This sets the stage for an epic battle, the theft of the *sampo* by Väinämöinen, and the wild adventures that follow.

And so it goes for verse after verse. Along the way the reader encounters wizards, more beautiful maidens, magical eagles, a giant shaman, a really good ski chase, a lot of very bad weather (Louhi can't sing, but she can brew up a good storm), an enchanted kantele,* and a wild boat ride. Near the conclusion, the heroes are nearly wiped out by a plague, but, being Finns, they ward it off by immersing themselves in the best sauna ever.

---

* A thirty-six-string harp-like instrument, usually played on the lap, thought to have originated in Finland.

The First Reindeer

I AM THINKING OF LOUHI'S PROPENSITY to create bad weather as copious volumes of water stream off the eaves of my Kalevala Village cabin. It is midmorning, the day after my research at the Juminkeko. I am packed and ready to continue, but I cannot bring myself to leave the safety of the abode's tiny awning. Louhi is wreaking havoc, and I don't even have a shot at her fetching daughters, nor can I forge a *sampo*. Instead, my epic will take me a modest 27 miles down the road to Lentiiran Limaskya, where the ranger who warned me about being chased down by wolves and gulo gulos advised me to camp.

I stand and watch the dirt road connecting the cabins turn into rivulets of muddy water. I have already incorporated lessons learned from "the worst morning ever" and have prepared for my ride by sealing myself inside a waterproof, seamless barrier of rain pants and parka, with the hood tightly cinched around my neck. My maps are encased in multiple plastic bags. Lunch is packed in stages in my front carrier so I can retrieve food quickly without exposing other contents to the rain. But even with this Mannerheim line of rain defense, I am not eager to start the day in a deluge.

Around noon the rain lets up slightly. I step cautiously into the open, hoist myself onto the bike seat, and coast down the muddy path to the paved road leading to the village's fortress. Minutes after beginning my ride, another cloudburst lets go. Within seconds my shoes and socks, which I had carefully dried over the past two days, are again soaked.

The woman at the reception desk looks at me with what could only be pity.

"Summer in Finland," she sighs, as I surrender my cabin key to her. "Are you sure you don't want to stay?"

The prospect is tempting.

"I might be back," I reply, as water drips from my hood onto the counter.

I get back on the bike and coast downhill, serenaded by a chorus of wolf howls. It rains harder, as if Louhi herself is determined to stop this new incursion into her territory. Thunder rumbles in the distance. At the base of the hill, I find shelter under the porch of a building and watch the downpour with a growing sense of depression. Nearby is a running track, where, much to my amazement, a young man in spandex is roller skiing around the circuit, undeterred by the deluge.

At last the rain slackens. Yet I bike no more than a hundred yards when I see another dark cloud rapidly approaching. I dart back to the same visitor's center I sought assistance from yesterday and cower under the eaves. For some reason, Louhi is determined to drown me. *What have I done?*

With this latest downpour showing no signs of abating, I wander back into the building.

"Hello, again."

It is the ranger I spoke with yesterday.

By now she seems like an old friend. She had been watching when I pulled up and had already printed out the weather report.

"I'm afraid the weather will be bad for several days," she says.

She shows me the report. She's right. For the next couple of days the weather grows increasingly "unsettled." The mother of all storms is expected to hit in three days, on Thursday, judging from the graphic of a scowling cloud face hurling lightning bolts on the paper she has handed me.

"I guess I could stay here and finish reading the *Kalevala* in the library," I say.

"I'm sure they have many English books in the library," she assures me.

My friend wanders off to attend to some fishermen, leaving me to contemplate my situation. I do not want to stay in Kuhmo four more days. For all I know, it might rain forever. If I can survive the lesser storms during the next two days and make it to Suomussalmi, I can wait out the worst of the weather there—possibly in the comfort of another cabin.

Thunder rattles the building. I make a pact with myself. If the rain abates, I will bike five miles north. If within that distance I get slammed by another storm cell, I will return to Kuhmo and hunker down, perhaps for the rest of my life. That decided, I wander into the center's empty theater where I watch a different part of the same video I saw yesterday. This time the bear appears to be gorging on a reindeer. When I can watch no more, I return to the reception area, which seems curiously quiet. En route I pass a display depicting a small bear-like animal with a flat head and snout. I recognize it—it's a wolverine. Upon closer examination I notice the label, *Gulo Gulo*. The once-mysterious creature now seems less ominous. Outside, I notice the rain has stopped. Time to ride.

I set a slow but even pace, my eyes darting between the road and the odometer. At the five-mile mark, the sky is still leaden, but not a drop has fallen since I left the refuge of the visitor's center. But the Sorceress of the North is clever. She has held her fire, waiting for me to reach the point of no return. I cross a murky slough, which I dub "the Rubicon" and pedal on. No turning back now. As predicted, the skies darken again and the rain falls. I try to steer my thoughts away to something productive. I think of the desert. I think of my warm, dry house in Seattle. I invent a bike shoe, a sort of quick-drying sandal worn without socks that can withstand a monsoon. Despite the squalls I make steady progress, my mind now busy designing an entire line of waterproof clothes specifically for the Karelian summer.

The terrain flattens out. The forest opens to large meadows rippling with cotton grass and bisected by meandering coffee-colored streams. At any moment I expect to see a moose, elk, reindeer, or even a wolf, but none come into view. By midafternoon, as yet another dark squall rumbling with thunder and lightning bears down on me, I reach the turnoff to the campground, a farmstead that advertises itself as Lentiirua Lomakylä.

The place is deserted. A knock on the door of the big yellow house that serves as reception produces nothing, not even a barking dog. I consult the map, but quickly dismiss any thought of continuing. There is nothing but 60 miles of dense forest between where I stand and Suomussalmi.

After about thirty minutes, a woman emerges from an adjacent hay field. She wears hip boots and carries a pail. She does not speak English, and my attempt to inquire about a cabin in Finnish is met with a puzzled expression. I try the word for tent. She brightens and beckons for me to follow. She shows me a pleasant patch of lawn, not far from a river. Nearby is a cook's cabin and shower room. I am the only guest. For $12, I can't complain.

Later that afternoon, the sun bursts through the clouds. After hanging my wet clothes on the tent lines, I follow a trail through glistening blueberry bushes to a floating dock on the shores of the Lentiiranjoki. Here, I bask in the sudden warmth, watching birds dart in and out of the wide river, while trout surface to snag low-flying bugs. The reversal in the weather is astounding. But I know enough about the fickle Finnish climate to realize this is merely an interlude. I enjoy it while I can.

Later that evening after I have eaten and taken a shower, I wander back to my camp and am surprised to see a tall, young man unfurling a tent not far from mine. A bike is parked nearby. I bound up to him and introduce myself. Between shards of English and Finnish, I learn that his name is Sam, and he is heading to Espoo, the Helsinki suburb that I very much enjoyed a few weeks back. Sam has been cycling south for three days. But Sam, like his fellow countrymen, is a man of few words. I ask where he started from, but the name is one I don't recognize. After exchanging pleasantries and road information, he returns to the task of erecting his tent.

In the morning, all traces of the previous day's brilliant late afternoon sun have disappeared. Low clouds, like a fog, hang from the sky. But it is not raining. I quickly pack, and by seven I am rolling past Sam's tent to the dirt road that leads back to the main highway. Sam does not stir, so I silently say good-bye and pedal on. The rain holds off for two hours before it comes slanting down again. By now I have institutionalized my rain garb. The drops drip off my pants and parka and my head stays dry and warm, though my ensemble does not necessarily make riding any easier.

The forest is pervasive, interrupted by clear-cuts and furrowed by gigantic trenches scooped through the muck by what I can only surmise must have been a giant with a hoe. Unlike some of the old-growth and second-growth forests of my home state, Washington, these lands have been logged continuously for hundreds of years. Nearly eighty percent of Finland is forest, but all wooded areas, save a thin sliver in east Lapland, have been carefully cultivated. The result is a coniferous sameness that makes for painfully monotonous viewing from a slow-moving vehicle like a bike.

With the constant rain, I cannot even take appropriate food breaks. The best I can manage is to stand, straddle the bike, fish out some food, eat, take a drink, and then continue. Part of my reluctance to tarry is the warning about wolves, which is still fresh in my mind. At each bend in the road, I peer ahead anxiously, alert for howling or the sudden patter of wild canine feet. In the flat, gray light, every stump looks like a bear, every stack of piled slash seems to be hiding a wolf pack. From the periphery of my vision, the forest elements transform into all manner of stalking phantom animals that dart back into the woods when I turn to look at them.

There is no traffic except for the occasional logging truck, whose roar I can hear coming miles away as it builds to a crescendo that climaxes as it passes me with a sudden suction of air, followed by a contrail of woody debris. Then I am again alone, except for the brooding forest, its shadowy creatures, and the rain. I try to hurry on, but I seem to get nowhere.

In the growing gloom of loneliness, I have begun to exhaust the imaginary conversations I have with friends, and daydreams about home and my plans for the future. It is as if I have been watching the same movie over and over, so much that I cannot bear to see it anymore. My brain increasingly turns to the minutiae of my second-to-second experience: the gravel embedded in the asphalt, the texture of the clouds.

I am angry at the rain, angry at Louhi for conjuring up endless storms. In the absence of constructive thoughts to occupy my mind, I begin to chant. But my chant is not mystical, not a holy chant; it's more of a sophomoric child rant because it is the only thing that I can get into a brain that has been numbed by rain and gray.

We want a reindeer. We want a reindeer. We want a reindeer. This is my message of desperation to the world. Just show me one reindeer, something I can talk to, something that proves this Expedition has some meaning, and I will shut up. I chant on, shouting to the woods and the moving shapes and the wolves that are not wolves. I chant on, even though I know I am at least 50 miles from the range of Finland's most southern reindeer herd.

Then, surmounting yet another hill, I see something that is neither phantom nor carnivorous beast. It is a reindeer with a gigantic rack. It crosses the road, not more than a hundred feet in front of me. I am stunned. The sight is completely unexpected and rather unnerving.

"I see you—thanks for coming out of the forest!" I yell. "Great rack!"

What else can you say to a reindeer?

After all, it is my first reindeer sighting, and perhaps it is his or her (both male and female reindeer sport antlers) first encounter with a folding bike. I stop and paw through the front carrier, looking for my camera. I don't care if it's raining and my camera gets ruined. I've got to photograph this milestone.

The reindeer, Rudolph, as I christen him, saunters toward the edge of the forest as I fumble with the tiny digital camera. He is not wearing a collar nor is there a bell around his neck. Have I stumbled upon a rare wild forest reindeer? He stops on the opposite side of the road and stares at me. I get off the bike and try to approach, but he retreats farther into the forest. I follow, stumbling over logs, my shoes sinking into the wet, mossy forest floor. The reindeer leads on, gliding through the thick woods. The tree boughs seem to part magically before its massive antlers, while I wallow behind. I cannot get any closer. Our little game of hide-and-seek abruptly ends when the startling roar of a car sends Rudolph bounding even deeper into the woods.

North of Kuhmo, the Expedition sights its first reindeer.

My reindeer has transformed the morning from one of misty gloom into one of ecstasy. The Riding with Reindeer Expedition has now actually seen a reindeer! I will not have to change the Expedition name to Riding with Rain, Mosquitoes, Bulbous-eyed Flies, and Other Varmints.

The appearance of the reindeer so soon after I began my chant leads me to think about the *Kalevala* heroes and how they not only sung themselves out of trouble but also created useful things with their songs. *Maybe there is something to this singing in the forest!* With this thought, the opening lines of the *Kalevala* seem eminently appropriate to the beginning of an epic, even my epic.

> *I am driven by my longing,*
> *And my understanding urges,*
> *That I should commence my singing,*
> *And begin my recitation,*
> *I will sing the people's legends,*
> *And the ballads of the nation.*

The rain stops as I pull into a combination gas station and store in Ala Vuokki. I pour myself a cup of coffee and select a donut, then take a seat in the back, near stacks of televisions, toasters, and microwaves still in their boxes. A young man, his wife, and a small child come in, and after looking at the televisions, sit nearby. The kid, who is wearing a baseball cap with the Porsche logo on it, cannot take his eyes off me. What he sees is an extremely disheveled man who is slowly sipping his coffee as if it were the last cup in the world. He peers intently at a map—his blue rain pants and matching parka slowly wicking away the morning's accumulated moisture.

"Porsche, yes!" I say, getting up and giving the wide-eyed boy the thumbs up, rousing a chuckle from his parents. Adding further amusement is my departure, or rather lack of departure, from Ala Vuokki's only commercial establishment. I can't find the exit. Two old men, sipping coffee in a corner, finally direct me to another door I had not seen.

By midafternoon, I round a corner and come to a strange sight. There in a large clearing stand thousands of rocks in expanding rings, enclosing a modernistic memorial that looks like a giant candleholder. At its base are wreaths with ribbons in the Finnish and Russian national colors. Upon closer examination, I see that the smaller stones represent the thousands of soldiers, both Finnish and Russian, who died in these woods during the Winter War of 1939–40. Nearby, a few rusting tanks and artillery pieces sit in the parking lot of a visitor's center and cafeteria. Half the parking spaces are occupied by cars with Russian license plates.

In one of the great ironies of history, the Russians and their rubles are now more than welcome in Finland.

A memorial honors thousands of Finnish and Russian soldiers who died during savage fighting in the Winter War.

The battlefield that I had come upon near Kuhmo three days ago was the Russian feint. Eleven miles to the east of where I now stand, Stalin had amassed another forty thousand troops under the command of General Vinogradov. While another Russian army attacked to the south, General Vinogradov was ordered to storm through the thin Finnish defenses and cut the country in half.

Opposing Vinogradov's divisions were fifty Finnish border guards with a few scattered companies of civil guards backing them up farther down the Raate Road. This was the sum of Finland's initial defense that lay between the advancing Russian columns, Suomussalmi, and the rest of Finland. During the next forty-five days, the outnumbered Finns, with no tanks and a couple of ancient antitank guns, scored one of the greatest tactical military victories of all time.

The Finns retreated to Suomussalmi, razed it to the ground, then withdrew to better defensive positions. Sensing his vulnerability, Mannerheim quickly sent more troops to the Suomussalmi front, assigning Colonel Hjalmar Siilasvuo, a lawyer before being called into service, to command what would be called Task Force Susi, or Wolf. One of the first units to arrive was a bicycle brigade, which helped stymie the Russian offensive about five miles from here. *I can barely function in the rain,* I think. *How did the Finns manage to maneuver bicycles in deep snow in subzero temperatures?*

By mid-December, enough reinforcements had arrived to begin a series of counterattacks. Gliding through the forest on cross-country skis, the Finns severed the Russian column in dozens of places, isolating and besieging pockets of soldiers and equipment that became known as *mottis.*[29] Their orders were to take out mess kitchens, officers, and food depots—anything that could provide their enemies with warmth and sustenance. To the Russian soldiers, most of whom were poorly trained conscripts, the attacks must have been terrifying.

During the first counterattacks, the Russians fired wildly into the woods, rarely hitting anything but tree branches. By late December, their ammunition was running low. Continued, frantic Russian counterattacks were repulsed by the all-but-invisible Finns, who gunned down the hapless Russians by the thousands. One by one, Russian units were annihilated. With temperatures often reaching 30 degrees below zero, the dead and wounded froze solid in grotesque shapes.

By late January, the battle was over. The charred remains of hundreds of Russian tanks, supply trucks, jeeps, and artillery pieces littered the Raate and Juntusraata Roads. Among the debris were thousands of pairs of skis, along with booklets illustrated with comic book characters showing how to use them.

The luckiest Russian soldiers were taken prisoner; the less lucky straggled back to Russia. Among them was General Vinogradov, who was summarily executed, along with three of his surviving officers. The charge: failing to protect the division's fifty-five field kitchens.

Highway 912 bends west toward Suomussalmi, passing Huakila, where more savage battles were fought sixty-eight years ago. What strikes me most about the monuments that I pass is their even-handed portrayal of the war. No judgment is placed on the Soviet Union's unprovoked attack against a lightly defended neighbor. The memorials are intended to honor both Finnish and Soviet soldiers. When English interpretations are available, they provide a dispassionate, journalistic account of maneuvers, tactics, and statistics, similar to Civil War memorials in the United States. While this seems consistent with the Finnish propensity for understatement, I wonder how much the tone also reflects unease about the still-sensitive and unpredictable moods of its colossal neighbor to the east.

I, too, have taken casualties during my visit to this land—namely, on my rear end. Saddle sores that began to fester a week ago are now in full bloom. The last few miles I try to ease the pain by standing in my pedals or shifting from one buttock to another. My agony ends when the forest thins and the outskirts of the now rebuilt Suomussalmi come to view. I find the Kianlajarvi Campground, rent a tiny cabin on the shores of Lake Haukipere, and prepare to wait out the monster storm that has been predicted.

North Karelia to Kittilä

21

Haunted Cabin

I AM GLAD TO BE OFF THE SADDLE, even if the Kianlajarvi Campground is a little worn around the edges. The camp road leads through a spruce grove that slopes down to Lake Haukipere. A couple of miniature ponies graze lazily in a small meadow. Among the trees in the scattered tent sites are old, clunky trailers that look as if they have been here for a long, long time. By the shore, campers gather wood near the open-roofed kitchen cabin, preparing to roast a pile of fresh fish.

I find my tiny cabin perched on a small bluff not more than twenty-five feet away from the lapping waters of the lake. The wind is already gusting, a precursor of the big storm I have anticipated for days. White caps churn farther out. The cabin is furnished with a bunk bed tucked against one side, two wooden chairs nested under a table, and a small refrigerator with a hot plate on top. There is barely enough room to turn around, but it is warm and will keep me from harm's way during the upcoming tempest. Before the weather can deteriorate further, I unpack, unhitch the wagon, and ride the three miles into town to buy groceries and check my e-mail at the library.

As I enter the town's outskirts, I realize that today is the last day of July, my thirtieth day in Finland, and roughly the halfway point of the Expedition. According to my calculations, I am a little more than halfway to my goal despite my glacial pace. I just need to keep grinding forward and hope the weather gets better.

Back at the camp, I begin preparing dinner by fetching a pot of water from the lake. Pasta highlights the menu tonight. After boiling the noodles for ten minutes, I take the pot outside to pour out the excess water. I keep a clothed hand on the hot pot handle and use my other hand to hold the clamp that grips the lid, which in turn keeps the pasta from sliding out of the pot. This is not normally a complicated procedure. But remember: this is an epic and things you least expect happen at inconvenient times.

I have a firm hold of the lid clamp, or at least I think I do. Just as I finish pouring, the lid seems to jump out of my grip on its own accord. It lands on its edge and rolls toward the lake. I give chase. The lid somehow winds its way around shrubs, rocks, and trees while gaining momentum on the downhill slope. Why it doesn't flip over and lay flat but instead continues to defy the laws of gravity is a mystery. I stumble after it. As it approaches the lake, the lid gains speed, caroms off a tree trunk, then bounces off a boulder before flying into the lake. I am in close pursuit, but when I get to the boulder, which slopes into the lake, I slam on the brakes.

Earlier, I had removed my soggy cycling socks and shoes and had luxuriated in wearing my only pair of wool socks and a pair of dry slip-on mocs. Anyone who has worn mocs knows they are not designed for steeplechases, let alone steeplechases in Finland. Despite my efforts to stop, my shoes keep sliding on the slick granite, launching me, my dry clothes, and shoes feet-first into the lake. I thrash my way out of the water, in the process gouging my left shin against the boulder. Blood seeps from the five-inch laceration. The lid, as if mocking me, glitters like a lost jewel at the bottom of the lake. I lie on my stomach on the boulder and try to grab it, but my arms are too short and the water too deep.

I need that lid. It isn't mine. I borrowed it from a friend back home. Plus, the lid doubles as a frying pan. It is indispensable. Yes, I can buy another one, but that would put another unexpected hole in the Expedition budget. More to the point, this little escapade of insubordinate equipment, followed by my leg wound, has really made me mad. It's one thing for the gods to drench me in rain; it's quite another thing to start screwing with the few miserable pieces of equipment I possess, then toss me into the lake. I know this is the work of Louhi, Sorceress of the North, and she's not going to get away with it, if I can help it.

I storm back to the cabin, tear off my clothes, put on my swim trunks, and march back to the lake. The wind has intensified by now, and what had been mild lapping against the shore has been replaced by the froth of waves. I lower myself into the water, then take the plunge. It's not nearly as refreshing as my after-sauna swim, but my sense of mission keeps me focused. The lid shimmers in the water. I stretch my arm and grab it before the Sorceress can turn me into a trout. I claw myself out of the lake. Shivering, I run back toward the cabin to towel off. A nearby fisherman, who has been observing this drama, shouts something in Finnish, but when he sees my blank expression, yells helpfully in English: "Better to take sauna first, then dive into lake."

"Thanks for the advice," I shout, as I scamper back to the cabin.

I do not think much of this incident again until later that night after I crawl into the top bunk and fall asleep. Something jars me awake in the middle of the night. *What time is it?* My reading glasses are out of reach on the table, so the digital readout on my watch is a blur. Outside, the wind whistles through the trees. Rain pelts the sides of the cabin. The mother of all storms has arrived. I lay still in the bed, trying to generate enough energy and nerve to get up, leave the warm cabin, and relieve myself—usually a once-a-night chore. I think about the lid and its strange journey, as well as my unfortunate associated mishaps. Was this an act of chance, or was something else at work?

I recall legends about supernatural beings that dwell in the forests of the Far North. These beings, often invisible to humans, sometimes take form during violent storms that occur at the periphery of civilization, such as a village like Suomussalmi. But are these legends, or are they based on a tiny speck of reality?

Years ago, an American bike rider who had pitched a tent in a deserted campground in Sweden during a violent storm told an interviewer he saw a furry creature with pointy ears and a humanlike face in his tent. When he reached for his flashlight, the creature rushed out.

Both he and his girlfriend, who was half-asleep at the time, felt the fur. But when they examined the area outside of the tent, they found no footprints or any other evidence of the creature's existence.[30] Could the supernatural beings encountered by the heroes of the *Kalevala* during tromps through the wilderness of what is now eastern Finland have some basis in reality?

For the first time in the trip I am afraid to go outside, and my fear isn't of the mysterious gulo gulo or the elusive European brown bear, but of something that might not even be real. As the wind howls and thunder shakes the tiny cabin, I start to believe that if I wander too close to the lake, whatever guided the lid at dinnertime might be waiting there, ready to shove me into the water.

Ridiculous, thinking of ghosts! I say to myself. I've come all this way, and I'm not going to let a little superstitious hysteria prevent me from peeing. I swing my legs out of the bunk and feel with my feet for the step stool. As I lower myself down, the stool flips to the side. I cling to the bed, barely averting a serious fall. Gradually, I lower myself to the floor. Now I am seriously paranoid. *Did something kick the stool out from under me? Or am I really just losing my mind?*

I put on my pants and shoes and shove open the heavy cabin door, making sure it will not slam shut and lock me out. As usual, it isn't completely dark. A luminous gloom that seems spookier than true darkness prevails over the forest. Tree branches sway. Pine needles and bits of bark fly through the air. Waves pound the shore. I find a tree not more than five feet away, perform my chore, and then scramble back to the cabin, slam the door, and scuttle unaided into my bunk. *Safe again,* or so I think.

An hour later I awake with a start. I had stashed nylon bags full of clothes, as well as my day pack, maps, and the other detritus in the lower bunk. What I hear unnerves me: stuff is being moved. I glance at the door. It is shut, still locked. The shuffling of bags continues. *Are mice rampaging through my things looking for crumbs?* I listen. *If it's mice, they are really big mice.* Then I hear tapping and scraping on the roof, as if something is trying to claw through it.

Petrified, I lay in the bunk as if in a nightmare, the kind where you can't move as the monster slowly approaches your bedroom. But this is not a dream; I am fully awake. Outside, the storm is in full fury. Thunder rolls, and I can see lightning flashes through the only window. I will myself to be calm, to be rational. But the noises below and the scratching from the roof continue. *Are tree branches brushing against the roof? That has to be it.* In the morning, I will confirm it. But I have no simple explanation for the shuffling on the bunk below. Too terrified to investigate, I burrow inside my sleeping bag, desperately thinking of a song to sing away the horrors occupying my lower bunk.

When morning comes and I open my eyes, the cabin is still and silent. Through the window I can see that the sky is a solid gray of unbroken clouds. I find the stool, get out of bed, and peer into the bottom bunk. My stuff is still in a disheveled heap, but whether a specific item has been moved, I cannot tell. No food is disturbed—none of my precious granola bars, perfect mouse food, have been tampered with. Beyond these observations, I am not going to stick around to conduct an investigation. I have one goal in mind for this morning and that is to get the hell out of here, even if I have to bike through a typhoon. There is no way I will spend another night with giant mice, forest spirits, ghosts, trolls, and God knows whatever else rolled through these parts last night. I pack as quickly as I can.

After I hitch up the bike to the wagon, I take one last look around. I remember the clawing on the roof. I back away from the cabin to get a good look at the surrounding trees. There isn't a branch within thirty feet of it.

I jump on the bike and pedal as fast as I can, which really isn't very fast. I don't look back.

The haunted cabin

Agony and Ecstasy

SOMETIMES TRAVELING ALONE IS SHEER JOY. Sometimes it is sheer agony. Today it is agony.

Shortly after leaving the haunted cabin, I scurry via a bridge across Lake Haukipere on Highway 9150, then pass another war monument—the scene of the decisive battle for Suomussalmi. I totter into the nearby village of Suomussalmen, looking for National Bike Route 5, which will take me deeper into North Karelia, bend me within two miles of the Russian border, then pop me safely into southern Lapland. This new 110-mile segment will take two days, with an overnight stay midway in the little village of Hossa.

Once again the bike route signs vanish when I most need them. *Why is this?* I wonder, baffled and irritated at the chronic inconsistency of signage. I pedal on what I think is the most sensible route, which drops down to the shore of yet another lake. The road narrows. For a main route to Lapland, there is suspiciously little traffic. I consult the map. Bike Route 5 does not parallel a lake. This can't be right.

Backtracking up a hill, I reenter town as the day's first cloudburst unleashes its fury. I cower under the awning of the local market across the street from a church cemetery where fresh red flowers mark the headstones of the Winter War dead. Twice I bike up and down the tiny town's main street looking for the bike route sign. In keeping with the epic's standing orders to minimize backtracking, I choose the only road heading north and plunge into the forest. There is no way I'm going all the way back to Suomussalmi and its haunted cabin.

For an hour I cycle on this lonely route, straining up rain-battered hills. The hills steepen. I dismount, feeling like Sisyphus as I push the bike and wagon up hill after hill. As has become my pattern, after summiting I enjoy a brief coast, then repeat the process for the next hill, which always seems steeper. My pace is not impressive. Occasionally, I come to a landmark, an old road sign or a dirt road branching into the woods. I consult the map, carefully shielding it with my body to keep it from turning to pulp in the wet weather. I check the names of farms, nearby villages—anything that can provide a clue that I am on the right road. The physical reality does not match my map, and yet this *has* to be the correct route. There is no other way to get to Lapland other than to plunge blindly into the woods and bushwhack. Or so says my map.

At last I come to a crossroads. A dirt road heads off to the north, while my route continues east. I have reached the great metropolis of Riihivaara. I only know this thanks to a wobbly sign that welcomes me. Only one thing is missing—Riihivaara.

I dismount and walk around behind the sign. Perhaps the village is hiding. I peer intently into the trees, but I see nothing that would indicate a settlement, not even a haystack or a barking dog. In the distance, I see a low-slung log cabin that looks like it was designed by hobbits, a thin curl of smoke issuing from its chimney. One thing is for sure: Riihivaara definitely has room to grow. But Riihivaara does have one thing going for it: it's on my map. I am on the right route. I relax. My position is reconfirmed thirty minutes later when I reach another Potemkin village, Pyyvaara, which is equal to Riihivaara in terms of its metropolitan grandeur, if not greater, because this phantom village stands at the crossroads with Highway 843. Finally, this is the road that will take me north to Lapland. A brief feeling of euphoria washes over me as I celebrate this evidence of my slow, but real, progress.

But what follows is pure torture. I crest yet another hill and see yet more storm clouds boiling toward me, a progression of dark veils of doom. By now, I have been exposed to so much "unsettled weather" that I could qualify as a Finnish weatherman. Even though I can see these clouds advancing, my other senses have become so attuned to the weather changes that I can *feel* when a maelstrom will hit. First, there is a gust of wind, then darkness, followed by a few big warning drops that burst like tiny water balloons on the road. Then Louhi, my nemesis, yanks the chain and the heavens open. Today's featured effect is big, Texas-style drops. Thankfully, I am spared the thunder and lightning—for now.

This routine is getting old, very old indeed. I have ceased becoming miserable and am now officially angry—angry at the rain gods, angry at global warming (for surely this is an end product of that), angry at myself for embarking on such a soggy epic. I want to vent, but I don't know to whom I can direct my venom, or even where to begin. My thoughts are as dark as the clouds. At some point, I begin to taunt the rain.

"Is that the best you can do? You call this rain?" I challenge, as yet another squall dumps on me. I laugh like a lunatic as the rain is flung from the clouds, my bike sloshing through water, my fists shaking at the sky. The gods respond to my taunts by steering squall after squall toward me, as if the sheer magnitude of the onslaught itself will finish me off.

Through this mayhem I wonder if I am descending into a kind of solo cycling madness. My lone source of reading pleasure, *The Race for Timbuktu*, describes the solitary agony of the early English explorers crossing the great expanse of the Sahara Desert for weeks without break, seeing nothing but sand and dazzling sun. I could use some dazzling sun as much as those early desert explorers could have used rain, but the end result on our minds is the same: a lack of human interaction, combined with a monotonous terrain and a constant battering by the elements, is a recipe for a slow decline into derangement. In a moment of lucidity, I decide that "solo explorer" is not a career path I wish to follow for the long term. If Kati, the reporter, had interviewed me now, I think my answer to her question about loneliness might have been much different.

When I tire of cursing I begin to sing. This is no hushed concert, but a full-throated bellow to the trees, stumps, and moss bogs that I slowly pass by. Instead of the epic verses of the *Kalevala*, most of my songs, not surprisingly, have a rain theme—"Singin' in the Rain," "Raindrops Keep Fallin' on My Head" and "Wouldn't It Be Loverly" (the second song in *My Fair Lady*, which starts out "All I want is a room somewhere..."). I only know a few words in each of these tunes, so I make up the rest with a Finnish twist or sing the first line over and over.

My pace slows to a crawl. There is little traffic. The forest is indeed unvarying, filled with Norwegian spruce of uniform height and girth, interrupted by massive clear-cuts with piles of Bunyanesque logs waiting to be hauled to the mill. Signs of logging activity are everywhere, but I have yet to see a tree actually being cut down. Sometimes, when the wind abates, I think I hear the distant buzz of a chain saw. But I never see the act. The Finns have perfected stealth logging.

Throughout the day, I see more reindeer wandering by the road. These sightings temporarily buoy my spirits as they confirm that I am closing in on southern Lapland. On the other hand, I can't help but notice that they seem as bummed about the weather and incessant buzz of mosquitoes as I am. Heads down, they trudge along, searching for tidbits of moss along the roadside. I stop the bike near one group to commiserate.

"This really sucks!" I yell to the leader. The big reindeer looks up and shakes his head, looking at me with big, sad brown eyes.

"Sorry—didn't mean to rub it in," I offer. It feels good to at least have an exchange with another living creature.

Except for the taunts of magpies and blackbirds, no other wildlife has manifested itself today, though maybe that's a good thing. I am an easy mark for wolves, as my pace is nothing more than a dawdle.

I'm pedaling hard to stay warm, but my saddle sores are aflame. To lessen the pain, I shift from one cheek to the other on the bike seat, trying desperately to stay off the hot spots. Nothing seems to work. At mid-morning, during one of my standing food breaks, I stuff a towel inside my undershorts to add padding. I christen this innovation "the Bicycle Diaper" but quickly decide the name is a marketing liability and change it to "the Cyclist's Friend." It does provide some temporary relief, and as a side effect, it provides me with a more robust masculine profile in a certain critical area. Meanwhile, the rain is incessant.

By midafternoon, I am within 20 miles of Hossa, which has now become larger than life in my addled imagination. I fantasize about fine restaurants, hotels, cabarets, open-air cafés, bowling alleys, and smartly dressed Hossanians going about their business. When I actually see Hossa, however, I am not surprised to find that there are no sidewalk cafés—or even sidewalks—but instead just a muddy crossroads and a big sign pointing to a campground with cabins for rent. I slog on for another quarter of a mile and arrive at a little store, a cozy café, and cabins. When I ask at the café about a cabin, I am told they are all booked. The campground has room, but a quick look reveals that the tenting area has turned into a mud wallow. The manager tells me that there is a hotel on the main road that may have room. I retrace my route to the highway and see the hotel a few hundred yards down the road.

The receptionist only speaks Finnish and Russian, but through sign language we manage to establish that they do indeed have an open room. It is not exactly the Ritz-Carlton, but for this wet and weary traveler, it will do just fine. An hour later, after a hot shower and a challenging exercise in draping my wet clothes on every available hook, hanger, and furniture edge, I am tucked in the hotel's empty bar, nursing a beer.

I wonder how the hell I made it through this day. I am also feeling somewhat sad that my new pals, the reindeer, can't join me for a round or two in this pleasant rain- and bug-free environment. So, instead of reindeer for supper, I order fish. Pictures of fish—trophy trout, pike, and whatever else they catch here—are everywhere: in the restaurant, in the bar, and in my room. If I were a fisherman, Hossa would be paradise. But the amenities here are rather meager, even for your average folding-bike expedition team consisting of one deranged epic seeker. As far as I can tell, there are no other commercial establishments besides the hotel and the aforementioned campground café and store.

I learn from the television news that there is a reasonably good chance the weather will be decent tomorrow, followed by—you guessed it—yet another storm. *Will they ever end?* I'm honestly starting to wonder. I desperately need a rest day, but Hossa isn't the place I want to lay over. My brain, which remarkably is still functioning, votes to press on to Kuusamo, a city of some size that is another 50 miles north. My rear end is voting, or rather screaming, for a down day here in Hossa. So I make a pact with myself. All of the United Body Parts of Bob (a new moniker I've just invented to show that my limbs are beginning to protest actions ordered by my brain) agree that if the weather is good tomorrow, we go; if bad, we stay. The promise to parts in pain is that I will layover for at least three days at the first available decent place.

෴ ෴ ෴

I awake to find a stripe of dazzling yellow light cleaving my bed in two. I fling open the curtain and see brilliant blue sky. Within an hour, I am pedaling north again through sun-dappled forest, the United Body Parts of Bob in harmony for the first time in a week. Even my rear end seems mollified with the new folding pattern I've tried with the Cyclist's Friend.

In the bright sun, the Finnish forest has magically transformed from the somber gloom of yesterday. The trees are so green and the lakes shimmer so brightly that they are almost blinding. Reindeer, sporting red collars or wearing bells around their necks, begin to appear at every turn as if to welcome me to their land and cheer me on to my next destination. I have entered the southernmost range of reindeer-herding territory. I am tantalizingly close to Lapland.

My mood has changed from yesterday's deranged curses to a sort of *Mr. Rogers Bikes through the Happy Forest* demeanor. "That red collar is really you!" and "Nice bell!" I yell happily to my antlered friends.

The reindeer in this region travel in small family groups that usually include a doe and a calf or several adults and one or two little ones. The calves are cute, with their ungainly gaits; clomping along with oversized feet, they look like they are wearing shoes that are four sizes too big. The reindeer's big, cleft hooves are adapted for walking on snow.

At one hillcrest, I come upon three adults with magnificent racks, standing their ground in the middle of the road. They peer intently as the Expedition's strange contraption slowly approaches. Every few seconds they turn to each other, as if in conversation.

The three amigos

"What the hell is that?" I imagine the first one saying.

"You've got me—I've never seen anything like it before," the second responds.

"Could it be a new kind of wolf?" offers the third.

The reindeer return their gaze to me.

"I don't think it's a wolf—there's only one."

"Is it a car?"

The reindeer, all three in unison, as if in a showdown at the OK Corral, start walking, then trotting, toward me as I strain up the hill, fishing for my camera in my front carrier.

"Going way too slow for a car."

"Maybe it's one of those old Russian cars. It's making a kind of grunting noise and is going real slow."

The reindeer and I are on a collision course. By now, I have pulled out my camera and am firing off shots of what I'm calling the *Three Amigos of Reindeerland.* I am now within ten yards of them. The reindeer halt. They analyze.

"Whoah, what's that thing in its hand, and what's that thing it's dragging behind?"

"This is just too weird—let's get out of here."

As I get closer, the reindeer saunter off to the roadside, and then shoot me wary glances as I pass.

"Could have been a gulo gulo, though I've never seen one," I imagine one murmuring as they ease into the woods.

The sun and reindeer infuse me with euphoria and energy. I gun up the next hills at a whopping 12 to 15 miles per hour. For reasons unknown and that completely defy the laws of physics, I feel stronger than ever. My legs are pumping away as if fueled by the copious warmth and sun itself.

By noon, I cross a shimmering river that connects two lakes. On a gravel side road I find a lean-to, called a *laavu*. It's the perfect lunch spot. Clouds are beginning to coalesce, though I linger long enough to enjoy my first real rest break in a while. I stretch out on a log bench, soaking up the sun, which is warding off the clouds. I think, *Yes, this is why I've come, to revel in moments like this.* The storms, the wet, and the solitude seem like they happened a million years ago. I am so in the moment, I can barely leave there. But the Expedition must continue.

Shortly after leaving the *laavu*, I hear a dog barking—a very big dog from the sound of the howl. This, in itself, is not unusual. Virtually every Finnish farm has a dog—either a husky, German shepherd, or some other herding or sled-pulling beast—which is usually tied up or kept in a fenced area. The dogs always sense my approach long before I come into view, so I have grown accustomed to barking in the distance and am not alarmed, as I've begun to trust the Finnish tendency to not allow their pets to stray.

But as I pass a dirt road leading off to a nearby farm, I see a mixed-breed collie in full yelp sprinting toward me. The last thing I need is a dog bite. I start cranking. It helps that I am on a gradual downhill grade. The collie rounds the corner and starts the chase, but I easily pull away from him. As soon as I begin to relax, I hear more barking just after passing a second dirt road, leading to yet another farm. I glance in that direction and see another, bigger dog—a giant wolfhound of some sort—sprinting toward the main road and me. *Is this the Valley of the Two Unchained Dogs?* I ask myself. *It's not on my map.*

I coax more speed from Friday, as the chase is accompanied by an entire cheering section of yelping dogs that has erupted from every farm in the valley. In yesterday's horrible conditions, the dogs would have caught and torn me to shreds. But not today. After rounding a bend, the dogs give up the chase. Good riddance. I wish them to the wolves.

Two hours later, after cycling past Kuusamo, I make a right turn at Santa Claus Lane and find myself at the Holiday Club Kuusamon Tropiikki. This name would be ironic under any circumstances, but it merits special status because I have now officially crossed into southern Lapland. The Holiday Club is a spa, a fact that reveals itself as I push open the doors to the vast reception hall and see men, women, and children lounging around in fluffy white bathrobes. I feel like Dorothy just entering Emerald City after her own harrowing journey.

I am not totally out of place, at least from a fashion standpoint, given that I am wearing my standard uniform of bike shorts (now enhanced by the Cyclist's Friend) and my bright orange Arizona bike jersey—the same outfit I have worn almost every day. Unfortunately, the Tropiikki is well beyond the Expedition's meager budget. My guidebook informs me that the spa handles bookings for the campground next door, which is where I will spend the night. No fluffy bathrobes for me, I'm afraid, though the friendly receptionist tells me I'm more than welcome to dine in the spa buffet.

Sadly, I leave the hotel with my key to the campground shower and head off to a stand of trees and a series of low mounds. I pitch my tent on one of these dirt hills, change into my only clean pair of pants, and head back to the hotel for dinner, taking the receptionist up on her offer to let me sample the buffet.

"Can I eat as much as I want?" I ask, maybe a little too greedily, as I look beyond the waitress manning the cash register and catch a glimpse of an epicurean paradise. I see mounds of food, with multiple varieties of salmon, pastas, and other delights. I speculate that the entire economic premise of the spa is likely based on the assumption that most customers will be judicious in their intake of food. After all, this is a spa. However, I'm guessing the economic model did not foresee one very calorie- and protein-starved cyclist.

As I consume piles of food, astonished waitresses huddle in the corner wondering, "How much is that little guy going to eat?" When not wolfing down food (the salmon is to die for), I glimpse down from my second-floor perch to observe a giant swimming pool grotto with water-falls, canals, and lagoons teeming with happy children.

I, too, am momentarily happy, marveling at how my fortunes on this trip change from hour to hour. My euphoria is somewhat subdued, though, knowing that I face the prospect of leaving this paradise to return to my tiny tent full of stinking clothes and dead bugs. After dinner I linger in the lobby, glancing at brochures and spa magazines, hoping to lessen the amount of time I have to spend in solitary confinement. In one magazine, I spot an advertisement in English for the "Klubi Apartments, fully furnished one-bedroom luxury apartments, only €50 summer off-season rate." I read on. "The apartments are located in the ski resort of Ruka, only a thirty-minute drive north of Kuusamo." An accompanying article describes how Finnish tourist officials are trying to lure more summer business to Ruka with inexpensive accommodations.

With sudden intense interest, I leaf through the rest of the magazine, encountering pictures of beautiful blonde women sipping cocktails on the terrace of one of many Ruka outdoor cafés. Others hoist day-packs through lush Lapland forests bursting with huckleberries, while still others lounge in the sauna. I think of my tiny tent, bedraggled and grease-stained clothes, and soggy maps. I think of my evening ritual of slaughtering mosquitoes before daring to fall asleep at night. I think of my throbbing butt, the incessant rain, and the barking chasing dogs that want to tear me to shreds.

I rip out the ad, startling a couple of fluffy bathrobe-wearers sitting nearby, and stuff it into my wallet. I don't know exactly where Ruka is, but I will find the Klubi Apartments if it's the last epic-like thing I do. The United Body Parts of Bob have spoken. They will not be mollified until they are basting in the healing warmth of the sauna, sipping beer on a sun-soaked terrace, and wallowing in their very own Klubi Apartment.

Lapland's Penthouse

ENTICED BY THE IMAGE OF THE EASY LIFE at the Klubi Apartments, I return to my tent and consult the maps. Ruka is closer than I thought, only 12 miles to the north, right on National Bike Route 5.

"Only 12 more miles," I tell the United Body Parts of Bob, which have been fooled by such promises before (as in the one I made just yesterday); in other words, one more day before they can rest.

I make this pronouncement knowing that the dirt mound upon which I have perched my tent is not exactly the Garden of Eden, though it is tantalizingly close to the forbidden realm of the fluffy bathrobes. *Perhaps the Klubi Apartments comes with fluffy bathrobes, too, I muse.* The United Body Parts of Bob will be mollified.

Another incentive for my need to move on tomorrow comes soon after I begin my nightly one-chapter ration of *The Race to Timbuktu*. Engrossed in a passage where the protagonist is dying of thirst, I become aware of a buzzing, not unlike the sound of a swarm of angry bees. Judging from the noise, the swarm is rapidly approaching.

Now what? I think as I unhook the clothespins holding the mosquito netting in place and poke my head outside.

A convoy of motorized tricycles with gargantuan tires approaches my mound. The machines are piloted by children (or very small adults) in Darth Vader-like jumpsuits. It looks like a *Saturday Night Live* rendition of a Mad Max movie. I watch in horror as the monster tricycles claw up an unclaimed neighboring mound, and then, with a cloud of dust in their wake, gun toward my hill. I emerge and let my presence be known.

The riders avoid cresting my mound and instead circle it like a pack of angry Apaches. They veer off down a dirt path, looping around other mounds, and then return, circling my mound again. I have pitched my tent in the middle of an informal off-road vehicle race course.

I watch this activity for a few circuits, concluding that there is nothing I can do except hope they run out of gas. At more than $6 a gallon, I wonder how long they can keep this up. By eleven, and long after I have finished my chapter, I lay in my tent listening through earplugs to the ebb and flow of many tiny motors.

〰〰〰   〰〰〰   〰〰〰

By midday, the Expedition is bobbing its way up and down steep hills, or fells as they are called in Finland. Formed by retreating glaciers from the last Ice Age, the fells I now see are mostly solitary hills, though later I am bound to run into a more daunting series of interconnected fells in north-central Lapland. In the distance, I can see ski lifts and swank condominiums perched atop the highest fell, egging me on, but my progress is very slow. After almost a week of steady cycling in foul weather, my exhausted leg muscles are stiff and sore. The logging trucks of the previous day have been replaced by lumbering dump trucks hauling loads of rock and dirt away from Ruka, while cement trucks, massive cylinders churning, rumble toward town. The forest is dotted with fancy homes, interspersed with meadows blooming with purple fireweed. The sun beams brightly as I reach a bike trail that passes a pleasant pond, then climbs the last few feet to the heart of Ruka Village.

I crest, expecting to see a magical town filled with happy villagers whiling away the day at sidewalk cafés, hoisting tankards of beer and discussing the latest developments in reindeer husbandry.

Much to my horror, though, I come upon a massive pit where the Ruka town square must have once quaintly stood. It looks as if a bomb has exploded smack dab in the middle of the village. Inside the pit, rivers of concrete flow from cement trucks. Pile drivers slam the earth.

Hard-hatted construction workers jackhammer at stubborn chunks of granite. Plumes of red-brown dust billow from the work hole.

The industrious Finns are at it again, transforming Ruka into something "bigger and better" than its former self. I don't know whether to laugh or cry as I walk my bike up a temporary road to a large lodge-like structure that houses the village's booking office.

One thing is for certain: I can ride no more. There is no other refuge, nowhere else to go, even if I could coax a few more miles out of my log-like legs and sore butt. I have survived more than 1,300 miles up to this point. But to go any farther, I must rest even if construction were to proceed twenty-four hours a day—which might just happen, given the need to finish projects before the short Lapland summer ends.

The cheerful, young woman at the booking desk takes pity on me.

"Of course, we have many kinds of accommodations," she says. "You can stay as long as you like."

I like her attitude.

She describes a number of possibilities, but nothing that sounds like the Klubi Apartments.

"What about this?" I ask, pulling the tattered ad out of my wallet.

"Oh yes, we have that," she says, as she punches it up on her computer. Then her brow furrows.

"Are you by yourself?"

"Yes."

"We have something smaller."

"Oh no, I want this…. Will I hear the construction noise?"

"All the units face the other way. They are very quiet."

"Good enough. Book me for three nights."

Ten minutes later, I punch in the code to my third-floor, $75-a-night apartment. The door buzzes. I push it open.

This must be a mistake, I think, recalling the description for a one-bedroom apartment. I had imagined some sort of efficiency unit.

I follow the entryway to a fully equipped kitchen featuring a wrap-around counter with a half-dozen sleek barstools. The counter faces a large living room with a big-screen television and a gargantuan leather couch that looks like it belongs in an IKEA showroom. A gigantic floor-to-ceiling window occupies the entire west exposure, providing an unobstructed 180-degree panorama of southern Lapland. Beyond the living room is a bedroom with a pair of antique wooden cross-country skis mounted above the headboard; adjacent is a walk-in closet the size of the entire haunted cabin in Suomussalmi. I wander farther, discovering a bathroom, then a second bathroom, then a fully equipped sauna. I find another large bedroom, then stairs leading up to two more bedrooms. I count at least six beds. I find a washer and a giant walk-in clothes dryer that resembles the orgasmatron in *Sleeper.* I am not in an apartment. I am in penthouse heaven.

By early afternoon, I have fully decamped. Two empty beer bottles stand on the coffee table. The television is turned to a drama about a doctor who moves to a small town on an Irish island. I have already been in and out of both showers, sweated in the sauna, and cooked up a cheeseburger with fries—the ingredients of which were conveniently located in a market one floor beneath my abode. I have already explored the village and found an Internet café.

Feeling invigorated, I bound outside—ready for an afternoon walk over Ruka Fell on the first part of the Karhunkierros, one of Finland's popular cross-country hiking trails that winds 50 miles through the last wilderness in Europe. I begin my hike by cresting the ski slope. The trail then descends steeply, where it enters Oulanka National Park, before starting another ascent of a neighboring fell. Though I am bike weary, I find hiking refreshing, using leg muscles that did not participate in the grueling work of cycling. I pass a score of trekkers, hunched over and shouldering huge backpacks, wearily hiking the last few miles of the trail.

I descend and the trail is now surrounded by a patch of ripening huckleberries. After grazing, I continue to the next fell and pass a lake with a *laavu* and a dock. Unlike the uniform forest tracts I have passed for days on end, this forest has the wild scraggly look of the untamed. Trees are bent and withered; other less lucky specimens are mere skeletons of brittle branches shaped like witches' brooms. I startle a family of pheasants, and for the first time since Helsinki, I see more than one squirrel in a day.

The ants here are as industrious as the people, constructing giant mounds of debris that would seem more appropriate in Australia than Lapland. At the top of the second fell, I rest and take in the sweeping view.

In most epics, there are key turning points, times when you realize that you have been so intent on overcoming obstacles that you fail to appreciate the slow, but steady progress toward your goal. Gazing over the forested hills and twinkling lakes of southern Lapland, I realize that I have come all this way on a little bicycle via my own power and pluck. It seems almost impossible, and yet here I am atop this hill, the known world stretched out before me. In the distance, still some 500 meandering miles to the north and west, lies my final goal: the Barents Sea. But for the first time in the journey, I begin to believe I can make it.

When I return to my penthouse, I punch in the code and push the door. It will not budge. I try again; no luck. I am locked out of my little piece of Finnish paradise! I need help, but it is Friday night. The Rukans have probably all gone home or are getting ready for whatever it is they do here on Friday nights. I have only my day pack, a water bottle, and a sack of granola with me.

"No, no, no," I whimper, clawing at the door. "How can you do this to me?"

The last comment is addressed to the gods who, I am now convinced, will relentlessly hound me to the epic's final day. They are so cruel. Beyond the thick metal door await a sauna, cold beer, a warm bed—six of them—and dry socks. I glance at my watch. It's about a quarter to six. There might still be time.

I dash out of the building, race around the construction pit, now eerily quiet, and bound up the stairs to the booking office, hoping against hope that it is still open.

It is, and she's there! My savior, the young woman who booked me in several hours earlier, is miraculously still manning her post, explaining in English the location of the nearest campground to an older German woman who clearly doesn't understand English. I want to shake her Teutonic frame and tell her that for only 50 euros you, too, can have paradise. Forget about camping; treat yourself. This is no time to be cheap!

But, of course, I say nothing while waiting patiently for the woman to finish. I really don't want to share the apartment building anyway. My savior deals with the woman efficiently. I am just grateful that unlike most of her countrymen, she has not yet left on her six weeks of vacation.

"Is there a problem?" she inquires.

I explain. She sighs and tells me this has happened before. She keys in a new number code and instructs me to try again. She also gives me the phone number to the night maintenance man, in case I should get locked out after-hours. When I return, I carefully punch in the code. Miraculously the door opens. I am readmitted to the magic kingdom. I vow never to leave the sanctuary again after five.

Snowman

TWO FULL DAYS IN RUKA DOES WONDERS toward restoring my strength and healing my sores. After my arrival day hike, I decide from that point on I really need to keep my promise to the United Body Parts of Bob and do as close to nothing as possible, at least for one day. Like Ahab searching the sea for Moby Dick, I stand in front of my panoramic window, gazing into the horizon with my binoculars in search of another great storm the weatherman has promised. I want to witness the maelstrom from the luxury of my rented living room while lying on the couch in my sweat pants. But other than a few scattered clouds and some drops in the morning, the storm never materializes.

Later that day, I venture outside for a leisurely stroll to see the transformation of the Lapland forest into a Finnish version of Aspen. At the base of the fell, bulldozers carve from the forest roads, bike paths, and drainage canals. As I walk along a dirt road that is being constructed at the base of the fell, clouds of fresh dust rise from dump trucks hauling rocks and gravel. When the traffic eases, reindeer mosey out of the woods. They appear as bewildered as I am by all the activity. "What happened to the last wilderness of Europe?" they seem to ask.

It turns out that I need to head farther north to find tumbling rivers, alpine canyons, and stands of old-growth spruce. On my second layover day, I bike 15 miles to Jumma, the starting point for the multi-day Karhunkierros (Bear Trail) and the Pieni Karhunkierros (Little Bear Ring Trail). These are hiking trails, so I lock my bike to a tree and shoulder my day pack. I decide that the Little Bear Ring Trail, an eight-mile loop, is just right for me, providing a one-day glimpse of what most of Finland looked like a thousand years ago. Most of the trail is within Oulanka National Park, a 270-square-mile patch of wilderness that stretches northeast to the Russian border. I had traversed a thin southern section of the park two days ago. The trail, dotted every few miles by spacious hiker's huts, meanders around lakes, crosses frothing rapids, and climbs mossy bluffs through habitat of brown bear, pine marten, ermine, weasel, mink, otter, and elk—none of which are in evidence during my hike. The trail is crowded with Sunday hikers, but we all space ourselves out nicely along the loop. By nightfall, I return to my Ruka refuge to study my maps and prepare for the last weeks of my trip.

vvv vvv vvv

The following morning, I am ready to resume the epic. My body, after numerous rounds in the sauna, is rested and relaxed. Calf and quad muscles that were tighter than bowstrings a few days ago are more pliable. At least I'm no longer gimping around like Grandpa McCoy.

As I gather and repack my equipment, I walk the bike into the hallway and carelessly lean it against the wall. Turning to resume packing, I vaguely recall my new vow to pay attention to detail.

Details *are* important. During the layover, I have had time to reflect on this often overlooked, but important axiom. I've already experienced what can happen when the wrong cotter pin is used or when the wagon axle is slightly off center. During my convalescence in Kuopio, I had carefully taken apart the axle and reassembled it. In doing so, I discovered that the spare cotter pin I had purchased at a hardware store in Seattle had a slightly different design from the pin that came with the axle assembly kit. The extra bend in the manufacturer's pin was intended to give it more strength. Early on, in my eagerness to assemble the wagon and get the Expedition under way, I had used the spare pin.

I had also failed to properly align the axle; it was off center a quarter of an inch—a mistake that added more stress to the cotter pin. I concluded that these two small deviations contributed greatly to the cause of the near-catastrophic accident on the road to Jyväskylä. This was my version of the "O-ring"* malfunction. I considered myself lucky to still have my bike, wagon, and self in reasonable working order. Since then, I have warned myself not to slough off on bike maintenance or on my morning round of checking bolts, screws, and other critical parts before heading out for the day.

Seconds after leaning the bike in the hallway, I hear a crash. The bike has fallen. The plastic arm that holds the rearview mirror bears the brunt of the impact. The arm snaps in half.

This is not good. I need the mirror to check on traffic. It allows me to focus most of my attention on the narrow shoulder of the main highway without constantly turning my head to see what's coming. Duct tape temporarily saves the day, but soon after I start the ride, the mirror droops out of view and becomes useless. *If only I had been more careful,* I admonish myself.

Not more than five minutes after roaring down Ruka Hill and joining Highway E63, the main road to Rovaniemi, capital of Lapland, I see a reindeer dash out from the woods ahead of me and right in front of a white van coming in the opposite direction. The driver swerves and slams on the brakes to avoid the beast, but there is a glancing blow and a strange bang, perhaps the hoof smacking the hubcap. The panicked reindeer turns and limps into the forest.

According to Finnish law, a motorist who crashes into a reindeer—a common occurrence in Lapland—is required to check the condition of the animal (by following it into the forest, if necessary) and then notify the police. I know this because somewhere I picked up the glossy brochure *Reindeer in Traffic,* which is shaped like a triangular "Caution" sign. If the reindeer is badly hurt the motorist must ". . . put the injured reindeer out of its misery or alert someone to the scene who will do it for you."

This last provision seems rather gruesome. Given the Finns' propensity for respecting the law, I have no doubt the act would be carried out

---

* Failure of an O ring, which seals the joints of the booster rockets, was believed responsible for the explosion that destroyed the Space Shuttle *Challenger* in 1986.

if warranted. Fortunately, this reindeer has plenty of life left in him. After the van screeches to a stop, the driver leaps out and gives chase. Both reindeer and man disappear into the forest.

vvv vvv vvv

I have planned to cover the roughly 132 miles between Ruka and Rovaniemi in three days, easing into the first day with a 40-mile ride to a campground at Morottaja. Refreshed, I ride almost effortlessly, heading northwest toward a rendezvous with the Arctic Circle. The fells that surround Ruka grow smaller by the mile. Soon I am in the flats, again passing lakes and small farms. The forest thins. Sun peeks from the clouds. There is almost no traffic. *This is almost too easy,* I think. By midafternoon I reach Morottaja, located next to a pleasant lake, but otherwise in the middle of nowhere. I pause. What will I do here all day? I've just had plenty of downtime. I feel strong, so I pedal past the campground and continue west.

About an hour later I see what appears to be the Pillsbury Doughboy looming above the woods and swaying gently in the breeze. I ride toward it and into the tiny village of Tonkeburo, which straddles the border of the Arctic Circle. The small sign designating this important geographic landmark is dwarfed by the doughboy—in actuality, a thirty-foot-tall inflatable snowman wearing a black top hat and scarf.

I congratulate myself, the wagon, and Friday for reaching this significant landmark, but the fact that I am the only human in my crew emphasizes the Expedition's greatest weakness when it comes to celebrating momentous events: I have no one to revel with. Well, almost no one. I do have the gigantic Frosty the Snowman, whom I perceive to be smiling down on me as he waggles gently in the Arctic breeze.

"Give me five, Mr. Snowman!" I yell, not feeling self-conscious because, as usual, no one is around to hear my shout, though I suspect a few reindeer are peering apprehensively at me from a safe distance in the woods.

The giant inflatable snowman is the only object to greet the Expedition when it crosses the Arctic Circle.

The snowman, of course, cannot give me five, or even one, because he's a snowman (a fake one at that), and snowmen, even in Finland, have sticks or stumps for arms. So I high-five him on the first big white balloon ball that comprises his base, and then I take a self-portrait, posing with my newest inanimate friend. Once the photo session is over, I look up at the big guy, wishing he were real so he could at least congratulate me. But my friend is a typical Finn: he is a snowman of few words. So I circumnavigate his bottom and walk into the small coffee shop that is nearby.

The shop is empty. I help myself to coffee and a donut, which seems appropriate fare for commemorating my arrival at the Arctic Circle. I wait by the cash register. At last a young woman emerges from a back room, looking somewhat shocked that a customer has arrived.

"I'm celebrating," I gush, now that I have someone real to talk to. "I just rode my bike from Helsinki, then to the Åland Islands—through storms, lightning, and thunder—and now I've reached the Arctic Circle."

The woman is sizing me up, and I'm not even certain that she speaks English, but I am hoping that she's understood the gist of my braggadocio. Oh, to have my epic be acknowledged by another human! I expect that at any second her face will brighten with a big smile, and she'll jump over the counter and slap me on the back and sing "For He's A Jolly Good Fellow." And then maybe she will yell to the back of the room where the rest of the population of Tonkeburo is monitoring the air compression equipment that keeps their giant snowman aloft as a beacon for lonely bike travelers, and that they will burst into the room, hoist me on their shoulders, and carry me triumphantly around the room.

This does not happen.

"Okay," she says.

Perhaps I have not made myself clear. Perhaps the achievement is so beyond the experience of these Laplanders that they cannot truly comprehend what I have just accomplished. Perhaps I need to explain that this epic journey is still not complete, that even greater distances will be crossed, more storms endured, and probably more silences encountered.

"I'm planning to go all the way to Kirkenes in Norway."

The woman smiles at me like a mother who has just observed her child doing a neat trick.

"It's a long way," she says wearily, as if the act of listening to someone who plans to bike to Kirkenes is cause enough for great fatigue.

Dejectedly, I gather my donut and coffee and find a seat, glancing outside at the gathering gloom. The day, which started out so promising, is deteriorating. Clouds have swamped the blue sky, and now rain is beginning to fall. My arrival here reminds me of one of my favorite chapters in Ray Bradbury's *The Martian Chronicles*. The story describes the excitement of the first astronauts from Earth to reach Mars. The space travelers bound out of the rocket and knock on the door of the first Martian house they encounter. But the Martians are unimpressed with this feat and believe that the astronauts are merely delusional Martians who have breached the limits of sanity. The Martians end up killing the astronauts.

This is not exactly the thought I want to conjure up at this moment. The giant fake snowman outside suddenly takes on a sinister look. *Ridiculous. He's just a snowman.* I open my map and stare at the long, blue line to Kemijärvi, the next city of any size and a potential overnight stop. It's about 25 miles away. After a while, I wander outside to tighten some bolts on the bike, thinking of details again.

The woman follows, lights a cigarette, and plops down on a wooden bench near where I tinker.

"Why did you bicycle all the way from Helsinki?" she asks. "You can drive. The roads are fine, but the weather. Uggh, the weather this summer is very bad."

It is as if someone has stuck a giant nail in the inflatable snowman, and he has collapsed into a pile of plastic. I cannot answer this question. At this moment, I cannot explain why I have chosen to ride a very small bicycle all the way to this remote spot anymore than this young woman can explain to me in one or two sentences why she lives here when she could be living the good life in Helsinki, Tampere, or even Ruka. My usual answer of being interested in Finland's history and the temperate conditions unique to this small part of the world that allows me to follow a paved road all the way to the Barents Sea seems rather lame at the moment.

She has a nice smile and speaks English well. I ask her how she manages to live here, especially in the frigid—and I'm assuming isolated—winter months.

She shrugs and says, "It's okay."

I tell her I've been trying to learn some Finnish, but cannot get beyond a few greetings.

"I've been here more than a month, and I can only count to two."

"You have ridden that little bicycle all the way from Helsinki, and you can only count to two?"

"I hope to count to five by the time I reach Kirkenes," I deadpan.

"Finnish is easy," she says. "Just pronounce the letters exactly as they are. Of course, we have that funny ä and ö, you know the extra vowels." She then pronounces a name written on the side of the coffee shop, which is about thirty-five letters long and completely incomprehensible to me.

"See how easy it is?"

I try to say the name, but get tongue-tied. My teacher frowns and takes another drag on her cigarette.

"Where do you go today?"

"I'm going to try to make it to Kemijärvi."

She tells me that 10 miles up the road at Suomun Helmi, a Dutchman and a Spanish woman had purchased a campground. When the sale occurred neither spoke Finnish, which was a source of amazement to the natives.

"Why do you think they came here?" I ask.

"Maybe to get away from everything," she says. "You can really get away from everything here in Lapland. There is nothing except the reindeer, and in the winter the blue nights and the stars."

"What about him?" I ask, motioning to the snowman.

"The snowman—he's okay."

Thirty minutes later I reach Suomun Helmi. I have been thinking about the Dutchman and the Spaniard and have thought seriously about stopping for the night at their campground. The trouble is, I still have strength, and Suomun Helmi is as isolated as the woman reported.

I press on. In another thirty minutes, I reach another Winter War monument. While the Finns managed to stop Soviet advances near Kuhmo and Suomussalmi in late 1939, a heavily mechanized Russian division roared over the border and threatened to take Kemijärvi. Unlike in the thick forests of North Karelia, the Russian tanks and armor could maneuver reasonably well in this region of meadows, well-spaced pines, and low-slung hills.

The Finns were led by Kurt Wallenius, a flamboyant commander who was not one of Marshal Mannerheim's favorites. When in the presence of western journalists, Wallenius had the macho habit of strutting around in subzero temperatures with his shirt open to his bare chest. Outnumbered as usual, the Finns, dressed in white, dug in near where I stand now and were all but invisible to the advancing Russians. The Russians came in wave after wave, but each one was mowed down by withering Finnish machine gun fire. Carl Mydans, on assignment at the Lapland Front for *Time-Life* magazine, toured the battlefield shortly after the fighting ended.

"They [the Russians] *lay lonely and twisted in their heavy trench coats and formless felt boots, their faces yellowed, eyelashes white with a fringe of frost. Across the ice, the forest was strewn with weapons and pictures and letters, with sausage and bread and shoes. Here were the bodies of dead tanks with blown treads, dead carts, dead horses, and dead men, blocking the road and defiling the snow under the tall black pines... Here the Finns met the Russians and stopped them."*[31]

Mydans, who found it difficult to take photos because his equipment froze, described how the wounded soldiers staggered like "dying insects," then froze to death in the half-light of the frigid Lapland winter.

By the end of December, with the Russian forces decimated, the Finns counterattacked, pushing their enemy back to the border.

Sixty-eight years later, a soft breeze rustles the pines around the stone monument, which depicts two Finnish soldiers on cross-country skis. It is hard to believe that anything remotely disconcerting ever happened here.

A middle-aged couple is having a picnic near one of the signboards that outline the military positions of each side in bright red.

"Would you like some biscuits and coffee?" offers the woman in heavily accented English.

I accept, welcoming another opportunity for conversation with someone other than a thirty-foot-tall snowman. She says she is originally from Lapland, but now she and her husband live in Lahti in southern Finland. They spend a few weeks here every summer at her family's cottage. Her husband, who doesn't speak English, asks questions through her about the bike, where I am heading, and how many miles a day I average.

By seven in the evening, I cross the causeway over the Kemijoki River. The sun's rays scatter behind a phalanx of cumulus clouds, giving my entrance into Kemijärvi, with its church steeple in brilliant silhouette, an ethereal glow.

"Are you with them?" asks the attendant at the Hietaniemi Campground, as I fill out my registration card. I turn to see that three pannier-laden bike riders—a young man and two older men—have pulled in behind me. I shake my head no as I wonder what it would be like to be traveling in a group.

Later, as I stake out my tent, the young man comes bounding over. His name is Timo, and he and his father and his father's friend started their trip in Nuorgam, the most northern town in Arctic Finland. When I tell him my ultimate destination, he puts his hand on my shoulder and says, "That is fantastic, but I must tell you about Lapland. It is a hard journey. There are many big hills."

25

The King of Lapland

TIMO IS A STOCKY, TWENTY-SIX-YEAR-OLD with crew-cut blonde hair and a ready smile. He's from the Turku area, where he works in a factory. After talking with him long into the night, it's clear that the idea of bisecting Finland on a bicycle odyssey is his father's dream, not his. His father had a heart attack a few years ago, so his family assigned Timo the task of keeping an eye on the two older guys during their journey.

"I trained for two years as a paramedic," he tells me, as we take turns using the stove in the camp cookhouse. He didn't elaborate on this, but I later wondered if the training was for his factory job or for this journey.

Like the handful of other cross-country bike riders I have encountered, they are riding in the opposite direction of the Riding with Reindeer Expedition. The north-to-south route makes sense due to the prevailing winds that roll off the Arctic Ocean and flow south down to the rest of Finland. But being a person of simple intentions, I decided early on that I would begin my trip where I first touched Finnish soil. This seemed in keeping with other historic expeditions, large and small, that did not have the luxury of modern plane, train, or bus travel to deliver them to a more convenient jumping-off point.

So far my plan has been working, though; I have not yet encountered sustained headwinds. I wonder how long this last shred of weather luck will hold.

Timo tells me his party hoped to be back in Turku in three weeks. The trio had bused to Nuorgam, which is perched on the Norwegian border about 50 miles from the Barents Sea. But the spokes and gear guards of their bikes had been bent when stuffed into the luggage compartment of the bus. They had improvised repairs and hoped the bikes would hold up. I gave a mental thanks for my hardy, but small, bike with its double-spoked wheels and stout frame.

From Nuorgam the trio had followed the paved Arctic Highway south, but one day out, they encountered the infamous fells of north-central Lapland. Finnish highway engineers, being of the no-nonsense school of road design, routed the highway directly over the hills. This isn't a problem for motorists, but for bike riders the fells present a formidable obstacle. The hills are particularly nasty south of the Sami town of Inari. One night, the threesome had failed to make their destination and pitched camp in the forest, where they were nearly eaten alive by mosquitoes.

"They say the mosquitoes are getting worse," sighs Timo, reliving that horrible night. "The more it rains, the longer the mosquito season lasts."

At Ivalo, the next major town south of Inari, the loose spokes on Timo's bike had become worrisome, so he tried to get help.

"But the bike shop was closed," he says. "The only bike mechanic in north Lapland had left town a few days earlier. They said he wouldn't be back until next year."

Unable to get the bike serviced, he had continued to ride until a spoke broke about six miles south of Sodankylä. Suddenly, the bike was unrideable. So Timo stripped off the panniers and loaded the bike on a northbound bus, backtracking to Sodankylä, where he was able to find a bicycle mechanic who had not yet abandoned his post. After he got the wheel repaired, he and his party had completed the one-day ride to this campground in Kemijärvi.

As we chat some more the next morning, which is bright and warm, he doesn't appear anxious to resume the trip.

"The road is very bad. Lots of potholes," he says. "And the fells, they are horrible. We call them the 'Hills of Bicycle Death' because the mosquitoes will swarm up and attack you as you struggle up the hills."

Like me, Timo says he is nursing a sore rear end.

This does not sound pleasant. Perhaps there is a way to circumnavigate the Hills of Bicycle Death. I recall that, according to my map, other roads besides the well-traveled Arctic Highway creep north, too. True, they are unpaved and penetrated miles and miles of uninhabited land, but it just might be worth venturing on the road less traveled to avoid what Timo's expedition had endured. I won't decide until I have studied the maps more thoroughly, but the idea of skirting the Hills of Bicycle Death is growing more attractive by the moment.

I explain my tentative plans, telling Timo I hope to reach Rovaniemi tonight, where I plan to resupply and rest for at least three days before continuing north to Inari and then farther up the right arm of Finland to Kirkenes in Norway.

"I'm not so sure anyone goes on those roads. If you break down, it may be a long time before you can get help. There are no buses. Besides, it can get lonely out there," he tells me as we shake hands before parting that morning.

I tell him the soreness in his rear end will eventually go away. "Then you'll have what we call in English a 'hard ass.'"

〰〰   〰〰   〰〰

It is a cloudless, windless day. By midmorning, the temperature has already reached the high seventies. *How ironic*, I think. *The farther north I travel, the warmer it gets.* Two weeks ago, I was battling the early stages of hypothermia. Now sweat rolls off my brow as I overheat while laboring up steep hills. Large tracts of forest are clear-cut and every few minutes a logging truck roars past. Interestingly, traffic, in general, increases to levels I have not experienced since leaving Helsinki. This may be because I am now back on the orange motorway and not on a designated National Bike Route. But I had no choice. This is the only road between Kemijärvi and Rovaniemi. Adding another element of intrigue, the map shows that I have entered a military bombing range. This is underscored near noon when several jet fighters zoom overhead.

While the military planes roar, enormous scmis that seem much taller than those in the states swoosh by, sucking my bike into their wakes for a few nervous seconds. To make matters worse, the shoulder contracts to a few inches, forcing me to ride in the road with the traffic. This is the worst kind of riding. I rivet my eyes to the road and make sure I keep as close to the edge as possible while glancing back for passing traffic. It is a nerve-racking day, and I vow to stick to the blue bike routes next time.

By midafternoon, I reach Vikajärvi, the junction where Highway 82 joins with Highway E-75. Rovaniemi still lies another 13 miles due west on the E-75. In contrast to yesterday's strong 75-mile day, I find myself exhausted after only 37 miles, my pace slowed by the hills and heat— it's now 90 degrees. Dehydration has replaced hypothermia as my new nemesis.

At the crossroads gas station, I buy a Pepsi, then buck myself up for the final push to Rovaniemi. *Thirteen more miles and then three days of rest,* I tell myself. The United Body Parts of Bob, appeased by the rest at Ruka and yesterday's big ride with little pain, are already protesting again. As bad as the traffic was earlier, it is now twice as bad—the result of the merger of Lapland's two major roads.

Slowly, the miles click by. Five miles east of Rovaniemi, I recross the Arctic Circle, as my route has veered slightly south since crossing the landmark yesterday. Here it is designated by a giant visitor's center and an entire village dedicated to Santa Claus. Mercifully, I find a bike path as the two-lane highway transforms itself into a full-fledged freeway— something I never suspected would exist in Lapland. Wearily, I pump my way across a bridge spanning the wide expanse of the Ounasjoki River, and shortly thereafter I straggle into Rovaniemi, the capital of Lapland. It is August 7, exactly thirty-two days after my departure from Helsinki.

I soon find myself in a pedestrian mall, squinting in the glare of the late afternoon sun. Sidewalk cafés are jammed with beer drinkers. An entire regiment of the Finnish army is decamped at one bistro. I walk my bike through this holiday atmosphere, looking for the Santa Claus Hotel, which handles bookings for the Hostel Rudolf. (I'm not making these names up.) But the hotel is not where it is supposed to be, so I wander aimlessly among the crowds, happy for the moment to be in a city surrounded by merry people.

Downtown Rovaniemi

I notice a man with unmanageable red hair drinking beer with friends at a sidewalk café watching me with unusual intensity. When I roll by his table a second time, he vaults over the low railing and runs toward me.

"Can I help you?" he offers.

I tell him I am looking for the Santa Claus Hotel. He points to a building that says Clarion Hotel and explains that the "Claus" was recently bought out, though the original name is posted on the other side of the building.

"Where did you come from?" he asks, breathlessly.

"Helsinki. I biked all the way from Helsinki." I impart this information without much enthusiasm. I've been gone more than a month, and

I'm tired of explaining myself or of thinking that I have done something special.

"This is totally amazing!" he yells. "I must congratulate you right now."

The man grabs my hand and shakes it vigorously. Then he slaps me on the back, nearly knocking me over, gushing about what a remarkable achievement I have accomplished.

"Tell me more!" he yells, then he turns to his friends who are drinking beer and says something in Finnish, which in my now-flattered state, I assume is along the lines of, "Here stands the greatest bicycle rider in Finnish history!"

I give a brief synopsis of the trip and my plan to bike to the Barents Sea.

"Fantastic!" he says, examining the bike and the wagon. "Look at this tiny bike with the tiny wheels. It's something you would see in a circus."

"Are you the mayor of Lapland?" I deadpan.

"Yes!"

One of his friends hoists a stein and says, "No, not the mayor. Eero is the king. Yes, Eero is the king of Lapland."

Eero will not let me walk alone to the Santa Claus, now Clarion, Hotel. The self-appointed king of Lapland pushes my bike for me as we cross the street and turn a corner to the entrance.

"Welcome to Lapland, my friend," he says, turning to me and shaking my hand once again. "I wish you a pleasant stay. This restaurant here is the best in the city. They serve the best reindeer. If there is anything else you need, let me know."

I'm left speechless as Eero abruptly turns down the street and disappears around the building.

In Search of the Christmas Stud Goat

THE HOSTEL RUDOLF IS LOCATED about a half-mile away from the city center, in a quiet residential area on Koskikatu. It brims with tourists from all over the world.

For some reason, my room's windowsills are at least six feet high, making it impossible to see anything outside except for clouds and tree tops. "Prison cell" are the first words that pop into my mind when I see this arrangement. I shove a chair against the wall to reach and open the windows to cool the place down.

Other than the window height, upon second inspection, the room isn't half bad. It has two twin beds and a bathroom. A closet-sized vestibule down the hall serves as a kitchen, although I'm sure its compactness would allow only one person to cook at a time. There is enough room via the unoccupied bed to spread out my gear and study my maps. It's not the Klubi Apartments, but it will do.

I keep myself busy during the next two days. I catch up on my protein consumption at the local Hesburger (Finland's answer to Burger King), find the modern and well-stocked local library, and inquire at the tourist office about routes heading north into central and northern Lapland. The city seems much larger than its population of thirty-five thousand. A renovation project is underway in the city center, as in Ruka's (although on a much smaller scale); the roads are torn up as workmen install new paving bricks. Other streets bustle with shoppers, tourists, and Finns scurrying around with cell phones attached to their ears like an extra appendage.

During one afternoon of errands to fetch groceries and retrieve e-mail, I hear a shout from across Rova Street.

"Bob! Hello, Bob! Remember me?"

I do not expect to be recognized in Rovaniemi, being about as far away from my stomping grounds as possible. A young man with short-cropped blonde hair bounds up to me. In tow is an attractive girl.

"Remember me? Timo?"

The perplexed expression on my face recedes when I hear the name.

"Timo, what are you doing here? Aren't you supposed to be biking south with your father?"

For the next ten minutes, Timo tells me a tale of biking woe. His rear wheel, weakened by its defective spokes, collapsed on a badly rutted dirt road about 50 miles south of where we parted company in Kemijärvi. He left his dad and his dad's friend, then took a bus to Rovaniemi, the closest city with a bicycle repair shop. That night, he wound up at the local campground but didn't have a tent. That's where he met his new friend. She let him burrow in with her for the night. The girl, who Timo did not introduce by name, is friendly and attractive with cascading red hair and a bright smile.

While we exchange stories, I marvel at the contrast of Timo's chance encounter with his new friend and my own strange reception by the pseudo king of Lapland and my prospective entombment at the Rudolf. I suppose the gods are saving me from such romantic distractions, reserving it for the province of youth, while allowing me to continue my epic, albeit in the company of reindeer and giant inflatable snowmen.

Timo seems in no hurry to part with his new friend and continue his trip. I really can't blame him.

"When will you catch up with your father and his friend?" I ask. I can't help but notice the parental tone in my question.

"Oh," says Timo, remembering that he, too, is on an epic, though reluctantly. "I think the bike will be ready tomorrow, then I'll probably take a bus to catch up. The roads are very bad, as you know."

I reiterate my plans to continue north until I hit the Barents Sea. A look of horror crosses the girl's face. She grabs my arm, as if she can stop this madness by holding on to me.

"You must be very careful. There are no bike shops north of here. Where will you get spare parts? Especially for that bike," she says, pointing to Friday. "No one rides a bike like that in Lapland."

ՍՄՍ   ՍՄՍ   ՍՄՍ

Even taking his lovely pal out of the equation, Timo's reluctance to part from Rovaniemi is understandable, as this arctic outpost bustles with activity and—for my stay, at least—sunshine. Home to a university, the northernmost terminus of the Finnish railroad, and a world-class museum about the Arctic, Rovaniemi has emerged from the devastation of World War II as a thriving commercial and tourist center, as well as a base for development of Lapland. The city was transformed uneasily into a quasi-German stronghold during the unholy alliance between Finland and Germany in World War II. During the height of the occupation, Germans—mostly soldiers—outnumbered the natives.

After Finland signed an armistice with the Soviet Union in September 1944 withdrawing from the war, German General Lothar Rendulic ordered his troops to destroy everything and anything that might fall into Russian hands. Rovaniemi was razed. Land mines were buried in the forests and roads. More than one hundred thousand reindeer were slaughtered, nearly half of the Lapland herd and the lifeblood of the native Sami. When the last of the German troops retreated into Norway in April 1945, Lapland was a ruined land with thousands of civilian refugees clinging to life.

As I bike through the city today, skirting modern apartment blocks before dipping down to the park-like promenade that runs parallel to the Ounaskoski* where the pleasant strains of polka music waft from tourist boats churning up the broad river, it is difficult to imagine Lapland's recent bloody past. I recall traveling by train through the former East Germany in the early 1990s shortly after the Berlin Wall fell, observing

---

* The Ounaskoski and the Kemijoki merge at Rovaniemi to form the Ounasjoki.

that Leipzig and parts of East Berlin still bore the deep scars of World War II. But here there is no trace of a wound, not even a scab. The ruins were bulldozed, redesigned, and rebuilt with the bright, functional practicality that has typified every Finnish city I have pedaled through.

Similar to the explanations inscribed in the various war monuments I had passed in Karelia, I again observe the Finnish propensity for objectivity. Yes, the reindeer herd was nearly wiped out. Yes, land mines were planted so effectively that they continued to blow up people and animals for years after the war's end. And, yes, there were monstrous war reparations that, incidentally, were repaid ahead of schedule. But nothing indicates that the Finns dwell on the past or even render an opinion about it, at least not publicly. Monuments and museums are bare of judgmental adjectives. Even Finland's heroic staving off of the colossal Russian army during the Winter War seems to fall victim to the Finnish habit of understatement.

While touring the Arktikum, a museum dedicated to the culture, climate, and geography of the Arctic, I linger behind a life-size stuffed bear while listening to a guide summarize (in English) the World War II experience of Rovaniemi. The guide, a young woman probably in her late twenties, explains almost apologetically that the retreating German army *had* to destroy everything in their path to keep it from falling into Russian hands. "No one knew at that time whether the Russians would invade," she says. I'm not sure whether this explanation was in deference to the German tourists in her entourage (and she felt she had to let bygones be bygones) or the guide's struggle to explain things diplomatically in a language not her own. Whatever the case, the Allies didn't buy the explanation that the destruction of Lapland was done for military purposes alone. For his lead role in this devastation, German General Rendulic was later convicted by a military war crime tribunal and sentenced to twenty years in prison.

\~\~\~ \~\~\~ \~\~\~

While Rovaniemi sprung from the ashes of its former self, the Finns realized that the juxtaposition of the Arctic Circle, reindeer, and the legend of Saint Nicholas presented an irresistible marketing idea. Why not make Rovaniemi the official home of Santa Claus?

Until now, I had resisted visiting the more garish commercial establishments Finland has to offer. Except for a dinner and the howling of the recorded wolves, I had for the most part avoided the fake Karelian villages in Kuhmo and Nurmes. But the prospect of visiting Santa Claus himself, off-season nonetheless, was far too tempting to skip, particularly when the Finnish name for Santa, *Joulupukki*, translates roughly into "Christmas Stud Goat." The name derives either from a folk tale of a kindly, gift-giving old man with a white beard who lived near the Russian border or from a pagan legend about an evil monster goat that rampages through the countryside demanding gifts from whomever it encounters. Of the two tales, I prefer the latter, wondering what I can do to propagate its dissemination in the United States as a hedge against the rampant commercialism of Christmas.

> *Look, kids. If you are not good, the Christmas*
> *Stud Goat is going to thrash down your chimney*
> *and take all your favorite toys away. Now, let's*
> *get with the program!*

The day after I arrive in Rovaniemi, I study the map and head out for my historic encounter with Santa, while still secretly hoping to find the Christmas Stud Goat. The map indicates that Syväsenvaara, better known in English as Santa Park, is about five miles east off the dreaded Highway E-75. In fact, I recall passing the place on my hectic ride into town the previous day, but I have no desire to retrace my route along that busy highway. Instead, I cross the Ounaskoski, then turn right at a sign indicating a bike path along a less stressful route. The path takes me through pleasant countryside dotted with new suburban developments carved from the forest.

About forty-five minutes into the ride, I begin to question my choice of routes. I find myself on a dirt road leading past some new construction and wonder if I have once again gotten my directions confused.

But, no, after surmounting a hill, I spot a tall building with a roof shaped like a witch's hat. Atop it flutters a pennant adorned with the white-bearded face of Santa Claus. I pedal into a large parking lot filled with dozens of recreational vehicles, tour buses, and trailers. *So, others are here to see Santa off-season, too.*

Circling one of the on-site restaurants, I come to a series of pseudo-log buildings. One of the buses disgorges Japanese tourists, the first such herd I have seen since Helsinki. They make a beeline for the Santa Claus Post Office. I follow. Being Santa Village, the post office is the epicenter of this commercial enterprise. The place is swarming with frantic tourists snapping up postcards and stationary. But the most coveted souvenir is an envelope postmarked from Santa Village on Christmas Day, and sent directly to some hopeful child. Carrying out Santa's business plan is an army of elves who are dressed in red pointy hats and red striped shirts. A fair number of these elves, almost all young women, are manning cash registers and other strategic money-making positions in the post office. One elf is assigned the important task of stamping hundreds of outgoing letters and postcards with the appropriate postmark. She grimly bangs them out with alarming velocity.

Indeed, the official statistics from 2006 reflect that Santa and his helpers are plenty busy. The Santa Claus Post Office receives an average of thirty-two thousand letters a day year-round from children all over the world, with the most prolific fans residing in the United Kingdom, Italy, Poland, and Finland.

I cannot bring myself to contribute to this scene, given the precariousness of the Expedition budget and my mixed sense of wonder and revulsion. It appears as if the elves would benefit from a union contract. As for the customers—well, it's obvious that none of them have heard of the Christmas Stud Goat.

I step away from the frenzied scene and into a large courtyard surrounded by restaurants and shops. Helpful signs indicate that the three-story building, the one I had spotted earlier flying the official Santa pennant, is indeed the administrative headquarters of The Man himself. Leading directly to Santa's office is a prominent line etched into the cement. The etching also declares that the line represents the exact location of the Arctic Circle, the geographic point I have now crossed several times.

The headquarters of Santa Claus is not difficult to spot.

I join the line of humanity that snakes up the three stories to the executive suite. Santa's helpers have posted signs reminding the visiting hordes that no photos of Santa are permitted. However, for a fee, Santa's special photographer will be more than happy to take your picture with The Man. To emphasize the point, the hall is lined with photos of Santa posing with various dignitaries. A few appear to be of military strongmen from small Central American countries.

As the line shuffles slowly forward, I feel like I am entering the White House and that I will be gang-tackled by watchful elves if I make a sudden move to reach for my camera. The rest of the crowd seems to understand this as well. We keep our arms and hands clearly visible.

We wind up a spiral staircase. At the top, we arrive at a small, wooden desk cluttered with papers, unopened letters, wrapping paper, and other detritus. A handwritten sign thrown lazily on top of the clutter declares that Santa is out of the office for a few hours.

Are you kidding me? Was I supposed to call ahead and schedule an appointment? What about all these kids in the line behind me from every country in Europe, not to mention Japan, Korea, and India? And where is the "in basket" for the thirty-two thousand letters a day that he receives? Is he all caught up? The supposed onslaught of mail, combined with the feverish activity of the elves in the post office, does not seem to justify a three-hour lunch. On the other hand, he *is* the chief executive. He probably has important lunch appointments. Maybe the Easter Bunny or Tooth Fairy is in town. And it *is* August, probably a relatively slack time in the village, a chance to catch up on old projects and spend some quality time with Mrs. Claus.

We file slowly past the unoccupied desk, admiring it in hushed reverence. Our collective behavior reflects the same somber attitude that crowds display while shuffling through Lenin's mausoleum. After viewing the desk, we are herded into what can only be described as a high-class jewelry store. A woman hands me a little souvenir packet containing one- and two-cent euro coins, both of which are obsolete in Finland where all prices are rounded to the nearest nickel. Estimated value at the plummeting U.S. exchange rate: two-and-a-half cents.

"Where are the elves?" I finally blurt out. But the woman only smiles.

I need fresh air. The absence of Santa, the discovery of the long-lost euro cent, and the spiraling tower of Babel is all a bit overwhelming. *Perhaps I'll have a word with Santa's reindeer,* I decide. They're no doubt pastured nearby, grazing up for the big madcap ride in December.

I find the exit staircase and descend into Santa Square. Studying a large map nearby, I cannot find a reindeer pasture or even any mention of reindeer. This is strange, given all the free-range reindeer I have mingled with the past week while riding through Finland's bountiful forests. I expected Santa Village to be the mother lode of reindeer.

I wander across the courtyard into the Santa Food Shop. I see reindeer, but not in the form I had hoped for. I see a sign for "Smoked Salmon and Reindeer Meat," advertising the special of the day. I hustle from the store and blunder into a stack of reindeer hides piled in front of a souvenir stand across the aisle. Another shop a few feet away sells dozens of large knives—not exactly reindeer-friendly implements. A few steps away, reindeer sausage is for sale, while the shop across the aisle sells T-shirts emblazoned with "Good girls go to heaven. Bad girls go to Lapland."

An alarming trend is developing here. My view of Santa has been shifting from that of an indulgent, kindly old man with a beard to Christmas Stud Goat to an international business tycoon living in the land of "bad girls" (though I have yet to encounter any), and now it is transforming again. Santa, at least from the reindeer's point of view, is assuming the characteristics of Hannibal Lecter.

I leave the mall of reindeer horrors and return to Santa Square, now filled with the strains of "Silent Night" piped in from hidden speakers. I walk to the end of the village, but find only more restaurants and shops—and no trace of living reindeer. I decide that as the commander of the Riding with Reindeer Expedition, it is my *duty* to liberate any reindeer imprisoned here before they become next week's special of the day. But as I search every nook and cranny of the fake village, I begin to suspect that my plan is in vain.

Of course, it may be possible that reindeer are brought in during the winter, when they can pull sleighs. But these are no doubt lackey reindeer that have no clue what goes on here during the summer, as revealed by the Expedition's findings. Perhaps it is just as well. Smart reindeer, unlike the bad girls of Lapland, would do well to stay away from this place. *Keep to the forest, guys. And forget about the alleged celebrity perks that come with pulling a sleigh on Christmas. It's not worth risking your skin.*

I walk back to the village center where I pass a large fence surrounding a huge construction site. The sign says that "the corporation" is building Santa a new office with thousands more square feet and that the entire project will be finished in time for Christmas. I certainly hope so. Hungry, I treat myself to a Santa burger (reindeer-free!) that comes with fries, spending $15 from the Expedition's meager budget. Santa will make a little money off me after all.

Later, as I head back to my bicycle, I walk in back of the post office, where a couple of elves on break have doffed their pointy red hats and are puffing away on cigarettes.

Lapland

I SPEND THREE DAYS IN ROVANIEMI, resting, restocking supplies, and making repairs. This is the last Finnish city of any significance I will encounter until my return here hopefully later this month. So anything I need, or need to do, must be gotten and done now.

Between me and the Barents Sea lies the bulk of Lapland. Its thirty-eight thousand square miles of forests, bogs, and moss—not to mention the infamous fells, the Hills of Bicycle Death that Timo so painfully described—represent nearly one-third of Finland's territory. But most of Lapland's one hundred eighty-five thousand inhabitants live in Rovaniemi, Kemijärvi, and a handful of other cities and towns. Farther north, the province is largely devoid of people, making it the most sparsely populated area of Europe. The native Sami now number only sixty-five hundred in Finland, though they are more numerous in Sweden and Norway. Finland's Sami are scattered amongst the vast stretches of reindeer-wandering open space and in the small villages I will pass through in the next week.

I am the latest in a long line of curious adventurers who have come to this land of the midnight sun. Prior to the 1600s, the Sami pretty much had the place to themselves, save for the occasional wanderer, missionary, or oddball colonist seeking to settle new land in the North. For the most part, the Sami bothered no one and no one bothered them, though legends of Lapland being a land of flying witches and strange beasts fueled the popular imagination in Europe. One theory even suggested that the Sami and their strange language were remnants of the lost tribe of Israel.

Lapland gained widespread notoriety in 1671 when the thirty-six-year-old French sailor Pierre Martin de la Martiniére described his travels in *Voyage dais septentrionaux*.[32] Unfortunately, his descriptions of the Sami are colored by the patronizing tone of Christian ethnocentrism that then prevailed. He unilaterally declared that all Sami were sorcerers, an accusation that would be taken seriously a hundred years later when the Inquisition found its way north. We can also thank Martiniére for the term *hellcat*, an expression he used to describe the resident black cats. He was convinced the cats were agents of the devil.

Sixty years later, Swedish scientist Carl Linnaeus—the father of modern taxonomy—explored Lapland on horseback, conducting the first objective study of Sami culture. Among his many interests was their use of native plants as medicines and their relationship with reindeer. He was followed four years later by French mathematician Pierre Louis Maupertius, who led a geodesic mission to measure the length of a degree of latitude, a key to proving his theory that Earth's shape was oblate (slightly squashed at the poles) and not perfectly round.

Many others followed. In 1799, Italian lawyer turned adventurer Guiseppe Acerbi, whose path I intersected in the Åland Islands, made his way up the west coast of Finland, then through the heart of Lapland, to the North Cape. An American adventurer, Paul Belloni Du Chaillu, who had already gained fame by discovering the existence of gorillas in Africa, set out on a winter trip to Lapland in 1871, providing a colorful and detailed description of the land and people in *Land of the Midnight Sun*. Even the grandson of Napoleon Bonaparte, Prince Roland Bonaparte, was fascinated by Lapland and the Sami. During his 1886 expedition, he not only took scores of photographs of Sami (many of which I would see in the Sami town of Inari), but also made meticulous measurements of their heads, reflecting a popular interest in ethnology at the time.

The Sami need not fear that the Riding with Reindeer Expedition will conduct head measurements. Besides the epic quest of reaching the Barents Sea by bicycle, I hypothesize that Lapland is a plausible destination for the self-contained and somewhat frugal bicycle tourist.

The roads and facilities are reported to be good, and the people and reindeer friendly. These claims will be verified—or refuted—in the next few days.

In the meantime, the Expedition is still encamped in Rovaniemi with a growing problem on its hands. After resupplying, I can't cram all the stuff bags and packets into the wagon. Worse yet, I am alarmed by the load's growing weight. Petite sacks of supplies neatly arranged during trial packing sessions in Seattle have expanded into an amorphous mass. The tiny quantities of cooking oil, sugar, and coffee—long ago exhausted—have been replaced by family-sized containers. For a couple of weeks, I have lugged a quart of vegetable oil, a pound of instant coffee, and a half-kilo of laundry detergent that I am reluctant to ditch, given my propensity for getting grease on my pants.

I carefully portion out supplies required for the next two weeks. Sugar cubes are rationed at two a day, coffee at two spoonfuls a morning. Unfortunately, discipline breaks down in the apportionment of shaving cream, where the smallest replacement is a big can of foamy. I can't bring myself to grow a beard, fearing that the sudden appearance of facial hair in the vast plains of Lapland will cause a reindeer stampede. But I stick to my plan of using only one razor blade a week.

My library has also expanded. A parcel of reading material sent by friends and retrieved at the Rovaniemi post office has replaced my waterlogged copy of *The Economist*, the faithful journal that kept me apprised of world economic events and also served as a useful weapon against the continuous onslaught of mosquitoes. Lacking information on Arctic Norway—a region I will need to cross to reach the Barents Sea (Finland ceded its access to the Arctic to Russia as the price for ending the Continuation War)—I buy the Lonely Planet guidebook on Norway for the princely sum of $35.20. *Now is not the time to be cheap*, I reason.

I had already learned this lesson the hard way by purchasing a slimmed-down version of a Finnish phrase book that has proved mostly useless. I reluctantly part with *The Race for Timbuktu* (which I finished), leaving it for the next visitor to my room. It is replaced with the only other pleasure-reading I can afford, both in weight and in price: a slender volume from the children's section titled *Finn Family Moomintroll.** Admittedly, this is not exactly high literature, but I expect the Moomin characters—Snufkin, Sniff, and the Snork Maiden—and their zany exploits to lighten things up amid the vast stretches of Lapland isolation.

The proudest moment of my Rovaniemi hiatus comes when I devise a plan to fix the broken stem that holds my rearview mirror to the left side of the bike's handlebar. My hasty repairs in Ruka with duct tape failed. Borrowing a lesson from a first-aid manual, I treat the broken stem as if it were a fractured ankle. Mimicking a figure-eight pattern, I bind the mirror stem to the handlebar with dental floss. Next, I splint the fracture with an ice cream stick (found on the sidewalk near Santa Village) and a piece of rubber I scavenged from the roadside. I finish by wrapping duct tape around the splints and the floss binding. The mirror holds.

On Friday, August 10, the Expedition, with banner fluttering proudly from the rear of the wagon, is ready. The heat wave that descended on Rovaniemi the day I arrived has dissipated. A cool wind blows from the north, but the sun is out, blocked occasionally by puffy clouds scuttling across the sky. I pedal through the quiet morning streets, reach the river, and turn north on National Bike Route 4. This was not part of the original plan, and anyone tracking my progress back home would have been puzzled by this deviation.

During the layover I had pored over the maps, attempting to deduce the best way north. The obvious route was to backtrack on Highway E-75, the traffic-frenzied road that brought me to Rovaniemi, then turn north on the Arctic Highway to Sodankylä. But by now I have grown accustomed to the quiet, though sometimes maddening, serenity of the back roads. I also feel confident in my mechanical abilities and hoard of spare parts, should any breakdown occur. Even if I couldn't fix something, the Finns, though not particularly gregarious, had thus far proven

---

* Tove Jansson, one of Finland's most beloved children's authors, wrote a series of books featuring the zany adventures of the Moomin Family and their wacky friends. Recall that Finland's president in 2007, Tarja Halonen, is often referred to as Moominmama, the lovable matriarch of the Finn Family Moomin.

resourceful and, I reasoned, would surely help if I got into a jam. After all, this is an Expedition. It is time to get back to the road less traveled.

The first five miles are delightful. The dedicated bike path keeps me from harm's way. I pedal briskly through the outskirts of Rovaniemi, the wind slightly in my face. The broad swath of the Ounasjoki, Finland's biggest river, glints through the spruce.

The continuation of the forest is a surprise. My prior Arctic experience, a canoe trip down the Noatak River in Gates of the Arctic National Park and Preserve in Alaska, led me to believe that north of the Arctic Circle here, as in Alaska, the trees would get smaller, then disappear altogether in the harsh environment. But this notion was quashed during my visit to the Arktikum museum in Rovaniemi, where I learned that warm ocean currents from the Gulf of Bothnia keep Lapland relatively warm, compared with other Arctic zones. True, the dark winters can be harsh, with temperatures often below zero, but the twenty-four-hour summer days are still warm enough to keep the ground from permanently freezing. Despite its huge territory above the Arctic Circle, and unlike Russia, its neighbor to the east, Finland has virtually no permafrost or glaciers. The temperate environment makes it possible for the tree line in Finland to extend almost to the Norwegian border. Indeed, the trees appear to get bigger and healthier the farther north I pedal. Sprinkled amongst the forest are farms and dairies, which seems astounding because I am now above 67 degrees latitude, placing the Expedition roughly equal to the snowy crags of Alaska's Brooks Range or about a quarter of the way up Greenland's ice sheet. The Finns contend that the winters are getting warmer and the summers wetter—the product of a warming atmosphere.

After a pleasant lunch at a roadside picnic area near the river, I encounter hills, then a small town whose major attraction is a store advertising fresh, whole salmon. The parking lot is jammed, and for an indecisive moment I think about stopping. Then practical sense intervenes. What will I do with an entire salmon?

By midafternoon, my pace slows due to increasing wind velocity. So far, I have been lucky to avoid those stiff headwinds that I'd heard about.

The only winds of consequence I've encountered have been friendly tail-winds or the solitary but violent gusts preceding a squall.

By the time I reach the bridge crossing the Ounasjoki, I am being tossed around by hefty gusts. On the east bank, I must make a decision. Ahead, National Bike Route 83 peels off to the northeast via a narrow, lonely dirt road that stretches through a dense forest corridor that looks never-ending. Somewhere along that route, in the middle of nowhere, is the tiny village of Unari, which allegedly has a store and a summer camp.

Alternatively, I can stay on the paved Bike Route 4 (Highway 79) and head north for two days toward the town of Kittilä, about 110 miles north of Rovaniemi. I'll have to deal with the wind, but that seems preferable to heading off into the unknown. I know that Kittilä has a campground and a couple of hotels. I am not confident, however, that I can find a place to stay near Unari, despite the efforts of a helper at the Santa Claus Tourist Office in Rovaniemi, who called various farms in the area that function as bed-and-breakfast establishments in the summer.

"I sent someone on a bike out there last year, but I never found out what happened to him," Santa's helper told me. Now that I have reached the crossroads, my on-site observation tells me no one has gone down Bike Route 83 in a very long time. I fear I might find the bleached bones of last year's cyclist somewhere in the vast unknown. (It's true that I want to take the path less traveled, but not *that* less traveled.)

I point the handlebars north, sticking to the better-traveled Bike Route 4, knowing I will face more solitude-laden roads in the days ahead. My decision means, though, that it will now take me three, not two, days to reach Sodankylä. But thanks to my maniacal pace in North Karelia, I have actually gained a few extra days, adding to the reserve I had when I started the trip. I don't mind spending one now. The good news is that the map indicates there is a campground about 15 miles north, at a place called Ounasmö, about halfway between Kittilä and Rovaniemi.

But the wind god is determined to stall my advance. Large gusts slam into me head-on. This, combined with hills, slows my progress to a pitiful five to six miles per hour. When logging trucks pass, my speed increases slightly as the bike gets sucked into the vortex. But when they barrel down in the opposite direction, I have to brace for the shock wave, then fight to keep from being blown off the road. It's exhausting. To add further drama, the sky darkens ominously, its gray clouds fusing together.

As I struggle through the last few miles, I notice that I have been passed by several ambulances, first in one direction, then in the other. With sirens and lights off, the ambulances do not appear to be in a hurry. Normally, this wouldn't pique my interest, but the appearance of multiple ambulances *does* arouse my curiosity. When yet another ambulance passes me, I begin to suspect it's the same ambulance that I keep seeing. I speculate: *Is it normal in Lapland for the local ambulance to patrol a stretch of road, awaiting a call from one of the area's few inhabitants? Has my quest been reported to the local health district authorities, who have decided to keep an eye on me in case I need resuscitation from the heart attack that seems inevitable? After all, no sane person bikes due north. Maybe they think it's only a matter of time before I am sucked into the grill of a monster truck.*

I may need that ambulance yet. Each push on the pedal is now difficult. My eyes dart between the odometer, which slowly cranks off each tenth of a mile, and the shoulderless road. At last, I see a sign indicating a campground ahead. I turn down a dirt driveway to a farmhouse. The farmer has converted his field into a giant tenting area, with a few log cabins in the woods near the banks of the Ounasjoki. But other than the farmer himself, who is in a nearby field cutting the grass on a John Deere mower, no one is around.

I knock on the farmhouse door and a stocky, gray-haired woman answers. In my best Finnish, I request a *mökkit*—a cottage or cabin. She looks at me like I have just landed here from Mars. She says something that I do not understand. I ask if she speaks English, but she doesn't. I look longingly at the *mökkits* in the woods by the river and wonder if they are closed for the summer. Then I remember that I am in Lapland, where the indigenous Sami speak their own language, not Finnish. Although many Sami still herd reindeer, others are farmers or tradesmen. Physically, they tend to be short of stature, but otherwise they are indistinguishable from ethnic Finns. I had seen pictures of some Sami who bear a striking resemblance to Eskimos, while others are as blonde as a native Swede. Other than being short, I have no clue about the ethnicity of the woman, but it is clear I am not getting anywhere with my rudimentary Finnish.

I revert to sign language, forming a triangle with my hands. This gets instant recognition. She tells me through gestures that I can camp anywhere. The cost is $13. Then she disappears into the house and brings forth a giant guestbook for me to sign. While she goes to fetch change, I leaf through the book, noticing that the last visitor was from Holland. He had been through three days ago. I quickly scan through the remaining pages, going back several years. I am her first American.

The Expedition camps at Ounasmö on the banks of the Ounasjoki.

Even though I had my heart set on a *mökkit*, I am not disappointed with the campsite. I pitch the tent on a thick, grassy knoll overlooking the Ounasjoki. Nearby sits a set of lawn furniture and a trampoline, the latter of which seems to be common in Finnish campgrounds, leading me to conclude that liability law is rather undeveloped here. Although I am not in the mood for trampoline bounding, I drag some of the furniture over to serve as clothes hangers.

Upstream about a hundred yards, fishermen cast from a long, wooden boat. The sun breaks through the clouds, and the wind magically begins to dwindle. There is no kitchen for me to use, so tonight I take out the stove to boil water for one of the precious dehydrated dinner packets I have lugged across Finland. Tonight's repast consists of miso soup followed by turkey tetrazzini (spooned out of the bag), with a dessert ration of two biscuits. Entertainment is a rousing game of darts with myself and two chapters of the *Moomins*. The trampoline remains untouched.

Kittilä to Hammerfest and the Expedition End

Where Is Everyone?

I WAKE UP IN THE DARK, curled in a fetal position. Except for the soft murmur of the river, the early morning is still. I poke my head out of my sleeping bag, and the cold hits me like a slap in the face. After making a quick exit from the tent to pee, I return shivering. I pull on long underwear and fumble through my clothes bag for my head cap, last worn during the morning maelstrom I survived the day I left Nurmes. The temperature is probably in the high 30s or low 40s—a good twenty to thirty degrees cooler than when I went to bed.

Everything is wet—clothes adorning the lawn furniture, bike, rainfly, trampoline, grass, and probably the cows that are lolling in the pasture nearby—from the foggy dew that hangs in the air. This is not the kind of morning that inspires me to bound out of bed and sing of another glorious day. Even the mosquitoes are lethargic, sluggishly bouncing off the tent netting where they become an easy target for me. I want to burrow into the sleeping bag and indulge in my own body heat. But this strategy can last only so long.

By nine o'clock, I decide that Lapland will not get warmer. I extract myself from the bag, put on my cycling shorts, and then, for the first time in a week, pull on my leggings.

After coffee and pustajes—the little Finnish cinnamon rolls I'm now addicted to—I quickly fold the wet tent, pack, and begin my ride, turning north on National Bike Route 4 again. Unlike yesterday, the road is quiet, with not a car or truck in sight. The wind is gone. I grind on in silence, knowing that today's goal is only 47 miles away at the Sami town of Kittilä.

As I eat my hard-boiled egg snack at a roadside pullout, an old man wearing a colorful embroidered Sami tunic approaches on a dilapidated three-speed. He stops after spotting me. By now, I understand enough through sign language and a few key words to know when someone is asking where I am from and where I'm going. I explain. He gives me the thumbs-up, but he's bursting to tell me something else, if only I could understand him. He does a good imitation of a sous-chef sautéing fish on a pan, then gesticulates toward the woods and makes like he's picking berries, chopping wood, and starting a fire. *Is he inviting me to his cabin for lunch?* He motions for me to follow.

He gets on his bike and wobbles down the road in the opposite direction I had just come. I jump on mine and follow. He cycles about twenty feet, stops, and motions that I should turn off on a barely discernible dirt track that veers from the highway and disappears into the forest down a hill. Now I understand. He's telling me there is a good place to build a fire, cook fish, and gather berries down by the river. He appears emphatic about building a proper fire. Then he remounts, cheerfully waves goodbye, and pedals away. I call out thanks for this neighborly advice and turn the bike toward the muddy track that spirals down to the river.

Giuseppe Acerbi, the Italian adventurer who came this way two hundred years ago, also noted the Laplanders' fondness for a good fire. "We drew our boats ashore and walked about a mile into the country to visit the families of these two Lapland fishers, who had fixed their constant habitation there," he wrote. "We found fires everywhere kept up: the pigs had their fire, the cows had theirs; there was one inside of the house, and another without, close to the door." Acerbi observed that the fires not only kept people and animals warm, but the smoke also warded off the mosquitoes and flies.

The thought of fresh fried fish is almost too much to bear, especially after a nonstop diet of hard-boiled eggs, cheese, sausage, and a pair of biscuits for nearly a solid month. The old Sami put the idea of fish in my mind. Now I crave trout. Unfortunately, I am missing a few key ingredients—like a trout, for starters, not to mention an iron skillet and a hatchet. I walk the bike a few feet toward the track and wait for the old man to disappear. I don't want to appear ungrateful. When he's gone, I re-emerge and speed off in my original direction. I hook up my MP3 player for the first time on the trip and try to chase away visions of trout with the Gypsy Kings.

The day remains cool as I pedal north, making good time on the mostly flat terrain. I notice that the houses here are not as immaculately painted as in other parts of Finland. Many are unpainted. The few people I observe, however, are as industrious as Finns elsewhere. In the hamlets I pass, I see Laplanders on ladders fixing roofs, mending fences, hoeing up yards, and splitting and stacking firewood. The reindeer, too, have become more numerous, regularly strolling out from the forest to take a look at me or to hover on the edge of the road, daring cars to pass them.

Near the tiny settlement of Niskankangas, an unassuming place nes-tled along the banks of the Ounasjoki where one might figure nothing important has ever happened, a large stone monument reminds travel-ers that the wake of history has touched even this rather dull landscape.

The first ripple of consequence occurred in the 1870s when Lapland, like Australia, Siberia, Alaska, and the continental United States, expe-rienced a gold rush, on the Ivalojoki River, north of here. Since the area lacked roads, the only way the miners could get to the fields was by pol-ing upstream on the nearby Ounasjoki.

Forty-five years later, while Russia was preoccupied with World War I, young Finns imbued with the idea of helping the duchy achieve independence were hidden here from czarist police by local residents in a Finnish version of the Underground Railroad. When the coast was clear, the patriots sneaked into Sweden, then into Germany for military training. Later these Finns would form the elite Royal Prussian Battalion of Light Infantry, which would play a decisive role in helping Gustaf Mannerheim's White Army defeat the Finnish Bolsheviks during the 1918 Civil War.

Not far from Kittilä, at the few ramshackle houses that form the hamlet of Tiukuvarda, a boy on a bike suddenly merges onto the main highway. He is on the wrong side of the road, which means he is heading directly toward me. A school satchel is strapped to his back, and his head is down in rapt concentration on the pavement. A car thunders up behind me, leaving no room for me to move over and let him pass.

I yell. His head jerks up. Wide-eyed, he stares at me as if he has just seen the headless horseman. An instant before we collide, I inch off the shoulder onto a narrow strip of dirt. Our bikes clear each other by mere inches. I imagine how many times he has turned and encountered an empty and silent highway. But today, he nearly runs into a stranger riding a strange bike and clad in clothes no Sami owns, let alone wears. After the car passes, he darts across the road. Without glancing back, he hurriedly pedals around a bend.

I reach the outskirts of Kittilä by midafternoon. Though it has five thousand inhabitants, Kittilä is not highly touted in the Lonely Planet guidebook. The book notes that the town, although one of the major service centers for northwestern Lapland, "has little to recommend it to travelers except as a base or a jumping-off point for the ski resort of Levi" about 10 miles north. Named after Kitti, the daughter of a powerful witch from local folk tales, the town—at least according to the Expedition's initial foray—*does* seem bewitched. Signs guide me off the main highway onto a side road that winds through a neighborhood of modest homes and small farms. Laundry flutters from clotheslines and at one place is draped over a nearby hamper, as if its owner has just stepped away. Children's bicycles lay scattered in a yard, but the kids are missing. A tractor idles in another driveway, but there is no driver. Barking howls emanate from the back of every house as I slowly bike down the residential lane, but I see no dogs.

Near the banks of the Ounasjoki I spot the fluttering flags of the Scandinavian countries, indicating the location of the city campground. When I pedal up to the small hut that serves as the reception area and store, I am greeted not by a person but by a sign propped on a chair out front, giving would-be campers a phone number to call for assistance. I walk into the hut, but it is empty. I look around outside, but find no one. I pull out my cell phone and dial the number, but no one answers.

I remount my bike and take a slow tour around the campground. There are no tents pitched, and the only patch of ground that could accommodate one is occupied by a dilapidated trailer. I bike past this to a series of small decaying and deserted cabins. *Do I really want to stay overnight here?*

Finally, along the riverbank I hear the sound of shouting and loud whacks. I pull astride an open-sided kitchen where two grizzled men are whacking the heads off freshly caught fish with maniacal zeal. They glance up from their work. We exchange "ehs" while I search my thin Finnish vocabulary for something more useful to say. The sight of a bike rider does not impress the fish whackers nor does it inspire them to exchange additional pleasantries. They return to their task with a single-mindedness that is frightening.

In the mood for something a little more festive, I turn the bike around and head back to the highway, where the main part of town is located. Perhaps I will find someone else home.

In the town's center, I come to the Gasthaus Kultaisen Ahman Majatalo, a bed-and-breakfast—somewhat of a rarity in Finland. A friendly woman at the reception counter indicates that plenty of rooms are available. In fact, I am the only guest. The woman tells me she can bring the breakfast to my room in the morning. That clinches the deal.

Later that night, I am the only diner at the Hotelli Kittilä, across the street.

"Where is everyone?" I ask the waitress, as she brings me a plate of reindeer casserole. I feel a little guilty about eating reindeer, but my hunger and the fact that it's pretty darn good overwhelms my thin sense of morality. I guess I'm no better than Santa after all.

"School has started. The season is over. Everyone has gone home," she says. "Now, I go home."

Although it's only August 11, the seasons change rapidly in the Far North. In the last few days, I've noticed them becoming shorter and the nights darker.

I watch as she takes off her apron, shouts to someone unseen in the kitchen, then grabs her coat and walks out the door. I am left with my casserole, a mug of Lapland beer, and the company of forty empty tables. After I finish my meal, I sit patiently at my table, feeling like a student waiting obediently for the teacher to dismiss me. No one else seems to be on duty. The moments tick away. A fly, also eager to escape, buzzes desperately at the window.

I get up and look for someone I can pay. I hear the faint thudding of music with a heavy metallic bass pulsating from the kitchen. I wander back among the stoves and giant pots and find the cook chopping the heads off fish to the rhythm of some weird Euro-rap music. Is fish-beheading the national sport in these parts? I coax him over to the cash register, show him what I ordered, and settle up.

Outside, a cold wind blows down the main street. A pickup truck with monster tires roars down the road looking like a prehistoric beast and honks at a couple of chubby teenage girls smoking near a storefront. A block down the street, young men clad in black coats with silver studs protruding from the shoulders sit on a bench outside the supermarket listening to loud music and drinking beer. Well, at least the place isn't completely deserted.

Trapped in the Women's Shower

KITTILÄ SHOWS EVEN FEWER SIGNS OF LIFE in the morning than it did the previous night. Although the deserted streets may not provide evidence of its strategic location, the town sits at the crossroads of two major highways. As I eat the tasty breakfast, delivered as promised to my room, I ponder which of the roads I should take.

For the last two days, I've trekked steadily north on National Bike Route 4 (Highway 79), which continues to Sirkka before veering to the northeast, where it disintegrates into a dirt road and enters the empty quarter of north-central Lapland. There are no towns to speak of on this route and only a few places on the map that hint of human habitation at all. If I go this way, I will need to pedal a hundred miles and over the dreaded fells before reaching Inari, a significant settlement that is considered the unofficial Sami capital of Finnish Lapland. Inari is also where I would join the Arctic Highway for the final push north. My hope is that I could avoid the worst of the fells that Timo and his party struggled over.

The Expedition, however, still has the option of taking the eastbound road that branches from Kittilä and connects earlier with the Arctic Highway at Sodankylä, about 53 miles east from here. North of Sodankylä lie the fells I am trying to avoid. This detour has the advantage of being more traveled, but it would also add an extra 60 miles and at least another day to my journey.

The extra day does not bother me as much as my growing weariness of undertaking what is probably the most circuitous cross-county bicycle trip ever attempted in Finland. Had I gone in an imaginary straight line,

I would have already passed the North Pole and now would be making my way south down through Canada. Instead, I have crisscrossed Finland three times in a kind of upward spiral, with the first loop taking me west from Helsinki to the Åland Islands via Turku; the next loop northeast through the central lake district to North Karelia; and then a loop north to Ruka, before turning west again to Rovaniemi. The route via Sodankylä would add yet another mini-spiral. I am finished with backtracking. It's time to confront the Hills of Bicycle Death.

At nine o'clock, I saddle up. A light mist falls, hinting of heavier showers to follow. My rain pants are strapped by bungee cords to the top of the wagon for quick access. I point the bike north. I steel myself, focused on my new mission: I will zigzag no more.

The cozy room, hot shower, breakfast, fresh coffee, and probably last night's lonely reindeer casserole have all provided fresh fuel for my body—my engine—and my legs—my pistons. In almost no time, I pedal the 10 miles to Sirkka, cross over the gap between Levi and Kätkätunturi fells, and enter into a world very different from the one I just left. Banners draped from the suddenly present ski lodges and gondola lifts promote the Levi resort as the host for the Alpine Skiing World Cup men's and women's slalom event in November.* Levi Fell, which rises eighteen hundred feet from the vale, is crisscrossed with twenty-eight downhill ski slopes, some even lighted. Sirkka has no shortage of hotels, cabins, condos, apartments, restaurants, shops, and everything else that belongs in a world-class ski resort. But like Kittilä, what it doesn't have at this particular moment is people.

Signs proclaim weekend hotel deals for $50 a night, breakfast included. The Lonely Planet guidebook tells of similar summertime prices for cabins, condos, or apartments. As I cycle past the empty hotels and winter ski homes, I think this might be another Ruka: a perfect place to celebrate my return from the Barents Sea in a couple of weeks.

But thoughts of a sauna, a cozy couch, and a big kitchen dissipate as I wheel beyond Sirkka and reality hits: ahead still lie hundreds of miles

---

* The World Cup slalom scheduled for mid-November 2007 was canceled due to lack of snow.

of cold emptiness, a land of bogs and reindeer and not much else. North of Sirkka, Highway 79 splits. My route, Bike Route 4, juts to the northeast along Highway 956. And so I begin my long trek to Inari by crossing the Ounasjoki for the last time. This upstream version is considerably smaller than the broad river that muscled its way through Rovaniemi just a few days ago.

While pedaling across the bridge, I am overtaken by two other cross-country cyclists, a man and a woman. Their bikes are laden with bulging front and rear panniers. Pulling up alongside me, the man, who speaks halting English, says he and his wife are from Germany. He's been cycling on and off in Lapland for the past fifteen years.

"You are the first American I've ever met here," he tells me. "And you are one of the few who are going north. North is difficult."

"I know," I say. "What's the road like ahead?"

He says it is "very bad" and the "mosquitoes very big." But something else he says gives me hope that the next two days will be survivable: at a village called Pokka about 50 miles up the road, there is a campground with rental cabins. This is unexpected. All morning I have been preparing myself for a night in the woods, locked in a desperate struggle against the mosquito hordes that invariably breach my tent. As he scoots ahead to catch up with his wife, I shout good-bye and say I will see them tonight in Pokka.

As if on cue, the pavement ends and the road turns to dirt. My German friend was right: the road *is* bad. I bounce my way along, dodging potholes and rocks and trying to steer around the jarring washboard surface.

Within a few miles, the sleek ski shops, condominiums, and apartments of Sirkka are replaced by large log cabins and giant tepees, called *kotas*. In their nomadic days, the Sami used the *kota* as a portable house. The poles and outer reindeer skin could be easily dismantled, loaded on a draft reindeer, and hauled to the next camp. Today, the *kota* is used for ceremonies, a place for contemplation, or as a spare bedroom in the summer. The *kota* is a reminder that the Sami were the original inhabitants of Finland and the masters of sustainable living. For hundreds of years before the demarcation of national borders, they followed the migration of Lapland's vast reindeer herds. Much like the buffalo sustained the North American Plains Indians, the reindeer provided the Sami with meat, milk, hides, and, once domesticated, transportation.

Kotas, the traditional portable tepee-like structures, of the Sami.

No one knows when the Sami first arrived in Finland, but evidence suggests that the initial settlers moved here from Siberia after the retreat of the last glaciers ten thousand years ago. Later, the docile Sami were pushed north by new waves of immigrants from northern Europe. These newcomers would eventually become the Nordic majority in Scandinavia. In Lapland, the Sami lived in relative obscurity until a trickle of Christian missionaries began showing up in the seventeenth century. They built churches and made a major push to introduce God to the Sami; by the nineteenth century, most of the Sami had been converted to Christianity, while still retaining vestiges of their old animistic beliefs.

Early travelers, such as Acerbi, observed that the Sami lived in an environment of plentiful game. They seemed to be remarkably healthy, free-spirited people who let their children run wild, but did not measure up to the European standard of industriousness. This latter observation was probably a product Acerbi's ethnocentric cultural viewpoint. Clearly, the ability to survive above the Arctic Circle required planning but also economy of movement—something that I could appreciate on my bicycle journey.

Despite the harsh winters and pesky mosquitoes, the environment provided the Sami with everything they needed, which may have contributed to their welcoming and friendly behavior toward outsiders. The historical record shows few incidents of resistance displayed by the Sami, even as their lands were increasingly settled by pioneers from the south and visited by nosey travelers.

Acerbi's journal provides clues about how the Sami actually looked.

"The girl wore pantaloons and boots of the same shape; but her clothing was of wool and her cap, which was made of green cloth, was pointed upwards. They were most of them very short; and their most remarkable features were their small cheeks, sharp chins, and prominent cheek bones. The face of the girl was not unhandsome; she appeared to be about eighteen or nineteen years of age; her complexion was fair, with light hair approaching a chestnut color. Four out of the six men had black hair; from whence I conclude this to be the prevailing colour amongst the Laplanders, distinguishing them from the Finlanders, amongst whom, during the whole of my journey, I did not remark one who had hair of that colour."

Intermarriage with the Nordic majority has, over time, dulled the lines of a distinct Sami look. With settlers and modernization encroaching into Lapland in the late nineteenth century, the nomadic traditions of the Sami began to disappear, too. The cultural destruction continued into the twentieth century with the devastation caused by the retreating German army during the Lapland War. Afterward, the opening of new roads and the invention of the snowmobile also conspired to end the Sami's nomadic lifestyle.

Recently, however, Sami culture has revived. Today there is a Sami radio station, a newspaper, and a growing list of books published by Sami authors. The Sami language, distinct from Finnish, though based on the same roots, is taught in schools where the majority of students are Sami. Traffic signs and place names in Lapland are written in both Finnish and Sami. And now, as I pass more farms with *kotas*, I often see the Sami flag with its distinctive yellow, green, blue, and red blocks of varying sizes intersected by a circle.

〰〰 〰〰 〰〰

I come to a ramshackle grocery store with a gas pump. I judge that this might be the last place for a warm cup of coffee and, if I'm lucky, a pastry—any kind will do. *Why not one last treat before riding into the unknown?* As I set foot inside, I see an old man sitting at a small, round Formica table, reading a newspaper. The room opens into a larger store, which is closed, but the part I have entered—a small antechamber with knives, wool hats, thread, and pastries for sale—is open. As I puzzle over the goods, the man, sensing what I'm looking for, points to the coffee pot. Next to it sits a tray of donuts. I'm in business.

A woman shouts from somewhere within a backroom apartment. The man grunts, gets up, and wanders through a door, leaving me alone. On an adjacent table, I see a guest book and flip through its pages. The previous entry, from yesterday, is signed by Amber and Claire, bicycle riders from England. I imagine two flaxen-haired English beauties, gliding effortlessly across the velvety plains of Lapland, golden in the afternoon light, herds of reindeer scampering behind them. This rather pleasant thought leads me to think that I might be better off spending this time pedaling, perhaps gaining a chance to catch up with the two beauties, rather than sitting here at the last store on Earth, stuffing a donut into my mouth. Reflexively, I look out the window at the bike. A raven perches on the handlebars, staring intently back at me and my donut. The bird caws.

"Beat it!" I yell with little conviction. But the bird remains, like a premonition from an Edgar Allen Poe tale that does not end well for the protagonist. I do not have the willpower to leave my morsel and shoo it away. We stare at each other through the gray gloom, now accented by a gentle rain washing away my last bit of motivation to catch Amber and Claire.

I look through the book for evidence of a fellow countryman or woman, but most visitors hail from southern Finland. Two years ago, a lost soul from the United Kingdom wandered in, then a couple from Holland, who were followed by a pair from Hungary. At 2004, I stop turning the yellowed pages. It's time to head back out.

The rain turns steady. What was once just a wet road slowly transforms into mud. My tires skid on the slick paste. I slosh in and out of mud holes. I lurch around rocks. And now my skittering has awoken every dog in the district. Fierce barking echoes through the woods. When I do see a dog, it is the size of a small bear straining at its leash or rearing within its wire enclosure. I do seem to bring out the best in man's best friend.

I decide to arm myself, just in case. I stop and look for a stick but settle for a rock. *This is ridiculous*, I think, after cycling for a short distance with my stone-age implement. I hurl the rock into the woods. *Should one of these beasts break loose, I'll take my chances.*

By midmorning, the rain slackens and all vestiges of civilization along the roadside have disappeared. The barking ceases. Every thirty minutes or so, a car or a camper-truck passes, then the road goes silent again. But I do not feel lonely. Instead, the solitude fuels my strength and adds to my resolve to complete the epic. Each revolution of my mud-encrusted tires brings me a few feet closer to my goal, still more than 200 miles away. One lesson among many that I have learned on this trip is that no matter how slowly I move, I still make progress. Even on my worst days, when I walk up countless hills, I gain ground. *Just keep moving*, I tell myself.

At noon, the sun peeks out. I find a clearing, steer the bike off the road, and prepare to have a picnic. But shortly after pulling out my food bag, I am engulfed in gnats and mosquitoes. I eat quickly while swatting away the pests, then jump back on the bike.

A wooden fence, about six feet high, now runs parallel to the road. The fence continues for miles, though in some places it is splintered, like a large animal has burst through it. Then I remember that the road cuts through traditional Sami reindeer-herding territory. I wonder if this fence is intended to keep the reindeer from wandering into the path of oncoming cars and trucks, particularly at night. As many as four thousand reindeer a year are hit by motor vehicles. On the other hand, in a reindeer-bike collision, I would probably be the worse off.

The bugs are also a problem for the reindeer. The swarms have been known to drive reindeer crazy, causing them to run and thrash about blindly. My biggest danger is not cars, wolves, or even dogs, but being bowled over by a berserk reindeer running recklessly through the forest and onto the road.

En route to Pokka

The first reindeer family I encounter seems oblivious to the swarming critters. Mom, dad, and two calves daintily cross the road, striking a pose of the perfect nuclear reindeer family. I creep closer, but just as I'm about to stop and get out my camera, the adults turn tail and jog up the road a few hundred feet. The calves are reluctant to follow, lingering for a few seconds to stare at what is probably the strangest creature they have yet set their young eyes upon. But at last, I sense the communiqué of the reindeer mom, the equivalent of: "Comet, get

your hindquarters over here, right now! You don't know what that is
or where it has been."

This game continues. Each time I get closer, the adults break into an
easy trot, while the youngsters linger. When the calves do retreat, I catch
sight of their enormous feet, which make them run splay-legged. I notice
that one of the adults has a prodigious bulbous nose, white instead of red.

The road twists up hills. At first, they are short and steep, and I
walk to conserve my strength since I don't know what lies ahead. Later,
others are long and constant, allowing me to gear my bike down and
grind along at four miles per hour. From each summit, I see a forest that
stretches forever.

By five o'clock, I reach the Kitineri River, the site of Pokka, whose importance to me has reached fantastical proportions. Pokka, or what I think is
Pokka, in actuality consists of a few ramshackle outbuildings, snowmobiles,
barking dogs, and a building called the Tieva Baari, which serves as a combination restaurant-tavern-store. I walk into the dimly lit building, which
like the store I stopped at in the morning sells knives, thread, and beer. A
few men and women sit quietly in the room's smoky recesses. The chatter
ceases when they see me. I feel like the new guy in a B-grade western.

Behind the bar, a bearded young man with penetrating dark eyes
is talking to another man in a flannel shirt and wool hat. I am not sure
whether my few words of Finnish will work here. I'm not even sure he is
Sami, though I notice that everyone is kind of short.

"Hello," I say. "Speak English?"

"Yes, I do my friend," he says in an accent that sounds Russian.
"Where are you from?"

I tell him an abbreviated version of my story, which seems to impress
the crowd. I ask if he's seen two German cyclists today, but he says no. I
ask about camping.

"I have something better," he says. "You have come a long way, and
tonight the weather is cold and maybe there is rain. The mosquitoes
are going to kill you anyway. You do not want to be like a wild and
crazy reindeer."

I shrug my shoulders. It's true; I do not want to be like a wild and crazy reindeer.

"I have a big cabin with a refrigerator and stove. It is very warm. You can stay there for $40," he says.

This sounds like a good deal to me. I shell out the euros. The man jumps out from around the bar and leads me out the door to show me the cabin. We wander to the back of the tavern amid a repository of snow-mobile parts, all-terrain vehicles, and big tires strewn about in the moss. A kennel holds two barking huskies, which take an immediate dislike to me. The cabin is the largest one I've stayed in to date, and even though there appears to be a chicken coop on the roof, I observe that the chickens are missing.

"What about a shower?" I ask.

"The only shower is in the women's bathroom in the tavern," he says. "But you can use it. Remember to lock the door and sweep the water down the drain. It will be okay. There will not be many customers tonight. Not many people live in Pokka."

Later that night, I stroll over to the tavern for my shower. The place is packed. Every woodsman and woodswoman in the district is here, slugging down beer and whatever else is available. The friendly chap who showed me around earlier is gone, so I sneak into the women's restroom and lock the door as instructed. I hurry, but while I'm rinsing someone pounds on the door.

A woman's voice booms from the other side. While I am prepared for many emergencies, I had not foreseen a scenario in which I would be harassed while stark naked in a women's bathroom in a tavern in the middle of Lapland that sells beer, knives, and thread. The middle item on that list is the Expedition's chief concern at the moment, particularly when combined with happy hour. I myself am not altogether happy, though somewhat cleaner.

I do not know the Sami words for "I'll be out in a second, and the bartender said it was okay!" Although Sami has several hundred words for reindeer, the language probably does not have sufficient traction to rescue me from this situation. Perhaps if I were washing a reindeer, I could better explain myself.

The pounding continues, with more emphasis. A bladder needs to be emptied.

"I'll be out in a second," I shout in English.

A moment of silence ensues. Then a female voice bellows. The tone and emphasis suggests that it translates into something like, "There's a fucking man in the women's room! Get the hell out of there!"

For good measure, I'll suggest that she may have added: "I'll huff, and I'll puff, and I'll blow this door down!"

In this moment of panic, there is little time to waste on speculation. The door shudders from a crash that sounds like it's sustained a full-body blow, followed by more cursing. I do not think the door can withstand another slam.

By now I am dressed. I grab my stuff, including a ripe towel that could probably ward off an assailant for a few precious seconds, and prepare to launch myself out of the room as quickly as possible.

When I open the door, there is no one there. I glance around the smoke-filled tavern. Music pumps out from a boom box. In the haze, I see big bulky men and women drinking, smoking, and talking. *Where did all the little people go?* I wonder. I guess that my antagonist has either sought refuge elsewhere or is buying one of the big knives. I do not stick around to find out. I scamper out the door and into the forest, but my retreat is quickly signaled by barking dogs. Groping around in the twilight, I find the cabin, slam the door, and vow not to leave again until morning.

Later, as I inventory my meager possessions, I realize that I have left my only bar of soap in the shower. In my tattered yellow notebook, I add "soap" to my lengthening shopping list.

30

Hills of Bicycle Death

IN THE MORNING, THE TIEVA BAARI IS DESERTED, last night's rambunctious crowd having dissipated as unobtrusively as the Lapland mist. I say a quick good-bye to the dogs, who acknowledge my greeting with another crescendo of "I want to tear your head off" barking, then I pedal off. Mercifully, the dirt road turns to pavement.

Today's 73-mile route will take me through the "empty quarter"—a lonely land of thickets and swamps—then to the Hills of Bicycle Death. *Yes, I know I am violating the 50-mile rule, but I have no choice.* There is nothing between me and the village of Inari—my destination for tonight—except those damn fells. Despite my attempts to find a route around them, the fells cannot be avoided. But after scrutinizing the map contours, I believe the path I have chosen will be less horrible than the one taken by Timo along the Arctic Highway. I will soon find out whether this is based on a realistic interpretation of map data or just wishful thinking.

I make good progress as the challenging hills of yesterday transform into a plain dotted with marshes and bogs. For a while, it feels as though I am the only object moving in this landscape of dull green and gray. Then the honking of bean geese suddenly springing from a pond and flapping south reminds me that this seemingly empty land is filled with wildlife. Looking skyward, I notice more geese, flying in V-formations across the pale sky. A few miles farther, I come upon two stately, black-necked swans lounging in a swamp, in no hurry to go anywhere.

By midmorning I reach Repojoki, the traditional reindeer roundup grounds for the Sami. Until the nineteenth century, most of the reindeer that roamed Lapland were wild. Gradually, the Sami expanded their herds by using decoy domesticated reindeer to capture their wild cousins. Soon families controlled large herds, and by the late 1800s, all the reindeer roaming these plains were, in theory, owned.

How can you tell? The reindeer I have encountered thus far appear to wander haphazardly, moving about at will. Some wear collars, others bells, but it's the ears that serve as their identification card. Each animal bears a distinctive ear notch that identifies its owner. The notch is administered by wrestling the calf to the ground, then using a knife to carve the appropriate pattern onto the ear.

I pull over at a series of interpretative signs that explain what went on near here in the old days of the Sami reindeer roundup. A trail heads off into the bush, leading to a place called Sállivári, where there once was an elaborate series of corrals where reindeer were shunted and separated according to ear notch. Special foremen were posted at the first corral to count and separate the reindeer. Other Sami lassoed the animals and dragged them to smaller pens assigned to each family.

Much like old North American cattle roundups, the reindeer roundup featured a lot of good old-fashioned haggling as reindeer were pinched to test for fat content and fur thickness. Reindeer meat, milk, and cheese were all essential parts of the Sami diet. Hides were used for blankets, mittens, and clothes; antlers were fashioned into tools.

The gathering was more than just a reindeer auction, though. For the nomadic Sami, who lived a self-sufficient existence in small family groups, this was the social event of the season. Families came from throughout the region, pitched their *kotas*, and joined in music, singing, and dancing that usually lasted all night.

Soon after World War II, permanent homes and log cabins replaced the *kotas*. Snowmobiles and all-terrain vehicles replaced sleds and reindeer-pulled sledges. Finally, the paved road connecting Rovaniemi to Inari was the death knell for the old Sállivári roundup. By the 1960s, it had become another quaint relic of the past.

Today, the roundups continue during the darkness of December.

After resuming my ride, I soon pass the modern pens, corrals, and light standards of the new Sállivári Cooperative's roundup grounds. This particular cooperative, one of fifty-seven in the Lapland and Oulu provinces, is owned by one hundred twelve families who today manage herds totaling nine thousand reindeer. Reindeer meat, and to a lesser extent the cheese and hides, remains an important commercial product in Finland.

\vvv \vvv \vvv

Ahead I see a line of low-lying hills stretching across the horizon, blocking my path to the Barents Sea. *The fells; at last we meet!* With each crank of the pedal, the hills draw closer. When I reach the first slope, I gear down. My strategy is to conquer the fells with a slow, disciplined, and methodical pace.

After surmounting the first few inclines, I use my now-expert strategy of gathering momentum on the descent and using that speed to sling myself almost effortlessly to the top of the next hill. The process repeats itself again and again, and the only hard pedaling is near the top of the ascent, when my momentum is finally subdued by gravity.

At about the time when I begin to think the fells are overrated, I notice that each new hill is getting steeper and longer. On the descents, I now shift into my highest gear, then pedal ferociously to capture as much momentum as possible—but this output of energy still leaves me far short of each summit, requiring more hard and steady pedaling. Near the tops of the hills, my speed diminishes to four miles per hour.

I see now that I was fooled by the first line of low-lying hills; these were mere decoys hiding the bigger rises beyond. Now the road doesn't even bother to descend—it leads exclusively and relentlessly upward, into the gray sky. Rounding a bend, I finally see a descent—followed by a climb straight over the top of a monster fell whose grade is much steeper, at least ten percent. *Is this the king of the fells? Does salvation, or at least easier pedaling, lie beyond?*

So far on this trip, common sense has largely overruled my occasional impulse to take on ridiculous physical challenges—the glaring exception being the day I bypassed a perfectly good holiday camp and ended up in the woods near Lake Pyhäjärvi (and perhaps the day after that, come to think of it). But I am also aware that the monster fell, like a mythical dragon guarding the castle in which the fair maiden is entrapped, is stirring some primitive competitive impulse within me. This urge is particularly dangerous to anyone beyond the age of fifty.

Counterbalancing this instinctual urge are the words of the well-known distance cyclist Fred Matheny, who provided the very same warning that I ignored a month ago: *Do not overreach.*

For weeks I have stuck to my rule about walking the bike when the slope of the road became excessive or when my speed dips below four miles per hour. After all, I can walk uphill at nearly three miles per hour and save a lot of stress on my legs and knees, not to mention give my butt a rest. The strategy has worked up to this point. I have reached Lapland. I have suffered no chronic knee or leg pain. Why mess with success?

I slowly begin to ascend. My speed quickly drops to four miles per hour, then three. I know I should get off the bike and walk. But I do not get off. I continue to think about dismounting. Nothing happens. My brain has been taken over by enemy forces.

Far ahead, on the summit, I see three tiny figures standing next to a parked car. They are watching me, probably taking bets on whether I will make it or collapse. I am not going to disappoint my fans. I will put on a show of middle-aged power biking.

I pump on, grinding away ever so slowly up the hill. There is no traffic, no sound except the grating of my lowest gears straining against the chain. Perspiration drips from my face and falls to the pavement. The muscles in my legs ache. Slowly, ever so slowly, the three figures grow larger, the gray sky nearer. My muscles scream *No more!* But the voice in my head is shouting *You're going to make it!*

Beyond all expectations, I do make it. Panting, I pull up to the three watchers, who have turned their attention to the car's trunk, which contains binders, charts, and instruments of some unknown kind.

"Hello!" I shout to the two men and one woman, all of whom appear to be middle-aged.

The woman speaks some English. The crew works for the government. They are conducting a survey on the health of the vegetation in the area. I explain myself.

"Helsinki is a long way," deadpans the woman, after I tell her where I started my epic.

This, of course, is not exactly news to me, but at least I am no longer being told that Lapland is far away.

"Is this the highest hill before Inari?"

I ask this question only to confirm what must be the truth. There is no way in hell that higher hills are ahead. It just can't be possible in flat Finland.

But the answer I receive is typically Finnish. Where an American would have sugar-coated the truth with a "You're almost there" or "Just a little more," the Finns give it to you straight, no matter how far from Helsinki you are or how many tendons you just yanked out of their sockets. The Finns will not burden you with small talk, not even among the Hills of Bicycle Death.

"There are many more hills ahead," says the woman.

"You're kidding!" I blurt, the disappointment in my voice translatable into any language. "Are you sure?"

The woman confers with her colleagues. An earnest conversation ensues. The trio pores over a large, detailed map that has materialized from an attaché case. Fingers point to contours, then the thin, black line that represents the road. Calculations are performed, exact altitudes determined, measurements and distances debated.

I stand to the side, dripping with perspiration, my heavy breathing slowly dwindling back to normal. They glance back at me as if to size up the exact number of calories I have left in reserve and whether the sum of this energy equals or slightly exceeds that which is required to reach Inari.

The woman turns to me. She clears her throat as if rendering a verdict. "Yes," she says. "There are many more hills."

"Ugghhh." I feel like a balloon that has just been pricked.

Then she grants me a small concession. "But this might be the highest hill. We cannot determine this for sure."

I thank them for their careful analysis.

"You know," says the woman, as if in passing, "a big storm is coming in the next few days."

This last bit of news is the final straw. The triumph over the monster hill is a Pyrrhic victory. If the fells don't finish me off, the next big storm certainly will. It will not take much more of nature's huff and puff to blow me down. I wonder if Gustaf Mannerheim had similar thoughts of "How long can I hang on?" as the Russians hurled attack after attack against the thinly manned Finnish fortifications during the Winter War.

Too tired to find a decent lunch spot, I drag the bike onto the shoulder and hunker down near a patch of scraggly pines to quickly eat my typical ration. Unfortunately, I am out of bananas, nature's remedy for muscle cramps. This does not bode well.

Slightly refreshed after lunch, I drag the bike back to the road, begin my well-earned coast down the other side of the monster fell, and behold a sight that justifies my earlier scream. Ahead, the road continues into infinity, bobbing up and down hills until it disappears into the horizon. The melody to "Stairway to Heaven" plays through my head, but with words Led Zeppelin never composed.

There is nothing else to do except carry on. But this soon becomes problematic. On the next ascent, I feel a painful twinge in my left knee. With each push on the pedal, the twinge becomes more pronounced until it transforms itself into a genuine pain. I had experienced a similar malady during my week of winter training in Arizona, particularly during a long ride from Tucson to Sierra Vista over 5,200-foot Sonoita Pass. I had attributed that bodily malfunction to a combination of overreaching on my first day and being out of shape.

Today, the assault of the big fell must have pushed my knee, which until now had performed heroically, over the limit. I've learned that once you are over that threshold, there is little you can do but rest and apply ice, which here, a couple hundred miles above the Arctic Circle, seems to be curiously in short supply.

I am still at least 20 miles south of Inari. The Expedition grinds on. The pain grows worse on each successive fell. Finally, unable to bear it any longer, I stop pumping with my left leg. I pedal with only the right leg, giving my left knee a free ride. I wonder how long the right knee, now bearing twice the load, will hold up. My pace slows to a crawl.

During a downhill lull in the relentless trek, I am distracted from my knee problems by a sharp pain in my neck. *Now what?* I reach back and pull off a wasp. I stare dumbly at the creature before casting it away. I feel more pricks on my neck. I stop the bike, and yank off more wasps. Dozens of them are sticking to my jacket, slowly marching up to my neck. The Expedition flag is covered with them. I look around and see a swarm of these critters buzzing frantically around the banner. It's the honey, the vat of honey that exploded next to the flag, courtesy of the U.S. Postal Service, when my sister shipped it to me. The wasps are clearly attracted to the smell that must still permeate it. This is no time to marvel at this synchronicity of events. What were the odds of me biking through a swarm of wasps with the equivalent of a honeycomb flapping from the back of my bike? For a moment I think about taking down the banner, but no—the symbol of the Expedition must remain aloft. I brush off the wasps as best I can and wobble back into the saddle, with one good leg pedaling and my neck stinging.

Within 10 miles of Inari, I cannot pedal uphill any more. The same twinge that started in my left knee is now afflicting my "good" knee. I cannot risk further injury, so I dismount and walk up every hill. I take solace in the fact that the Expedition is still moving forward, despite the attack of the wasps and the relentless fells. I have to admit that Timo wasn't kidding about the Hills of Bicycle Death.

While preoccupied with my state of misery, I had not noticed until now the change in scenery. The boggy marshlands have given way to forested fells, which have now morphed into honest-to-goodness mountains. *Flat Finland—what balderdash!*

After passing a large lake, Solojärvi, the road skirts the tumbling Juutuanjoki that courses through a narrow valley bordered with stately spruce. Road signs indicate fishing and camping spots. I also observe some strange roadside debris. Earlier in the day, in a ditch in the middle of a vast marsh, I passed a manual typewriter, sitting primly by the edge of the road as if the writer had placed it there and just stepped away. Now, I see a full-sized refrigerator standing upright next to a dirt road. Could this be another act of divine providence blatantly delivering ice to me in a full-sized Frigidaire®? I open the fridge, but alas it is empty. The plug, like a tail, dangles from its back.

At last I reach the outskirts of Inari, passing the Sami radio station and school. I turn briefly south on Highway E-75, the Arctic Highway, then head straight toward the Uruniemi Campground.

By Lapland standards Inari, population five hundred and fifty, is a metropolis, which sports the usual business district with a gas station, restaurant, hotel, gift shop, two grocery stores, and something I have not seen in awhile: a bank with a cash machine. At the campground, I waste no time renting a small cabin. I quickly unload the bike, then with little enthusiasm ride the one mile back into town to resupply with groceries and replenish the Expedition cash supply.

When I return, I lie listlessly on my bunk. From the window, I see the afternoon sun glinting brightly off massive Lake Inari, whose watery fingers stretch 50 miles, filling most of the northeast quadrant of Finland all the way to the Russian border. Offshore islands appear to float on the ice-blue surface like a mirage. The Sami considered the lake sacred, its islands and waters the dwelling place of spirits. On this brilliant late afternoon, it is easy to imagine this land through the lens of its original inhabitants.

The campground fills with the usual assortment of trailers, camper vans, recreational vehicles, and motorcycles. I arise from my prone position and now watch this orderly activity while I prepare my evening feast of pasta, this time treating myself to a meat sauce (having mastered the Finnish word for ground beef), and, of course, my nightly ration of one beer. The caravans and recreational vehicles here are much smaller than their behemoth cousins in the states. This may be due to the $6-per-gallon gas or perhaps just the Finnish penchant for using space efficiently. It is also clear that the Finns, as well as their neighbors in Sweden and Norway, enjoy being outside as much as possible. Near my cabin, the owners of a small recreational vehicle crank out awnings, unfold chairs and a table, and set out plates and a bottle of wine. As the wife brings out some food, her husband erects a separate tent (larger than mine) for the family dog.

After eating, I turn my attention to my injuries. The throbbing in my left knee has abated for now. I know that I need to ice it, but I forgot to buy ice at the store, and I am not about to ride over a hill back to town again, not after logging a brutal 73 miles today. The welts on my neck caused by the wasp stings have also diminished. I hope for the best as I take two aspirin, curl up in my bunk, and thank the spirits for allowing me to survive the crossing of the fells. With a good night's sleep, a layover day or two, and perhaps a little magic from some friendly lake spirits, I plan to will myself to a speedy recovery and resume the Expedition.

Magic Drums

AT THE MERCY OF NATURE AND STRANGE TWISTS OF FATE, I seem to be saved from the brink of disaster each time the Riding with Reindeer Expedition is about to implode. Proof, albeit circumstantial, keeps accumulating. Brilliant sunbursts spring from darkened skies just before I am driven insane by incessant rain and traumatic thunder and lightning. The wagon tire flies off the axle and stays in one piece when it could have just as easily been pulverized by an oncoming truck. A log shelter in the middle of the forest saves me from hypothermia. Clothespins, the perfect solution to my broken mosquito net zipper, lay before me like mushrooms freshly sprung from the moist earth.

Am I lucky? Or, is there something else at work here besides pure chance? If the latter, I wonder, what should I do to appease the gods so that my rescues continue? The mayhem has been relentless, and yes, I have made it thus far, but enough is enough.

The ancient Sami, plagued with problems of their own—such as "Why are the wolves eating my reindeer?"—turned to their shaman for answers. When called upon, the *noaide*, as the shaman was called by the Sami, would induce a trance with the aid of the syncopated beat of his ornate reindeer-hide drum.* From that point, the shaman would leave the physical world and travel to the spirit-filled underworld. The Sami believed all creatures were linked to a spiritual deity, which usually manifested itself in animal form. The gods of nature, water, wind, and hunting resided atop this complex pantheon. Gods, being gods, required

---

* A Sami shaman could be either a man or a woman.

animal sacrifices—which were usually performed atop a fell. In Inari, the Sami of old journeyed to nearby Ukonselkä, one of the mystical islands I spotted last night, to pay homage to the thunder god. The spirits, when properly approached, could apparently divine wisdom, make accurate predictions, and cure the sick.

〰〰 〰〰 〰〰

This morning, the golden glow of last night's magical sunset is replaced by mist, which cloaks the offshore islands. The covey of campers and recreational vehicles has disappeared. I am left with my thoughts and a sore knee that seems to have benefited greatly from a night's sleep.

I am thinking of the shaman's ability to travel metaphysically to consult the spirits. If I can't find a modern-day shaman, perhaps there is a magic drum somewhere nearby, and I can induce my own trance. At the very least, I would like to do *something* to placate the gods of wind, rain, and thunder.

After breakfast, I pedal to the other side of town where I find the sleek, modern building of the Siida, the Sami Museum and Northern Lapland Center.[33] After wandering through galleries full of artifacts and displays about life in Lapland, I realize that I have begun my search for a magic drum about three hundred fifty years too late.

Protestant missionaries, who first came to Lapland in the seventeenth century, were not exactly enamored of spirit world journeys. Fueled by the fires of reformation, the missionaries built churches and schools and set to the task of converting the Sami. Not surprisingly, church authorities viewed the sacred drums as symbols that perpetuated devil worship. In the late 1600s, the church began confiscating the drums. Once confiscated, they were burned or crushed. Many shamans who refused to give up their practices or their drums were declared witches and burned at the stake. Only seventy-three drums are known to have escaped the purges of the seventeenth and eighteenth centuries. Most are preserved in museums in various European cities. One drum still exists in Inari.

This morning I stand before its glass case in the darkened main hall of the Siida. Bowl-shaped, with reindeer skin stretched taut across the opening, the drum's membrane is decorated with symbols painted in blood red. Prominent among the drawings is the shaman himself, shown beating the drum and surrounded by reindeer, dwellings, and people standing on what appear to be skis. Below the shaman stretches an image of a passageway to the underworld, which is inhabited with animals and other symbols that fill the supernatural world.

I ask a docent sitting at a nearby desk whether shamans still exist. At first she doesn't understand the question, but after I rephrase it and beat on a pretend drum, she understands.

"No, that was in the old days. No more shamans," she tells me.

I have no reason to doubt her. She is a Sami, after all. But if drums do still exist, it would be logical to keep the location a secret. Why blurt out the information to a stranger in bicycle tights?

In fact, stories do persist of drums hidden in Lapland. The speculation is fueled by the occasional newspaper article. One Sami leader told a reporter in Norway that he knew of three drums, but would not even hint at their locations. A bus crash several years ago in Norwegian Lapland killed several Sami elders who were thought to have known of the secret location of some drums.[34] Another report, also from Arctic Norway, tells of a modern female shaman possessing and using a drum to undertake shamanic journeys.

Shaman or no shaman, visiting the museum is the perfect respite. The three-mile ride here was pain-free, though I wonder how my knee will feel when I try to pull a load uphill tomorrow. After spending the morning looking at the exhibits, then gorging on the cafeteria's specialty—reindeer stew with mashed potatoes served in a little caldron—I ride north to find the road to the Pielpajärvi Wilderness Church. The original church, built in 1646, represents one of the first permanent incursions of the Lutherans into Lapland. The building that now stands there was built in 1760 and restored in the 1970s.

The last mile of the road is a muddy lane. To reach the church itself, I discover I need to hike three miles on a trail that begins in a soggy meadow, then disappears into a grove of spruce. I contemplate the mileage, think of my knee and the concept of overreaching. I try to balance this with the nagging voice in my mind that tells me I may never be here again.

It starts to rain, small drops at first, but there is the promise of heavier ones to come, judging from the billowing dark clouds frothing in from the north. The gods have spoken. I cannot jeopardize the rest of my journey. I jump on the bike and retrace my route back to the main road. A few minutes after I reach my cabin, the heavens open up with a fury I have not seen for a week. I thank the rain god for sparing me, recalling the Sami tradition of performing sacrifices on high ground to appease the spirits. I am not about to kill an animal or seek a virgin's blood (people, let alone virgins, appear in extremely short supply in this part of the world), though the Sami found it quite acceptable to substitute the aforementioned with the juice from elderberries. In my tattered notebook, I add to my "to do list" the requisite ceremonies—as an insurance policy for the final push north.

On the morning of my third day in Inari, I emerge from my cabin, perform some knee bends, and declare myself fit for duty. A thick fog hangs over the area. All I can see of the massive lake are a few swells that disappear into the grayish white shroud. My neighbors are up early, industriously winding down awnings, packing away lawn furniture, and folding away the dog tent. I, too, pack. It *is* beginning to feel like the end of the journey; if all goes well, I will reach the Barents Sea in three days.

But before I pedal away, I need to make one last important navigational decision.

Until this morning, I had procrastinated about choosing a final route to the end of the world. My choices are to continue north on the Arctic Highway (National Bike Route 4) or turn right on the less-traveled Highway 971. The Arctic Highway heads due north to Utsjoki, then splits off to the east following the Teno River to Nuorgam, the most northern settlement in Finland and Timo's starting point. From Nuorgam, it's another 50 miles to the Norwegian town of Vadsø on the coast of the Barents Sea.

On the other hand, Highway 971 splits off from the Arctic Highway 15 miles north of Inari. It heads northeast along the shores of Inarijärvi. It crosses the border and ends in Kirkenes, in a small corner of Norway snuggled next to Russia.

In pre-trip planning, I told friends I would end up in Kirkenes, but now I am not so sure. Highway 971 is clearly a more remote route. The orange line representing it on the map radiates loneliness as it jiggles past what appear to be a thousand tiny lakes and ponds—prime mosquito territory.

In recent weeks, my ability to divine the landscape from map detail has become almost prescient. Highway 971 shows no towns to speak of on the Finland side, and only a few designated places where there *might* be a place to eat or camp.

I am not in the mood for another long soliloquy. I want to get to the Barents Sea as quickly and painlessly as possible, plant the Expedition flag, and go home.

I mull the choice over my morning coffee. Given that I had reached the southernmost tip of Finland, I decide that my journey needs to achieve its logical symmetry by staying on course for Finland's northernmost extremity. And from a practical standpoint, the Arctic Highway passes through two Sami towns that have stores. In the end, the stores win out. I change course and set out for Nuorgam.

As I creak up the first fell, the mist thickens until the landscape becomes positively fuzzy, as if I have cycled into an impressionistic painting. I pass a lake. In the distance, I spot a blurry glimpse of a solitary fisherman stoically standing in his canoe with his pole. The mist thickens. I stop to slip on my rain pants.

One glint of good news brightens this dull day. The knee pain does not reappear on the first climb. The United Body Parts of Bob are united once again in being relatively pain-free. Even my saddle sores seem manageable.

I soldier on in a kind of trance. The anger I once felt at the relentless bad weather has dissipated. Even the fells, which are greatly diminished from the behemoths that guarded the approach to Inari but are still grueling, do not elicit much of a reaction from me. I do not shout or curse or sing. I don't think about much of anything. Have I come to terms with the fells, the bogs, and mist? Ideas, places, and lists flare up in my mind, then recede so quickly I don't remember what I was thinking about. Other thoughts float in randomly and then eventually disappear, too, leaving my mind blank. I seem to take everything in without the pollution of preconditioned thoughts. I accept everything. It is what it is. I have become part of it.

Even this far north the forest persists, though the Norwegian spruce has been largely replaced by gnarled and weathered Inari pines, a slow-growing species that can live up to four hundred years. Other than the occasional swoosh of a car or a truck, the forest is silent, without even the chirp of a bird or the rustle of the wind. I pass a sign that tells me in Sami that I have reached the tongue-twisting locale of Buoiddeguelletjärrit.

North of the Sami tongue-twister settlement, I reach the cut-off for Kirkenes. I stay the course, my decision already made. I am firmly focused. I have 45 more miles to go to reach a campground called Kenestuvan Leiri.

Mercifully, the hills grow smaller. The rain relents, and the mist lifts as the road levels onto a vast plain of wetlands, ponds, scrub birch, and scraggly pines. I have not seen another cyclist all day. This is surprising because in Inari I saw several pannier-laden bikes outside the tiny information office and at the Siida.

Although this last section of the Arctic Highway wasn't completed until 1956, the route had seen its share of cyclists—most remarkably during the last days of the Lapland War. Following the armistice with the Soviet Union in 1944, the Finnish army, decimated from nearly five years of nonstop fighting, turned its guns on its former co-belligerents.

North of Inari, the Finns pursued the retreating German Mountain Corps on foot and on sturdy one-speed bicycles. By late October, the pursuers finally caught the German rear guard at a spot where I now stand, near the village of Kaamanen. It was the last skirmish of the war before the Germans slipped into Norway, still under Nazi occupation.

At a lonely, unremarkable spot marked by a monument, the old battlefield is a tangle of thickets and swamps. I stop to rest and contemplate what happened here, so far away from everything. This is the first monument I have observed where Finnish objectivity does not entirely blur out the sense of loss caused by the war. I read: "In its entirety the war in Lapland demanded from us a great sacrifice: 774 were killed, 262 were missing and 2,904 were wounded." [35]

By late afternoon, the landscape again transforms. The featureless plain gives way to a lovely alpine valley with a tumbling river, the Utsjoki, coursing through it. Now roughly 200 miles north of the Arctic Circle, I thought I had left the last of the trees behind. But Lapland is full of surprises. With each mile the trees, which had shrunk to stubby little witch's hats earlier, get taller as if in defiance of the extreme geography. As I pedal on, the valley grows deeper and the river wilder. *I must be dreaming. Am I in Colorado?*

As the clouds lift and sun momentarily lights the canyon, I arrive at the turn for Kenestuvan Leiri, the campground I had spotted on the map earlier.

As I pull closer, I see that the buildings are shuttered and the dirt road leading into the camp is barred by a locked gate. Although it's only August 15, I was warned that accommodations in remote areas might be scarce the later I got into the month. Judging from the lack of traffic today, I can't blame the owner for calling it quits for the season.

I have logged 60 miles—not a bad day's work, given my rejuvenated knee and general state of weariness. I take out the map and see that another camp is allegedly only five miles down the road. Experience has taught me to be wary of such promises, and sure enough, when I reach the spot, I find nothing, not even a building. I roll on, searching for campsites. About a mile farther down the road, I reach the trailhead leading into the Kevon Luonnonpuisto, a huge swath of land that has been set aside as a "strict" wilderness area.

There is no mention of this massive park in my guidebook, but I find the trail almost irresistible. It seems to disappear as it climbs over a ridge and into the wild. The sign board describes a 50-mile cross-country path that crosses fells, canyons, rivers, and bogs. I have the urge to abandon the bicycle and set off on foot.

It is almost seven. I calculate that I have another 15 miles before I reach Utsjoki. That would make an 82-mile day, the second longest of the trip after the miserable night in the woods near Eura. An apology to the United Body Parts of Bob is in order, but first I promise that in exchange for keeping all body parts functioning for the next hour and a half, I will not under any circumstances subject myself to another 80-mile day. I know this is another in a long string of promises—mostly broken—but I need to coax a few more miles out of my body. I will also keep a sharp eye out for places to camp. I know I am pressing my luck.

The road enters a narrow canyon. On my left, several hundred feet down, roars the Utsjoki. The growing shadows on the canyon walls remind me that the days are growing markedly shorter. What was once a land of almost unlimited daylight is now one of late-night darkness.

By eight, with the sun setting behind the canyon walls, I ride past an old stone church near the site of a school founded in 1751 to spread Christianity among the Sami. When I bump onto the town's bike path, I know I have reached Utsjoki, a tiny burg where Sami is the dominant language. The authors of the Lonely Planet guidebook are not keen about this Sami outpost, noting it "is not an attractive place by any means." I disagree. After a long day of riding, it looks wonderful.

And the campground is open. As I poke around for a place to pitch my tent, a wild-looking young man dressed in shorts and a T-shirt bounds from a nearby tent draped with drying clothes. I watch as he is pursued by a squadron of the biggest mosquitoes I have ever seen. A smile stretches across his mouth. He vigorously shakes my hand as if he is a shipwreck survivor and I have come ashore in a rescue boat.

"Welcome!" he shouts in a heavy accent. "We have been waiting for you."

The Top

"**DO I KNOW YOU?**" I ask, perplexed.

"The Germans said they saw you on the road to Karigasniemi," he replies.

"What Germans?"

This latest tidbit of information confuses me. I was not on the road to Karigasniemi, which lies to the southwest. That road follows the Teno River, and intersects the Arctic Highway here at Utsjoki, then continues northeast to Nuorgam. I will join this road tomorrow.

Is he referring to the two German cyclists I met several days ago on the road to Inari who told me about the cabins in Pokka? There is time to straighten this out later, but at the moment I am listening to my new friend while frantically yanking the tent from its stuff sack as the mosquito multitudes launch a full-scale attack. Amid frenzied swipes at the air, I introduce myself. The lanky youth pronounces a name that sounds vaguely like the acronym of my alma mater, OSU (Oregon State University) or, his being Belgian, I suspect it's closer to Orescu. As with most chance encounters that occur during the course of an epic, I do not think to ask for the spelling of his name until days after our encounter. At least I have an acronym to remember him by.

While Orescu helps with the tent, he breathlessly tells me that he has trekked across every national park and wilderness area in northern Lapland. Today is the first day in a week he's encountered anyone he can talk to. As we scramble to get the tent up, I hear snippets about a multi-day hike he took across the Kevon Luonnonpuisto, the wilderness area I passed earlier in the day.

"There was no one else," he says. "I think I start to go crazy. At night I hear strange sounds, so that is why I pack and hike all day and night to get to a road to get to a town to talk to someone. There is no way to cross rivers, so I swim." That explains the set of wet clothes strung out on his tent's guy lines.

Our conversation is truncated because every time I open my mouth, mosquitoes fly in. Every few seconds, I drop whatever I'm doing and windmill my hands to keep the pests at bay. Orescu (as I've now dubbed him), on the other hand, seems oblivious to the significant quantities of blood being sucked out of him. He's still excited about talking to someone, anyone, even me.

After the tent is pitched, I stand fidgeting while Orescu talks so rapidly and with such a thick accent that I can no longer understand what he is saying. All I can think of is that I am slowly being eaten alive. I need all of what's left of my blood to make it to the sea.

"Look," I say, "we should probably get back into our tents before the bugs kill us. We can talk later in the kitchen cabin."

With that, we both dive into our respective tents, where much swatting and thrashing occurs.

Later, in the kitchen cabin, I meet up with Orescu and the two German cross-country cyclists, Sebastian and Katherine, who arrived in the camp shortly before I did.

"So you decided to turn around and come back," Sebastian comments, as I enter the cabin. "I don't blame you. The road to Karigasniemi is difficult."

"I wasn't on that road," I reply. "At least, I don't think I was. I came from Inari."

"That wasn't you then? We saw a man pulling a wagon just like yours. But now that I think about it, he rode a full-sized bike."

The mystery is solved; just a case of mistaken identity. Perhaps I'm catching up to one of the phantom cyclists I've learned about during the past forty days.

The Germans are impressed that I knocked off 82 miles in one day. I am too, and I tell them that tomorrow I'm giving myself a break by limiting my distance to the 27 miles required to reach Nuorgam. I plan to stop there, at the very top of Finland, and rest before the final push to Vadsø, Norway.

Sebastian, who wears a neatly trimmed, graying beard and a warm smile, is about my age. Katherine, who is preparing a pot of noodles with carrots and cheese, seems a bit younger but also travel-wise. They, too, are hoping to reach the Barents Sea, by biking to Berlevåg, Norway—an ambitious undertaking given the mountainous terrain of Finnmark, Norway's northernmost province. My plans at the moment call for a less arduous route: a one-day ride from Nuorgam roughly east to Vadsø, which is perched on the shores of Varanger Fjord, an arm of the Barents Sea. As much as I would like to ride with Sebastian and Katherine, I know I could not possibly keep up with them. They started their trip two days ago and are fresh; they plan to blow right by Nuorgam tomorrow. I must keep my promise to myself to rest.

As we chat, Katherine offers me a portion of their dinner. I hesitate. I know how precious calories are. These two will need every ounce of food they carry later, when they tackle the mountains and gale-force winds of Arctic Norway. Katherine sees my hesitation and seems to read my thoughts.

"We made too much. If you do not want it, I will have to throw it away."

The thought of valuable carbohydrates wasted is too much to bear. I pull out my fork, take the pot, and contently shovel it down.

Sebastian says he traveled here 35 years ago with a friend when he was a young man. They had no money. In the evening, they would knock on the door of a cabin, hat in hand so to speak, and inevitably would be ushered inside, fed, and sheltered for the night.

"I do not think that would happen today," he says, noting the abundance of "no trespassing" signs and logs placed across roads leading to private cabins and homesteads.

"Everyone used to be so trusting of strangers here," he continues. "If you were alone in the winter, they would shelter you. It was part of the culture. But today things have changed. People are more wary . . . less open. I guess that is the way the world is going."

Orescu adds to this observation, saying that hitchhiking in Lapland is not easy.

"The Finns are afraid to stop for a hitchhiker because they think you might be a Russian criminal," he says.

I tell him I have not seen a single hitchhiker on my entire trip. I wonder how he got to Utsjoki.

The four of us talk into the night. Grateful for the company and that English is the common language, I seem to have found the magical moment when strangers, sharing the rigors of the road less traveled, intersect and become a community, if only briefly. For Orescu and me, it is particularly important because we've had so little social interaction. We are literally starved for conversation. Orescu, his English syntax diminishing as the night wears on, tells of being chased by demons across the lonely fells and waiting for hours for a ride. Sebastian unfolds his map. We trace routes. I ask the others for details about the coastal ferry, operated by the Hurtigruten line, which is the lifeline for the Norwegian fishing villages that cling to the north coast. The Hurtigruten may be the key to getting my Expedition turned back toward Helsinki, though I am unsure if the westbound Hurtigruten stops in Vadsø. I hope it does because it offers me a quick escape from the Arctic before harsher weather arrives. And I don't know if I can bike much more.

When we adjourn, the sun has set and cold permeates the valley. The mosquitoes have quit their attack. Tomorrow, we promise ourselves, will be a good day.

〰〰 〰〰 〰〰

From a meteorological perspective, the morning is not what I would call good. The mist has returned, leaving both my tent and bike moist. At least the mosquitoes remain grounded. I allow myself to sleep late—part of my plan to appease the United Body Parts of Bob, which are close to revolt.

When I finally emerge, I am surprised to see that Sebastian and Katherine are still here, busily packing their tent. I thought they would have gotten an early start. Orescu's tent is quiet, the clothes, wet again, still on the line. After coffee and a few cinnamon rolls I have managed to hoard for this final day of riding in Finland, I pack.

Sebastian and Katherine are the first to leave as I dawdle, packing slowly, hoping that Orescu arises so I can say good-bye, get his e-mail address and perhaps even the correct spelling of his name. By ten, my wagon is hitched and the Expedition is ready to roll. Orescu's tent remains quiet. I tiptoe over to it and call his name quietly, but he doesn't stir. For an anxious second, I wonder if perhaps he is dead, but then I hear snoring. I don't feel like disturbing him; he probably has not slept well for weeks. I say a quiet good-bye and slip out of the campground, which is quickly swallowed by the morning mist.

As my guidebook has said, there is not much to Utsjoki—just a store and a gas station before the road comes to a gleaming white ultra-modern suspension bridge crossing the Teno River into Norway. Highway E-6/E-75 on the Norwegian side follows the north shore, while National Bike Route 4 (Highway 970) stubbornly sticks to the Finnish side. I pass a chamber of commerce-like sign extolling the virtues of the Utsjoki District, chief among them "ample living space," which someone with some spare time on his hands calculated at one person for every 8,600 acres. In keeping with full disclosure, the sign concedes it is a bit more crowded for reindeer. One wonders how they manage to keep from bumping into each other at four per every 2½ acres.

The proportion of humans to acreage seems about right. Since rolling into Utsjoki last night, other than my fellow travelers, I have seen exactly one adult—the woman who took my money at the campsite. Is everyone else searching for those four reindeer?

Although travelers and traders have come this way since the Stone Age, the paved road on the Finnish side was not completed until 1983. Prior to that, residents in the winter drove vehicles and sleds on the frozen Teno.

After I pedal out of Utsjoki, the pavement narrows as it winds above the Teno, a broad river that cuts through a shallow canyon bordered by green-brown hills on its way to the Arctic Ocean. Prized for its salmon, the Teno is the last remaining sizable river in Europe where these fish still run wild. Like the great salmon rivers in the Pacific Northwest, Scandinavian rivers once teemed with the fish. Encroaching civilization, dams, pollution, and war ended the runs everywhere but here.

From the road I see fishermen in waders, while others in long-keeled wooden boats troll for the prized salmon, which after migrating as far as Greenland return to the Teno to spawn. Some weigh as much as forty-five pounds. Farther downstream, I see the *kotas* of Sami fishermen pitched on the gravel banks. Signs at roadside turnouts advise that all fishing equipment is required to take a "sauna." I puzzle over these signs, thinking that the Finns may have gone too far in their enthusiasm for these steam baths. Then I realize they mean that fishing gear must be sterilized before it can be used in this river. Biologists fear that parasites introduced from other areas will finish off the last of Europe's wild salmon. As an insurance policy, fertilized salmon eggs have been cryogenically frozen as further protection against extinction.

By noon, the mist has melted and the sun shines. The narrow road twists two hundred feet above the Teno. The pines have disappeared, replaced by thickets of birch and willow. The Expedition has finally reached the northern limit of where trees can survive.

Shortly after a leisurely lunch perched high above the river's bank, I come to a lonely monument that declares I have reached not only the northernmost point of Finland, but that of the European Union.* This seems a bit premature because the map indicates that the northernmost point of Finland is actually slightly east of Nuorgam. However, the Expedition is not shy about celebrating "great moments." In fact, it's about time I indulge myself in self-congratulation. It's good for morale.

I take out a tiny tripod and snap a few photos of myself triumphantly holding my helmet above my head in front of the sign declaring my

---

* Norway is not a member of the European Union.

position at 70°5' north latitude, roughly parallel with the great Greenland ice sheet.

As I pack my camera, I notice the small square National Bike Route sign innocuously pointing down a narrow dirt road that runs below the paved road and closer to the river. A sign nearby tells me that this is the original postal road used by the king of Sweden's couriers. The sign provides no details about why the king felt compelled to have a road cut through what was an even more desolate area in the eighteenth century, given that few people lived here. The Sami weren't big letter-writers back then either.

Of course, the king's postal road beckons me. Like the sirens of the sea, it taunts me with one last temptation for dirt-road adventure. *How bad can it be?* I am almost to Nuorgam. It is early afternoon. The sun is out. Wild Atlantic salmon are not yet extinct. What the hell!

I consult the map with the aid of my magnifying glass. I conclude that this old section runs no longer than a mile before it reconnects with the paved road. Then again, I've been led astray before. No matter. I wheel the bike to the sign and plunge down the narrow lane, hoping that a camper van doesn't come barreling down the blind bend that is straight ahead. Thirty minutes into the journey, as I struggle to push the bike up a fifteen-percent grade, I realize that the merry mapmakers have done me in again.

As I slip and slide in the mud slope, I have the sensation that I am being watched. I look up and see at the crest two big reindeer bulls, standing like sentinels in the middle of the road. But these reindeer are special because they each sport not one, but two sets of antlers. One set, perhaps last year's overgrown pair, juts like elephant tusks three feet into the air before branching into a more familiar antler pattern. Behind these is a fresh pair of regular-sized antlers. I stare up at the bulls and their double-barreled racks and swear they are both grinning as they stand smugly with their big goofy feet on the high ground.

I stop dead in my tracks and stare back, much in the way a man would react if he were suddenly to come upon a very beautiful woman. I am in awe. They are, after all, magnificent—the antlers, that is. But then I quickly remember that I am pushing nearly one hundred pounds of bike and wagon up a steep, slippery incline at the top of Finland, where on average the nearest living person can be found somewhere among the surrounding eighty-six hundred acres.

"Oh, you think this is funny, do you?" I yell up to them. "Why don't you get down here and lend me an antler? I could use a push!"

The lead reindeer—let's call him Donner—nods, then strolls into the forest, nipping away at sprigs of moss. They have concluded that I am neither car nor wolf, and therefore of no concern to them. By the time I reach the top, my friends have disappeared as quietly as they appeared, though I am not sure how they manage to steer their monster racks through the thicket without getting hung up.

For an hour I struggle up grades, then fly down slopes attaining speeds that are downright scary, before mercifully merging back onto the main road. I swear to never fall for the National Bike Route trick again.

Shortly thereafter I reach Nuorgam, a village of two hundred, almost all of whom are Sami. I pass a grocery and a hardware store, and then much to my confusion, I see a large sign announcing that I have reached the northernmost point in Finland—again. Not wanting to take a chance on missing the real northernmost point, I dismount, pull out the tripod, and wearily raise my helmet in yet another pose for posterity.

Then the Expedition does the next logical thing. It finds the northernmost campground in Finland, rents the northernmost cabin, then goes to the northernmost store and buys, for the sake of the moment, an extra large bottle of the northernmost beer. Soon thereafter, I cook and eat the northernmost meal, then I crawl into my bunk and sleep like someone who has biked the length and width of Finland for the past forty-one days, while outside yet another rainstorm of Biblical proportions begins to rage.

The Expedition reaches Nuorgam, Finland's most northern settlement.

33

The Barents Sea

IN THE MORNING, I feel the tingle of excitement that greets a special day. On this, the forty-second day since leaving Helsinki, only 57 miles remain between me and the Norwegian town of Vadsø. If my calculations are correct, by early afternoon I will cross the hills separating the Teno River Valley from Varanger Fjord, then catch my first glimpse of the Barents Sea.

Naturally, I am anxious to get started. I roust the bike from the cabin's porch and quickly pack. But in my haste to get the Expedition under way, I forget one of the fundamental lessons the universe has so patiently tried to teach me over the past two months: pay attention to detail.

As I gather my stuff from the cabin, I have again carelessly parked the bike at an awkward angle. When I strap on the sleeping bag, the bike starts to keel over. It's as if I am witnessing an exact replay of the "morning of the broken mirror." I reach out to grab the back of the rack, but miss and instead clumsily grab the flagpole. The pole snaps in half. The Riding with Reindeer banner crumples to the ground.

I stare at it, as if a sacred relic has been desecrated. I am not a particularly superstitious person—at least I wasn't until this trip—but I am thinking superstitious thoughts as I look at the wrinkled symbol of the Expedition lying in the Lapland moss. Is this an omen?

The dowel is broken beyond repair. Neither broken piece is long enough to work as a makeshift pole. I pick up the banner. I will not leave until it is repaired. My momentary carelessness has come back to haunt me.

Think, I tell myself. *What else have I learned on this trip?* I ponder the broken pole. What we need here is a stick. *Think Bob, think.* I am in Finland, one of the most forested countries in the world, even though I am currently in probably the least forested part of it. But I don't need an entire tree; a good-sized branch from one of those scrubby birches will do. I walk behind the cabin. Within seconds I find a birch stalk neatly broken into a four-foot length. Will this do? I slip the banner's sleeve over the sapling. It fits snugly.

Now I need something to secure it to the bike rack. *Aha!* I've got just the thing—another gift from the road, like the magic clothespins. During yesterday's lunch break, as I had lolled by the roadside admiring the broad Teno and watching the fishermen, I glanced at the ground and saw a length of nylon rope. I didn't know why at the time, but I picked it up and stashed it in the wagon. *It might come in useful later*, I had thought.

The rope is just the right length and thickness to bind the new flag-pole to the back rack. The banner flies again. I am ready to roll.

This little lesson, which dunked me into despair but then inspired the improvised repair, has shot my confidence to the moon. I now believe that I can do anything. If rubber trees grow by the roadside, I can mold my own tires. If the roadside rocks contain iron ore, I can forge my own bicycle parts. I have become a character in my own rendition of the *Kalevala*. But instead of the *sampo*, the magic mill forged by Ilmarinen, I create or magically find accessories for my bicycle, allowing me to travel ever onward through the mystical Northland. Louhi, the Sorceress of the North, only has a day left to marshal her forces against me. But I think she is too late. I have strength. I have confidence. And best of all, I have a full repertoire of songs to get me through the day.

In ten minutes, I reach the border separating Finland from Norway. I had expected at least a "Welcome to Norway" sign, but instead I am greeted by "National Border"—hardly a greeting at all, as if the border officials assumed that the travelers in these remote regions should bear the responsibility of knowing which country they are entering or exit-ing. As a consolation, another sign a bit farther along announces that I have entered Finnmark, Norway's northernmost province. Other than this concession, there is no customs house, no gate, no officials—nothing except a couple of bushes, a tall pole with a video camera mounted on top, and the faint barking of a dog. I wonder if some sleep-deprived official in faraway Oslo is watching the border activity, or rather lack thereof, on a monitor. I say good-bye to Finland and cycle into my new country, the land of Ibsen, fish, and fjords.

A few hundred yards down the road, I reach the tiny village of Polmak. Not much is happening here this misty morning, and probably not much has happened here for a very long time. I pedal past a rundown store that appears as if it hasn't been open for years. A few houses are scattered about, but no one stirs. Cows graze lazily in fields of stubble.

I was hoping to find a bank here because Norway, unlike Finland, is not a member of the European Monetary Union and thus does not use the euro as its currency. But these do not look like the kind of cows that can change euros for kroner.

Since leaving Utsjoki, I have noticed embedded in the asphalt a lot of small squashed rodents covered in brown-yellow fur with black stripes. These are lemmings, I am told, and during certain years when their population explodes they do what lemmings are famous for: literally heading for the hills in a frenzied mating migration ritual. The lemming's most formidable obstacle is not the highway, however, but rivers and streams, which they mindlessly scamper into and, more often than not, drown.

At the village of Skipagurra, I turn east onto Highway E-76. The road immediately starts up into the hills that separate the Teno River Valley from Varanger Fjord. For the first time in days, I shift to the mountain gear and begin the last grind up.

During the course of the morning's ride, the vegetation has changed rather dramatically. The pines have disappeared and the birches, which grow in thickets, have bright yellow at the tips of their stalks—nature's indicator that fall approaches. With each mile the birches become smaller and fewer. When I reach a windy plateau, the landscape is nothing but sedge and moss. I skirt a lonely lake with a solitary cabin perched on the shore. A chilly breeze blows in from the north. I slowly make my way around the lake, afraid to stop, fearing I will reach the end of the world before I reach the sea. In the distance, I see nothing but barren hills, stretching endlessly north into a white sky.

At the end of the lake, the road descends. The descent is gradual at first, then begins to steepen as the highway loops down among the folds of the brownish-green hills. As my speed increases, I concentrate on the road, head bowed, hands gripping the handlebars tightly to make sure I take the turns safely. The little bike is now shooting down at close to 30 miles per hour. I'm holding on for dear life, the cold air whistling by my ears. The speed, like an illicit drug, is both horrifying and exhilarating, a final release of freedom from all the hours of walking the bike up fells or slowly grinding along while my bottom seared in pain.

On straightaways I glance up, hoping to catch a glimpse of the fjord, and by extension, the Barents Sea. *It should be there; right over there*, I tell myself between snatches of observation. But I see nothing except more barren hills stretching into eternity. I descend farther, gaining speed, hurtling around bends, gravel flinging from my tires.

At last, after a hair-raising curve, I see water. *Is it another lake or the real thing?* I wonder excitedly. I had expected a grand expanse of ocean, not a thin finger that looks more like a river. I pull on the brakes, the bike slows, and I coast to a wide spot in the road. I need to know for sure. This is too important to guess. I yank out the binoculars, map, and compass. I take a bearing.

The line of travel shows that I am heading directly to a tiny finger of Varanger Fjord. It's official. I can see the Barents Sea and, by extension, the Arctic Ocean. I pump my fists in the air and shout "We did it!" but my words drift away in the breeze. A car whizzes past.

The moment I have been waiting for, the supreme moment of triumph has arrived. I should be doing more to celebrate, perhaps popping the cork from a bottle of champagne or hugging someone. Other than my steady but solidly inanimate Expedition companions, Friday and Wagon, there is no one to share the achievement with. On this headland at the top of the world, where witches were once hunted and polar bears roamed in cooler times, I learn the last great lesson of the solo epic. Until this moment, I have enjoyed complete flexibility, faced uncertainty, risen to the challenge of improvisation, and learned the importance of attention to details. I expected all of this, more or less, but now I am confounded with something I cannot solve by searching the ground or with rational thinking. After my brief euphoria, I am unable to halt a more powerful feeling—a matter of the heart instead of the head—from ruining the celebration. At the penultimate moment of triumph when trumpets should be blaring and banners fluttering, I stare at the distant sea and feel an almost unbearable loneliness. Have I come all the way to this little roadside turnout in Finnmark to realize just how social a creature I really am? What good is a triumph if you cannot share the moment?

Perhaps it is just me. Maybe real epic-seekers don't feel lonely or sad. But I am me, and no one else, and on that barren headland where the wind and endless sky have scraped away pretense and excuses, I finally allow the ache to breach my last wall of defense. I allow it to hurt, but then it fades as my anti-party-pooper survival defenses kick in—though I know a residual scar is imprinted in this indelible moment.

I coast for miles, sliding down the back of the last hills to Varangerbotn, a tiny village at the end of the fjord. I stop at a gas station. There is one salvation left to me. I can at least celebrate with a donut.

But when I enter the well-stocked gas station store, I remember that I have not a krone to my name. Thus, my first historic words upon reaching the Barents Sea are not pearls of wisdom or a philosophical phrase that will have scholars pondering its meaning long after I'm dead, but instead merely, "Where is the nearest cash machine?" The follow-up is equally less profound, though serves as a commentary on the commercial times in which we dwell: "Do you take Visa?"

Fortunately, the answer to both questions, provided by a bored teenage girl manning the counter, relieves me of my immediate anxieties. There is an ATM in Vadsø, and everyone in Norway takes Visa. Lingering

by the counter with my muffin (they are out of donuts) and coffee, waiting for the credit card machine to spit out verification that I still exist, I
am bursting to tell someone.

"I just rode my bike all the way from Helsinki to here," I declare.

The girl looks at me dully. There is an awkward silence.

"You rode a bicycle from Helsinki to come to this petrol station in
Varangerbotn?"

"No, not that," I say, realizing too late how ridiculous the literal
meaning of my statement must sound. "I'm going to Vadsø, but the point
is that I made it all the way from the Gulf of Finland to the Barents Sea
on that little bicycle over there." I point to Friday.

The girl does not appear to be impressed by this accomplishment. I
make a mental note not to ask her to come along on my next epic. I need
a little bit more enthusiasm here.

"It is such a long way," she sighs, handing me my receipt.

The road to Vadsø hugs the coast, wrapping around cliffs and skirting untrammeled beaches. East of Varangerbotn, I find another pullout,
park the bike, and clamber over rocks to the sea. Because of the mystique
it has held on me for so long, I half expect to see icebergs and polar bear
tracks. But it looks like any other seashore. When I dip my hands into the
water, it feels no colder than the Pacific Ocean.

Named after the Dutch cartographer and Arctic Ocean explorer
Willem Barents, the southern part of the sea, which includes the Russian
and Norwegian coasts, is ice-free throughout the year due to warm currents that push up from the North Atlantic. This was a theory in Barents's
day, and his voyages were intended to prove it. Barents was the first
European to observe a polar bear; in fact, he and his crew got a real good
look during his third voyage when a bear climbed onto his ship, causing
mayhem before it was shot.

The sea is calm. The water laps gently against seaweed-covered rocks
exposed by the low tide. Gulls wheel and squawk overhead. Guillemots
swim offshore. I am lucky there is little discernible wind. The collision of
warm air from the south and cold air from the North Pole often causes

ferocious gales in the Barents Sea. The second-to-last thing I need is a 75-mile-per-hour headwind.

Farther up the fjord, I again park the bike and climb down rocks to find a quiet spot for lunch on the sand, wedged between driftwood, torn fishing nets, and boulders. As I munch away on my usual repast, I notice that I am lounging next to a collection of bleached bones scattered among the rocks. These are not the bones of a small animal or a fish. I pick out a backbone and ribs, but the rest of the bones are helter-skelter. At first, I think they are from a whale. After a closer inspection, I rule out a sea creature. It looks like the remains of a cow. How did it manage to get down here by the sea?

The bones, combined with the squawking of scores of gulls, give the scene a spooky, Hitchcockian feeling. I eat quickly and resume my ride. The sky has turned gray, but the wind remains gentle. The road hugs the coast. Scores of waterfalls tumble from the barren highlands. In the distance, framed against the sea and mountains and resting forlornly on a narrow spit, is a simple white church. A sign directs me to an archaeological site where evidence of Stone Age dwellings have been discovered. I hike down the stony path, but after inspecting a few rocky remains, I decide the Stone Age can wait. I fear another storm is brewing. I am anxious to finish the day.

Near the shore by the village of Jakobselv, I see giant fish-drying racks resembling the unfinished frame of a long, A-frame house. The nearby houses themselves are painted in solid primary colors, brightening an otherwise dull landscape. I consider camping in Jakobselv, but the place is Ibsen bleak. I press on anxiously for Vadsø.

By midafternoon, I am only a mile from the city. From a curve in the road, I can see the harbor and spires of a church rising grandly in the distance. *I'm almost there—just a few more minutes in the saddle.*

I am beginning my second mental celebration of the day when I hear a sound that terrifies all bicycle riders: the shrill screech of tires on asphalt. In the instant it takes me to process the sound, divine its direction, and begin bracing for impact, I realize that the skid is behind me and the sound is receding. The screech is followed by the terrified yelp of a dog. I turn and see blue smoke rising from the tires of a white sedan halted in the road. A dog darts away toward a farmhouse, apparently unhurt but as scared to the bone as I am.

I have biked nearly two thousand miles on country roads and highways that have virtually no shoulder and have not had a single close call with a motor vehicle. The drivers, particularly in Finland, are uniformly courteous, giving me a wide birth even when it was unnecessary. Not once have I heard an angry horn blast. Even the drivers of logging and other trucks would patiently lollygag behind me, waiting until it was sufficiently safe to pass. Prior to the trip, I had worried about the combination of long isolated stretches of highway and the Finnish reputation for drinking. But the driving I witnessed—and I witnessed a lot—was done expertly, with diligence and care. The reindeer of Finland and Norway—as well as the cyclists—are lucky.

The screech of the tires, however, is one last reminder not to take anything for granted. I glance up at the roily sky and smile to Louhi about this final reminder that I should not celebrate prematurely. I hunker down for the last mile.

I should not be surprised that things are not as one would imagine in Vadsø. Because Vadsø is located more than 200 miles north of the Arctic Circle, I expected to see a town full of taciturn, blonde Lutheran fishermen and women hardened by the long Arctic nights. But as I merge onto a bike path at the edge of town, I pass a park bench where two darker men, who look like me, wave hello as I pass. *Have I found the long-lost homeland for Mexican-Jews?* Farther on, I pass a group of black teenagers playing soccer.

Vadsø, I soon discover, has become home to refugees from Kosovo and West Africa. One enterprising Liberian exile has organized his countrymen to form Vadsø's very own gospel choir. I had missed by a week a rousing performance they had given to appreciative townspeople during Polar Jazz, the world's northernmost jazz festival. The absorption of refugees is not without precedent. About half of Vadsø's fifty-two hundred inhabitants are descendants of Finnish immigrants who came here in the nineteenth century to escape famine.

For its size and isolation, Vadsø is surprisingly robust. I bike through a bustling business district and past a church with twin towers overlooking the town square and the harbor beyond. After withdrawing 3,000 kroner (about $525) from a cash machine, I confront my most immediate problem. Where to stay? There is no campground in Vadsø. There are hotels, but the cost would deal a severe blow to the Expedition budget, which still needs to fund the retreat south.

Earlier in the day at a rest stop, taped to an outhouse, I spotted an advertisement for a furnished apartment near the city center for $65, a reasonable rate by Norwegian standards. (Norway, warned Sebastian last night, is more expensive than Finland.) I am not normally prone to make queries gleaned from outhouses, but given that this is an epic and I am in Norway, I make an exception.

I call. No answer. I try another apartment recommended by Lonely Planet, and connect. The woman on the other end speaks only a few words of English, but I manage to convey that I need a place to spend the night. Within thirty minutes, I rent a fully furnished apartment—a cozy one at that, with a bed, small kitchen, and overstuffed couch—in a residential area west of the town center. I become Vadsø's newest immigrant, if only temporarily.

I unload my gear, then take a quick ride to the town market, returning with ingredients for dinner and a celebratory beer of mysterious origin. I flip off my shoes, turn on the television to my favorite show (the weather news in both Norwegian and Swedish), and pop the cap off my beer.

I have done it. I am finished heading north. The happy moment is brief but without the angst suffered earlier in the day. After all, I still need to return. Outside, Louhi hurls another tempest at me. Rain pelts the roof. Wind, as if trying to get at me one last time, rattles the window. Lightning flashes. But the Sorceress of the North is too late. I have won. I curl up on the bed and wrap myself up in thick wool blankets, snug as if I'm in my mother's womb. I hum "Somewhere Over the Rainbow" and fall asleep.

The Hurtigruten

TECHNICALLY, I AM NOT AT THE END OF THE ROAD. Highway E-75, which led me to Vadsø, continues another 50 miles northeast to Vardø, a forlorn fishing outpost at the tip of the Varanger Peninsula. But do I really want to go there?

Besides being Norway's easternmost town, Vardø had gained notoriety as far back as 1691, when local church authorities, not to be outdone by witch hunts in Vadsø, embarked on their own witch-burning crusade by torching ninety local women accused of satanic deeds.

If that wasn't reason enough to avoid Vardø, there are safety reasons for not performing an epic encore. Vardø is on an island, which for me is reachable only via the two-mile-long Arctic Ocean Tunnel. The prospect of riding underwater while towing a wagon seems to be pushing my luck. Then there is the idea of overreaching—a lesson that I have repeatedly ignored and suffered from as a result. I had mentally set Vadsø as the end of my journey because I can connect with the Hurtigruten, the coast ferry, which conveniently leaves here in the morning. Still, I can't help but want to journey down that last segment of road just to say I did it.

In the end, the tie-breaker is the weather. I dodged a storm last night. Another is forecast for today. I know Louhi is lurking, waiting for me to make one last error in judgment. I'm not going to let it happen.

I declare Vadsø the official Expedition turnaround point. The United Body Parts of Bob, Friday, and Wagon are pleased. The madman has come to his senses. It is time to go back.

In the early morning, the deserted streets of Vadsø are shiny black with wetness, but no drops fall from the sky. I cross a bridge to an island. In the distance, I see a large ship approaching the harbor. I pedal to the quay next to a giant warehouse, but except for a forklift driver, not another soul is around. Searching the warehouse and neighboring buildings, I look for a ticket office. Finding none, I return to the bike and watch the MS *Vesterlåden* nestle into the quay. Ropes are secured around divots by a few dockhands who have suddenly materialized.

This is no ordinary ferry, at least not the big flat-bottomed, car-carrying kind I am used to riding in the waters of Puget Sound. It is more like a combination ocean liner and freighter.

The MS Vesterlåden *arrives in Vadsø.*

I stand before the great vessel like an earthling welcoming an alien spaceship. On the deck I see the captain, or at least someone who looks like a captain, judging from his uniform and golden epaulets. He strikes a captain-like pose, hands clasped behind his back. As if by magic, two panels on the side of the ship slide open. From each panel emerges a giant mechanical arm, which extends to the ground like the segmented leg of an enormous insect. The arm nearest me unfolds into a covered gang-plank. The arm near the hold opens a ramp to the freight compartment in the hull. The forklift darts from the warehouse to the ship, loading crates of fish and other supplies.

Other than this activity, the dock remains devoid of other humans. I stand expectantly before the gangplank, but no one appears. Finally, a few passengers straggle off and wander to the warehouse, where a souvenir shop has opened for business. Minutes tick away as I ponder the mystery of how to buy passage. I had expected someone with a portable ticket machine to set up shop in front of the ship, but that clearly is not going to happen. The passengers straggle back from the souvenir store. The forklift driver finishes loading. The captain looks at his watch.

I am beginning to contemplate stowing away, when an old pickup truck lurches up beside me. The driver, who looks like the Old Man from the Sea, clambers out and makes a beeline for the gangplank. He looks like he knows what he is doing. I abandon the bike and follow.

Just inside the ship, the captain and a fellow officer are chatting.

"Where do I buy a ticket?" I call out.

"Right over there," he says, pointing to an on-ship reception area with a marble countertop that could have passed for the lobby of a four-star hotel. *Of course*, I think to myself, *why make things complicated?* Like most public transportation in Scandinavia and Europe, tickets are purchased on board. Why would the ship be any different?

When I explain that I want to head west to Hammerfest, the woman at the ticket counter tells me that only eastbound ships stop in Vadsø. To go west, I would need to board this boat, which ends its journey two hours later in Kirkenes, then board the westbound vessel for Hammerfest. It is circuitous route, but consistent with the Expedition theme of zigzagging in an upward spiral. Now I will zigzag down. *Funny. I will end up in Kirkenes anyway, as originally planned; if not by land, then by sea.*

Within minutes, I am issued a plastic ticket that hangs from a lanyard around my neck. I ask about the bike and am instructed to drive it into the cargo hold. I run down the gangplank as the crew prepares to cast off, jump on the bike, and ride into the hold, parking next to what appears to be at least one thousand tons of mackerel. I imagine I will be popular with cats after I reach Kirkenes.

Despite a biting wind, I spend most of the two hours en route on the deck watching a bleak landscape that would have provided another perfect setting for an Ibsen play. The *Vesterlåden* makes a beeline across Varanger Fjord, then enters a narrow strait that leads to Kirkenes. Stark granite headlands are covered with a veneer of moss, grass, and heather. Water cascades in a multitude of rivulets from unseen heights as the mountain tops are obscured by clouds. Tiny log cabins hidden inside little bays come into view, leading me to wonder who in their right mind would live in this treeless land of gray stones. A decrepit Russian fishing ship passes; its hull is red-brown with rust, and it belches thick smoke from its stack.

During World War II, convoys of American and British ships plied these waters in a desperate attempt to resupply Stalin's beleaguered forces. By 1942, German armies had reached the outskirts of Leningrad and had nearly surrounded Stalingrad. The only supply line open to the Russians was the railroad linking the ice-free port of Murmansk (about 240 miles by road east of Kirkenes) to the rest of the Soviet Union. In June of 1942, the Allies' bleakest month, twenty-three of thirty-six Allied ships were sunk in these waters by German submarines. From that time on, Allied sailors used the term "death convoy" for Barents Sea duty. Despite high casualties, the Allies managed to get five thousand tanks and seven hundred airplanes to the Soviet Union. The ships returned with Siberian timber.

On land, General Eduard Dietl, who was in command of the German Mountain Corps, was appalled by the primitive conditions he saw in the Varanger Fjord area and the rest of Finnmark. He viewed the area as totally "unsuited for military operations."[36] Dietl must have thought Hitler was out of his mind for ordering a land attack to cut the Russian railroad line from Murmansk. But he had no choice. To achieve this seemingly impossible objective, Dietl's army would have to cross the roadless, barren, boulder-strewn headlands crisscrossed by mighty rivers in subzero winter temperatures, and then survive plagues of mosquitoes in the summer. The Germans never made it. For three years, they were bogged down in a bloody stalemate against stubborn Russian forces.

At midmorning, the *Vesterlåden* steams into Kirkenes Harbor. The city looks much larger than its population of thirty-three hundred suggests. I, along with the mackerel and a few cars, wait in the hold for the doors to swing open. When it's my turn, I emerge into cool dampness. I wind my way along the wharves, which are full of rusting fishing boats, and then enter the city center, which is crowded with shops, banks, restaurants, and office buildings. The first thing I notice is that the street signs are in both Russian and Norwegian. The border is only six miles to the east. Judging from tourist posters, trips to the Russian Arctic and to Murmansk are popular.

I wander around town, stalling for time, for I have no clue what to do. I've already missed the day's westbound boat. The next one doesn't leave until tomorrow. Should I camp or splurge on a hotel? As rain pelts down, I dart into the tourist information office and ask about my options. The friendly clerk convinces me to take a tour of the network of underground bomb shelters that honeycomb the city. I leave the bike at the office and hike up the street to the entrance of the Andersgrotto.

The discovery of iron ore in the nearby hills gave Kirkenes a strategic importance that inevitably led to the city's destruction during World War II. The Germans, following their swift invasion of Norway, quickly occupied the city to secure the mines. Eventually, one hundred thousand German troops were stationed here, rotating in and out of the Arctic battlefront to the east. This area was the site of several prison camps for Russian soldiers, women with venereal disease, and Norwegians—mostly teachers—who did not display proper enthusiasm for the German occupation. Russian bombers pulverized the town three hundred twenty times, giving it the distinction of being World War II's most-bombed city.[37] To add insult to injury, the retreating German army razed what was left of Kirkenes in 1944 before it was captured by the Russians. But the citizens of Kirkenes were fortunate in two regards: they were not forced to evacuate along with the retreating German army, as were most other residents of Finnmark. And Kirkenes was returned to Norway after the war.

I can see the hulking remains of the steel mill on the west hills that dominate the town. The mill closed in 1996, but rumors persist that it will spring to life once again.

"When the newspaper has nothing else to write about, they publish a story about how the steel mill is coming back into operation," quips the Finnish guide, who will take us into the bomb shelter. I have been joined by two German tourists.

The guide leads us out of the rain into the bowels of Kirkenes, where a virtual underground city existed during the war. The shelters were effective. Only seven civilians were killed by the relentless air raids. I wonder what the young German couple is thinking, as we sit through a short film that shows goose-stepping Nazi soldiers symbolically ready to overrun Europe. These scenes are interspersed with shots of tranquility in Kirkenes and the surrounding land—the innocents unaware of the evil that is about to engulf them.

When we emerge back into the light of day, I linger and ask the Finnish guide how she came to have this job in Norway.

"I live in Inari, but I come here a couple of days a week to lead these tours," she explains. "It is good to live in Finland and work in Norway because wages are higher here, but the cost of living in Finland is much less."

I tell her I heard that Norway is expensive.

"It is very, very expensive to live here," she says. "If you are a Norwegian, you can afford it because they have such good pensions. With all the oil and gas, they are a very rich country."

This fact is reinforced when I glance at restaurant and café menus. My lunch food supply is exhausted, so today I will eat out and restock later. I settle on a fast-food restaurant, where a chicken sandwich and a soft drink set me back $25. I never thought Finland would seem cheap, but after carefully sucking up every morsel on my tray, I calculate my krone burn rate. I conclude that to avoid bankruptcy, the Expedition cannot linger in Norway. After lunch, I head to the campground.

I bike over a hill, past the rusting hulks of old railroad cars that once carried iron ore to the mill. On the outskirts of Kirkenes, I find a bike trail that winds pleasantly around a lake to the village of Hesseng. I turn right on Highway E-6, the same road that would have taken me from Finland to Kirkenes had I stuck to my original plan. After grinding up a hill, I see the flags marking the location of the campground. On the door to the reception office, I am not completely surprised to find a note telling me that it is closed until five and to please call the number below.

Aboard the MS Nordkapp

I AM LEANING AGAINST THE RAIL, watching the sun glint off scores of waterfalls cascading down the slate-gray mountains that form the Russian coast. They shine like beads of molten silver. The warmth has drawn passengers from the innards of the MS *Nordkapp*. The deck chairs are full. *What are the odds of actually basking in the sun while shipping across the Barents Sea?* But nothing lasts for long here. Soon, it is cold and cloudy again.

That morning I had boarded the *Nordkapp*, another ship in the Hurtigruten line. Since the trip to Hammerfest is an overnight one, I decided to splurge on a cabin. Given that I dropped $25 on a chicken sandwich yesterday, I thought the $380 for the cabin and passage, excluding food, was a relative bargain. The United Body Parts of Bob finally got their reward: twenty-four hours of eating, drinking beer in the piano bar, or scanning the horizon from one of the big, executive-style lounge chairs on the observation deck. As for the cabin, it includes two portholes, a bathroom with a shower, a writing desk, and a television that picks up the British Broadcasting Corporation.

The *Nordkapp's* route would take me from Kirkenes, around the tip of Finnmark, and deposit me the next morning in Hammerfest, where my little bit of shipboard luxury would end, and I would resume my hermit-like existence in the tent and cabins until I reached the first railroad line heading south. That would take at least a week, starting on a narrow road that snaked out of Hammerfest and over monster mountains the size of which I had not seen in Finland. Adding further to the impending return drama was, of course, the deterioration of the weather. Every day it got noticeably colder. The momentary blast of sun on the deck is an aberration. But I don't really want to think too far in advance and ruin the next twenty-four hours aboard the ship.

vvv   vvv   vvv

We stop at Vardø, and I am instantly glad I did not ride the extra 50 miles to this town. Wood-framed houses, brightly painted in solid primary colors, cling to this island where nothing larger than a blade of grass grows. Vardø sets a new standard for picturesque grimness seen on this trip, and there has been a lot of that lately in the Far North. As we enter the harbor, three men clad in eighteenth-century pantaloons and waistcoats, resembling Revolutionary War characters, march down to the quay to greet the ship. One beats a drum, the second plays a fife, and the third holds a standard with the town's coat of arms. As the ship docks, the trio plays on until the first people wander off. Followed by a growing line of passengers trickling off the ship, the drum and fife corps leads the procession down the main street to the town's fort and museum. The pied piper, however, cannot lure me from the comforts of the ship.

By evening, we round the Nordkinn Peninsula. The sky is again crystal clear. Late evening sun highlights the cliffs and rugged green mountains that line the shore. Flecks of last winter's snow cling to the higher reaches. Just as I am ready to conclude that no one has ever trodden these lands, I spot piles of rocks on top of the highest peaks. They appear to be either cairns or the remains of watchtowers. I can't be sure, but they appear to be man-made. I notice that the cairns are on the highest peaks, several miles apart. I wonder if they are the ruins of the fabled watchtowers that Northlanders erected as lookouts for approaching Viking ships.

At sunset, the *Nordkapp* steams into Bätsfjord Harbor. A perfect double rainbow frames the red-brown sedimentary cliffs opposite the town. Arctic terns swoop among the harbor pilings, while gulls cry out to the approaching night. Bätsfjord itself, however, is not exactly jumping with activity on this Sunday. From my omnipresent vantage point on the observation deck, I see a few lights on inside the houses and even catch a glimpse of one family watching television. But the only movements in town are from the few intrepid souls from the *Nordkapp* who have ventured ashore to stretch their legs. Beyond the town, a road serpentines into the hills, and a pair of headlights flickers as a solitary car heads out of town and is swallowed by the night.

After leaving Bätsfjord, the *Nordkapp* resumes its northwest voyage as the skies turn purple and the barren mountains black. We cross 71 degrees latitude, roughly equal with the top of Alaska. But unlike those ice-bound places, here the sea ice is still 300 miles north of us and receding more each year.

I had hoped to catch a glimpse of the North Cape, the alleged northernmost point of Europe, but the *Nordkapp* cuts through a strait south of this landmark in the early morning darkness. This shortcut not only saves the ship time, but also shields it from the fickle seas that usually batter the cape. It also raises an obvious question. The North Cape is not part of mainland Norway, but rather is part of the island of Magerøya. I do not want to pick a fight with the geographers, but this small detail would seem to disqualify the North Cape as the northernmost point because it is not connected to the mainland. This means that the *actual* northernmost point in Europe is probably Nordkinn, which we will also circumnavigate in the dark.

No one, of course, is buying into my theory. The ship's purser has been announcing over the loudspeaker that passengers wishing to set foot on the North Cape have the option of debarking in Honningsvåg at six in the morning and boarding a bus to the fabled landmark. There is great interest among my fellow passengers, some of whom are enjoying the round-trip excursion from Bergen and taking advantage of all opportunities to explore the land. I, on the other hand, have seen a lot of the land and have no desire to see more at the expense of leaving the luxury of the ship.

The elusive final goal of early travelers to Lapland, the North Cape has devolved into a tourist trap of the first magnitude. The Lonely Planet guidebook does not mince words by referring to it as "Europe's northernmost rip-off—an opinion shared by the regular letters we receive from our readers who've felt exploited." The lonely rock promontory, lashed by waves and wind, sports a five-screen theater, bar, restaurant and, believe it or not, a Thai Museum.* The toll to even approach this mecca of geographical commercial exploitation is $35. I find none of this attractive. Half-asleep, I vaguely hear the last call to board the waiting buses.

I roll over and go back to sleep, content with Giuseppe Acerbi's lyrical description of the landmark: "The North Cape is an enormous rock, which projecting far into the ocean and being exposed to all the fury of the waves and the outrage of tempests, crumbles every year more and more into ruins. Here everything is solitary, everything is sterile, everything sad and despondent. The shadowy forest no longer adorns the brow of the mountain; the singing of the birds, which enlivened the woods of Lapland, is no longer heard in this scene of desolation; the ruggedness of the dark gray rock is not covered by a single shrub; the only music is the hoarse murmuring of the waves, ever and anon renewing their assaults on the huge masses that oppose them."

By midmorning the next day, the *Nordkapp*, mostly empty now except for me and a few other killjoys, has completed its grand arc north and is churning south. The mountains are larger, though no less barren and gray, their peaks shrouded by squalls that march across the horizon, obliterating the view of everything in their path. Perched on an island guarding the entrance to Hammerfest harbor are tall smokestacks spouting yellow flames, as if guarding the lair of an all-powerful Nordic deity. The tanks and labyrinth of steel pipes that comprise the Snoehit liquefaction plant is a reminder of the wealth that Norway is extracting from the earth. The Arctic is thought to hold twenty percent of the world's untapped natural gas.

Hammerfest, which bills itself as the northernmost incorporated city in the world, clings to a narrow shelf of bay bordered by steep, barren

---

* The King of Thailand visited in 1907. Apparently, he was a big hit.

mountains. With the aid of binoculars, I scan my new debarkation point with the same intensity that the American traveler Paul B. Du Chaillu viewed the town in July of 1871—which then had a population of thirty-five hundred—from the deck of a steamship that had sailed from Alta, Norway.

"There are few towns in the world, if any, built upon a spot more barren, or surrounded by such a dreary, desolate landscape; not a tree to be seen, but only bleak, dark rocks. No road leads out of the place, for there are no farms to be reached, and no wood to be brought from the surrounding country; the streets are narrow, the principal one following the bend in the bay," wrote Du Chaillu.

That description pretty much applies today, though Hammerfest now has almost twice as many residents. Since Du Chaillu's time, a road has been built, linking the town to the rest of Norway. I see the line of the one narrow route, rising steeply along the escarpment. It clings to the mountainside before twisting out of sight. This, according to my map, is Highway 94—the only way south. It does not inspire confidence.

As I walk the bike out of the ship's cargo hold, I am nearly knocked over by a vicious gust. I glance at the harbor and see another squall advancing. I run up the street, pushing the bike, and park it next to the library. I dart inside just before the rain hits. I spend the next few hours dodging these ministorms. I visit the church and town museum and eat another $25 chicken sandwich. When the sun emerges, I ride to the town's only campground, located past a residential area and over a gap in the hills. Located next to Lake Storvannet, the place is deserted, with the usual sign urging any wandering travelers to check back after five. I call the phone number and leave a message. I notice some bungalow-type cabins and decide they are the solution for surviving what promises to be a very cold night.

In the meantime, I have time to kill. I decide it's probably time to read up on the attractions of Hammerfest, so I roll the bike over to a picnic table and take out the Norway guide. I am joined by a herd of five enormous reindeer, sporting antlers with enough capacity to hang-dry all my clothes. They approach en masse, look me over, and sniff the air. They appear to be wondering what strange beast dares to trespass on their campground.

Something is different about these reindeer. Perhaps it's the way they walk or hold their racks. Clearly, these are city reindeer, tougher customers than the Bambi-like goofballs with the bells around their necks that gamboled around in Finnish Lapland. The leader approaches and checks out the bicycle, while his compatriots relax on a patch of grass. I point out the more interesting aspects of the Bike Friday and wagon assembly. He seems unimpressed.

"Hold it right there while I get my camera," I say.

The reindeer takes a nip of moss, then strikes a Hartford insurance-like pose in front of the bike while I snap away.

Reindeer at the Hammerfest campground

"Can you tilt your head a bit to the right, please?" I ask.

When I'm done, the reindeer saunters back to his pals.

I stash my wagon, sleeping bag, and tent next to the camp office and ride back to the bay, bucking ferocious headwinds. Cod is still king in Hammerfest, though fortunately for me the town is no longer infused with the odor of cod-liver oil, which Du Chaillu observed was "by no means pleasant; but, as one of the leading merchants observed, the smoke that brings money is never unpleasant." I get as far as the Fuglenes Peninsula, where I park the bike and climb a small hill commanded by an old cannon pointing into the bay. This is all that remains of the Skansen Fortress, built by the citizens of Hammerfest in 1809 after the British brigs *Snake* and *Fancy* sailed into the harbor and pulverized the town. At the time, Norway was allied with Napoleon. The British attacked because they wanted to stop the French from importing Russian grain through Hammerfest.

Ten years earlier, a little cannon fire would have left a favorable impression on Acerbi, who stopped here on his way to the North Cape. Acerbi notes with disappointment in his journal that the townspeople did not fire a cannon honoring his departure, though he does concede the oversight might have been due to the lack of a cannon.

On the ride back into the town center, I am slammed by another frigid squall that swooshes into the town. It lasts only a few minutes, thankfully, then I continue to the town center, passing a Sami woman dressed in a richly embroidered, native tunic and hat. On the bay, I can see more squalls—dark shadows of mayhem above roily seas, advancing toward the town. I load up on groceries at the market and quickly retreat to the campground.

By evening, I am safely ensconced in one of the cabins. The woman who rented it to me mentioned that the season was about over. The place would shut down in a couple of days.

"Winter comes early here," she says. "You are lucky we are still open."

As I cook dinner, winter tries to bash down the door. A cold wind whistles through cracks in the cabin slats. Hail bounces on the roof. As I boil pasta, keeping warm from the steam, I watch the atmospheric show through the window: more dark squalls, hail, and wind, followed by bright sun. Not more than fifty yards from the cabin, two young men in shorts play tennis, while the reindeer nonchalantly nose for moss in the background.

Unlike the Finnish cabins, which spoiled me with utensils, pots, pans, dish soap, blankets and pillows, their Norwegian counterparts— both here and in Kirkenes—contain the bare minimum: a hot plate, refrigerator, and heater, but nothing else. I'm not complaining—I feel lucky to have any shelter for less than $100 a night here—but given the enormous wealth of Norway, the austerity surprises me. *No matter. This is why I have lugged seventy-five pounds of gear to the top of the world.*

After dinner, I lay bundled in my sleeping bag and swaddled in my thermal underwear. I shine the headlamp on a bus schedule and a map. I circle the town of Alta, about 100 miles south. But I fall asleep before I can decipher the Norwegian on the schedule, my last thoughts focused on escaping the clutches of the early Arctic winter and the sound of swatted tennis balls flying through the frigid twilight.

36

Where Are Your Reindeer?

THE ONE-LANE ROAD SNAKING OUT OF HAMMERFEST provides affirmation that riding a bike to Alta would have been suicidal. I am not sure how the bus driver manages to squeeze past oncoming traffic without hurtling us into the fjord that drops steeply on my side of the bus. Reindeer stick to the mountainside, snacking on moss. We pass through a tunnel that seems a million miles long, then emerge to cross the fjord over a narrow suspension bridge. I note with some satisfaction that there is no room for someone to ride a bike, let along one towing a trailer. The bus, now clinging to the opposite side of the chasm, gradually moves away from the freezing wind and rain of the northernmost city in the world. I am glad to be heading south.

After an hour, we turn away from the fjord and ascend a high mountain valley bisected by a tumbling river fed by gushing tributaries. Sadly, storm clouds obscure the higher peaks but spruce reappear—a sign that I have entered a more hospitable climate. The road climbs over a pass, then drops into a luscious valley carved by the Alta Fjord. As if on cue, the sun emerges, glinting off the city nestled at the end of the fjord, against a backdrop of snow-capped mountains. The fjord itself is as calm as a lake, unlike the seething sea that bashed Hammerfest.

The bus drops me off near the center of Alta. Whereas Hammerfest had reluctantly retained the bleakness ascribed to it by travelers throughout the ages, Alta, with its twelve thousand residents, seems to brim with the confidence of a thriving resort and commercial center. I quickly reassemble the bike, which had made the bus journey tucked in its case. I ride to a pedestrian mall lined with smart shops and restaurants, stopping at the information office where an impeccably dressed young man who speaks flawless English shows me the location of the town's three campgrounds. He also explains where I can catch the bus south to Kautokeino the next day.

Giuseppe Acerbi, after having traveled steadily north for more than a year, was also grateful to reach Alta, which in 1799 consisted of just one house—the home of a Norwegian merchant. It would take the hearty Italian traveler another month to reach the North Cape, but at least he was well supplied. "By way of provisions," he reported, "we had everything that was good, such as white wine, claret, brandy, fresh salmon, roasted fowl, veal, hams, coffee, tea, with the necessary utensils; and, in a word, all that we could possibly have occasion for."

Acerbi's bountiful kit, perhaps explained by his Italian origins, put to shame the pitiful remaining provisions of the Riding with Reindeer Expedition. While I manage to thaw out by riding through the pleasant streets of Alta, I am still shell-shocked over Norwegian food prices. I decide to make do with my customary gorp, cheese, and hard-boiled egg for lunch. I am not looking forward to dinner, which will be a bag of freeze-dried stew that has lain buried at the bottom of the wagon for the past two months. Eating, however, is not my top priority at the moment. There is something I want to see six miles south of Alta.

Near the shore of Alta Fjord, carefully pecked into smooth granite, are some of the world's best-preserved petroglyphs. Some of the five thousand carvings at this UNESCO World Heritage site are thought to date from 4,000 B.C. As I wander the paths, I see elaborate pictures of hunting parties stalking reindeer, bear, and elk. Others show human-like figures in boats catching fish and spearing whales. One carving depicts a solitary man standing on two thin, parallel lines—perhaps the oldest recorded use of skis.

Later, with the sun shining, I turn south on Highway 93 to the village of Bossekop, where several campgrounds are perched along the Alta River. Before turning off the highway, I find the stop for the bus to

Kautokeino. I need to be here early the following morning to continue my retreat south.

ᰀᰀᰀ ᰀᰀᰀ ᰀᰀᰀ

The next day, while I am aboard the Kautokeino-bound minibus, it stops in the middle of a spruce forest for no apparent reason. The bus driver, a middle-aged Sami woman, turns to where I sit, which is directly behind her.

"Are you in a hurry?"

She asks in English, for it's obvious that I am not a native of this region, and the three other men who have crammed their bikes into the small bus are speaking quietly in Norwegian.

I am not in a hurry; in fact, I am glad to have found this comfortable ride south to Kautokeino. The small Sami settlement is the end of the line, as far as bus service is concerned. Earlier in the summer, another bus would have continued into Finland. But as the driver explained, no one goes to Finland this late in the season. This means the Expedition will need to pedal the additional 200 miles from Kautokeino to the train station in Rovaniemi.

But that is a problem for later in the day. This morning, I am happy to be heading south, where each mile seems to bring warmer weather. The sun beams through the forest. Birds flit and twitter. Nearby, the Alta River tumbles through this broad valley that could be easily mistaken for the North Cascades of the Pacific Northwest. Who could possibly be in a hurry? I still have twelve days before my flight from Helsinki departs.

The driver, a stocky woman with close-cropped hair, asks if I'm sure about the pace. I am sure. She thanks me for my flexibility, though I am still puzzled why we are stopped here.

"A Sami woman said she will meet us here in twenty minutes," says the driver. "She will sit next to you. You better hope she doesn't have a reindeer."

Because of the three men and their bicycles, there is only one available seat: next to me. The small baggage compartment is stuffed to the

brim with my bike case (with packed bike) and my duffel. I'm wondering
where they are going to stuff the reindeer. And will it be alive or dead?

Fortunately, the woman arrives on time and does not have a reindeer. Then we are off again, climbing into a narrow canyon. The Alta
River gushes through a series of cataracts. At the top of the canyon, we
emerge onto a broad plain that resembles eastern Montana—a big grassy
expanse dotted with lakes and bordered by distant hills. More herds of
reindeer munch on moss. The cyclists are let off at a small camp area. The
women babble.

"We are talking in Sami," the driver tells me. "She was my neighbor
when I lived in Kautokeino. She has many reindeer. I drive a bus, so I
don't have reindeer."

I ask, "Does she know where her reindeer are?"

"They are at the coast," the woman says, as the driver translates
for me.

I have a vision of reindeer basking in the sand at a luxury hotel at the
coast. Then I remember what Hammerfest was like. The image dissipates.
Perhaps I had seen her herd yesterday when I took the bus to Alta.

I tell the driver I am interested in Sami culture.

"You know if you took the top parts of Sweden, Norway, Finland,
and the northwest of Russia, that would be the Sami nation," continues
the driver. "It would be a very big land."

The Alta River, which we follow, was a recent flashpoint of alienation
and provided the setting for the only acts of violence in modern times
over Sami issues. In 1980, the Norwegian government began building
a hydroelectric dam on the Alta, despite protests from local Sami who
argued that the resulting lake would submerge ancestral hunting and
pasture lands. Construction equipment was sabotaged and a bomb was
set off, leading one Sami activist to flee to Canada to avoid prosecution.

The bus driver and her friend, who chat quietly, seem like anything but
dam bombers. The mention of the vast territory that their people roamed
was the only statement that came vaguely close to having political over-
tures that I heard during my entire stay in both Finnish and Norwegian

Lapland. If I had not dug up this other information about Sami history, I would have concluded that they had lived a carefree, happy existence for the past several hundred years, and now went about their business with no complaints except for the occasional stray reindeer being run over by a tourist. If nothing else, the Sami seemed to be people who did not wear their past on their sleeve, but kept it tucked away out of view—certainly as well hidden as the handful of sacred drums rumored to have survived the witch hunts of the seventeenth and eighteenth centuries.

The driver turns to me and asks if I would like some candy. I nod. She takes out a bag of licorice-tasting stuff and passes it around. She turns to me apologetically and says, "I like to talk to my friend in Sami. It's our language, and since there are not a lot of us, we speak it amongst ourselves when we are alone."

She asks me about my trip and relays the highlights to her friend.

"You are like an old Sami because you like to move every day from one camp to another," she says. "And you're short, too. You just need some reindeer and a Sami wife."

I actually thought that at five feet, seven inches, I was rather tall for a Sami, and if the Sami Nordic Council ever organized a basketball team, I could volunteer to play center. Both Acerbi and Du Chaillu observed the small stature of the Sami during their respective journeys. Du Chaillu took measurements of one family; all except for one man were under five feet tall.[38]

The mention of a Sami wife brought to mind a rather elaborate explanation of the Sami courtship ritual that I had read about at the Arktikum, Rovaniemi's museum. Should I, in the next few days, see a Sami maiden who catches my fancy, I would need to do the following: recruit a bunch of friends who can sing; buy, borrow, or rent a bull reindeer; then ride it around her house three times while my friends sing a distinctively repetitive song called a *yoik*. The object of my affection would have only a short time to consider my advances.

The beauty of this ritual is its quick resolution. There is no dilly-dallying with the Sami; you're either in or you're out. If the maiden doesn't say yes immediately, but hesitates (like she has to think about it), I am out of luck. At best, I can repeat the whole ritual in a couple of months, perhaps recruiting other friends with better singing voices or renting a handsomer reindeer. If the answer remains no, or she can't decide, I should return the bull reindeer to the bull reindeer rental agency and go home. If the maiden says yes, then there is more singing and (I'm not totally clear on this part) more riding of reindeers around houses. There's more. On my wedding day, I will once again ride my trusty bull reindeer a final three times around my bride's house to seal the deal. And yes, there's a lot more singing of *yoiks*.

The minibus leaves the main road and detours to the tiny village of Masi, on the chance that someone there might be waiting for a ride. Farther along, closer to Kautokeino, we make one more stop at a pleasant little cottage with a *kota* in the backyard. The reindeer woman gets off.

"She lives here," says the driver. "She has invited me over for coffee and fish after I drop you off. Besides I need to come back to get the fare. Where should I take you?"

I didn't realize that the bus service here provides door-to-door service. I am tempted to say "Helsinki," but that would be stretching my luck. The truth is, I have no idea where to be left off.

I tell her that the city center would be fine, but as we roll into Kautokeino and pass a store, grocery, school, and a government building of some sort, I realize that might be hard to identify.

She asks, "What are you going to do today?"

"I'll put the bike together, then see how I feel," I say. "I might stay here tonight or ride to Hetta* in Finland. One of those Norwegian fellows on the bus this morning told me the road is mostly flat."

The driver leaves me at a dusty parking lot in front of a tourist office that contains very little tourist information. But the sun is out, and for the first time in weeks, I am actually warm. As I methodically put the bike together for the fourth time in the last twenty-four hours, Sami, some dressed in native tunics with blue- and red-fringed embroidery, go about

---

* Hetta is called Enontekiö on some maps.

their business. The place has a sort of Navajo reservation—or Mexican village—afternoon feeling to it. People stop and talk, and no one appears to be in a particular hurry. As I work, I find myself getting drowsy and would gladly take a nap if there were a patch of grass or a hammock nearby.

After assembling the bike and wagon, a task I can now do in less than thirty minutes, I wander over to the store to buy food.

Passing through in the summer of 1871, Du Chaillu found this same village nearly deserted as the Sami were out herding their reindeer. When he returned the next spring, the place was a beehive of activity. Houses were bursting with extended families reunited during this brief rendezvous, while outside thousands of reindeer passed through the village on their way to summer pastures. Strangely, Du Chaillu does not mention what has become known as the Kautokeino Rebellion. It occurred here twenty years prior to Du Chaillu's arrival and certainly must have still been in the minds of village elders. The rebellion resulted in the death of a local merchant and the police chief, and the whipping of a priest and his servants. In the aftermath, two of the alleged Sami instigators were tried and executed.[39]

It is only one o'clock in the afternoon, too early to stop, though I have the urge to stay here in this Land of Nod. I ride to the local campground. It's the same old story: I am to follow the written instructions, which tell me to go to the blue house next door and knock on the door, or come back at six. I find the house, but no one is home. I really do not want to ride today. I want to stay and absorb some of the local culture, perhaps for the last time. But the sun is out and the road is flat, and I've lost my excuse that I have a place to stay. Finland beckons just 30 miles to the south. Reluctantly, I get on the bike and lumber up a grade onto a vast plain speckled by a few lonely hills.

I pedal listlessly for about an hour when a car with two bikes tethered to a rack quietly passes, then suddenly pulls over and parks on the shoulder about twenty yards in front of me. A man and a woman emerge. They are smiling. The woman holds a shiny apple out to me. *How nice, I think. They are going to give me food.*

"Bob, how did you get here?" the woman says.

Amazing! They even know my name.

The synapses begin to fire in the correct order. I remember the voices. It's Sebastian and Katherine, the German couple I had met a week ago in Utsjoki, Finland. This instance of serendipity proves that a traveler can never truly be alone forever on a journey, particularly one that is rather circular.

They tell me they battled ferocious winds while trying to get to the Barents Sea. "We couldn't even coast downhill; we had to pedal," says Sebastian. He says his rear derailleur failed, reducing him to the use of the three gears on the front chain ring. Now finished cycling, they are on their way to Sweden for some good, old-fashioned car touring.

"You know," says Sebastian. "This is a special spot for me because when I was a young man, I hitchhiked here in the winter. A Sami gave me a ride on the back of his snowmobile, but I was so cold, I got off and ended up hitchhiking again."

The area looks desolate enough in late summer. I can't imagine what it would be like in the around-the-clock darkness of winter. We exchange e-mail addresses and part for the last time. I watch the car climb a hill, then disappear. It's hard to watch them go because I am reminded what it is like to make friends on the road. They come and they go; sometimes you don't even get a name. But the brief exchanges are priceless. I sit by the side of the road, staring at the fathomless plain, munching my gift apple. I imagine I am the last person on Earth because that's what it feels like right now.

At the 30-mile mark, I cross into Finland with the same lack of ceremony as when I crossed into Norway. A mile from the border, I come to a one-shop village, Tunturikestus, which is not on my map. The shop is a restaurant, gas station, and office for a campground with cabins.

I had hoped to reach Hetta, but I know I do not have the strength today. I see storm clouds gathering in the far reaches of the plain. I rent a sturdy Sami cabin built with two-foot thick logs. After I register with the petite Sami proprietor, I go outside to fetch the bike. A man is peering intently at it. He asks where I'm from. He's impressed by the distance I have covered. I am grateful that he does not remark that it is a long way.

"I am a Sami," he tells me proudly. He says he lives nearby and likes to come to this restaurant because they serve excellent reindeer. I am not sure what prompts me to ask the next question, but out it pops.

"Do you own reindeer?"

He looks at me like I've got to be kidding.

"Oh yes," he says. "Many."

"Where are they?" I ask, because I have not seen a single reindeer during my afternoon ride.

"Oh, they are over there," he says, pointing in some vague direction on the limitless expanse. We both gaze across the road beyond, to flat land disappearing into the horizon streaked with pink and gray. Lower in the sky a bank of dark clouds, like a precursor of evil, creeps forward. A chilled breeze rustles the Sami nation flag waving from a pole at the entrance to the camp.

"Are they at the coast?"

"Oh, yes, but they will come home soon. They always come home. It's near the time for them to come home."

"I think I know the feeling," I say. "It's time for me to go home, too."

Last Ride

THE MORNING IS DISMAL, making it doubly hard to rip myself away from the warmth of the Sami cabin. Once I saddle up, I know the day will be difficult. Within the first hour, my leg muscles seem to cry out "No more!" I coax them to keep pumping, reassuring them that, at most, only two more days of cycling remain—even though the Expedition was under the impression that the trip had ended in Vadsø.

The new plan is to head south to Hetta, then east to the Muoniojoki, the river that borders Sweden. Not only will this certify my circumnavigation of Finland from south to north, as well as east to west, but it also provides a final shadowing of fellow Lapland travelers Giuseppe Acerbi and Paul B. Du Chaillu. Today, I need to ride 65 miles to reach Muonio, then tomorrow another 40 miles to Sirkka, home of the Levi ski resort. In Sirkka, I intend to duplicate my penthouse experience in Ruka. The vision of endless saunas, beer, and watching the Muppets in Finnish from a comfortable sofa keeps the Expedition from collapsing into a lump of inertia.

What had been a featureless plain begins to transform into low, rolling hills. Fir trees reappear. The birches are bigger. After 15 miles at an abysmally slow pace, I reach a smattering of sad buildings and end-of-season cabins that look like they have seen better times. But Hetta has one thing that cheers my soul: a gas station with a café. It has been a while since I have indulged in my newfound passion, but there is some weird, undefined quality about a cup of coffee and a donut served in a Finnish gas station that will always cheer me up from now on. After my repast, I don gloves, a sweatshirt, and my head warmer to defend against the cold.

I'm still grinding along at seven miles per hour, exchanging pleasantries with local reindeer, when two young men pull up from behind me. Their bikes are loaded with panniers; tents and sleeping bags are strapped to their rear racks. One of the men, Tomi, speaks almost flawless English. He tells me that he and his buddy are taking a two-week tour up the "left arm" of Finland—this being the narrow appendage that juts into Sweden and Norway. Finland once had a "right arm," a similar narrow corridor that stretched to the northeast to the port city of Petsamo on the Barents Sea, but the right arm was severed in 1944 when it was annexed by the Soviet Union as part of the armistice that ended the Continuation War.

Tomi is a chemistry student at the University of Jyväskylä, but he plans to take time off next year to study Spanish in Cuernavaca, Mexico. I tell him that I am half Mexican-American.

"You are surely the first Mexican ever to ride a bicycle to the polar sea and back in Finland," he tells me. "And you are probably the first person ever to do it on such a small bicycle."

I tell him I am in awe of the multilingual abilities of the Finns.

"No one else speaks Finnish," he says. "We must learn other languages to succeed in the world. English is mandatory in school. Almost everyone under thirty speaks some English."

For the next forty-five minutes, we cycle side by side, talking away while his buddy keeps a sharp lookout for approaching cars. The conversation is like an energizing tonic. I pump hard to keep up with Tomi, but my legs find new muscle energy from somewhere—perhaps from the recently consumed donut. I hardly notice the miles or the hills. Tomi peppers me with questions about my trip, the bike, and my daily routine. I tell him that I've noticed the cold increasing in the last two days and that there are fewer reindeer by the road.

"If you stay here another few weeks, you will see snow," he tells me. "Winter is coming. The birds are gone, and the reindeer moss is no longer by the side of the road."

At Palojoensu, we part company. Tomi and his companion turn north on Highway E-6, the road that follows Finland's left arm. I turn south. Tomi warns me of another approaching storm and the potential for fierce headwinds along the Muoniojoki. I wave good-bye and brace myself for the final storm.

Acerbi was luckier than I was, arriving at this junction in late July of 1799—and one of the first Europeans to do so. Instead of the cold, he complained of the heat (84 degrees Fahrenheit) and mosquito swarms so intense that his expedition traveled at night. The mosquitoes weren't the only thing bugging Acerbi. In his journal, he declares that the geographical boundary of Lapland begins here, with the territory to the south belonging to West Bothnia. Because Lapland was such an elusive goal for early travelers, ensuring that one actually reached it was an important distinction that enhanced bragging rights back home. To this end, the Italian adventurer's journal displays annoyance with the geographical claims of the French mathematician Pierre Louis Maupertuis,[40] who published an account of his travels in Lapland in 1736. "He constantly confounds Lapland with West Bothnia," writes a clearly ticked off Acerbi. "...All other travelers after him seem to have fallen into the like mistake, and fancied they had been in Lapland, when they got as far as Tornea."[41]

The Expedition rolls into Muonio at five o'clock. In short order, I find a market, stock up on food for the evening and tomorrow's ride, then rent a cabin for the bargain price of $23, the best deal yet. My little abode overlooks the Muoniojoki, which broadens into a lake near the town. Once again, I am in a cozy environ. I cook dinner and sip a beer as the skies darken and the rain falls. *If it's raining in the morning,* I decide, *I will stay put. I am in no rush.*

Lingering is not necessary. The morning bursts forth with a brilliant blue sky, a gift for the final ride. I have only 40 miles left, but as usual there is a catch. I must recross a line of fells that separate western Lapland from the central part.

By midmorning, I slowly make my way east on Highway 79. The glare off the wet road is almost blinding. The forest here is teeming with reindeer. I'd like to think they have come out in force this morning to say good-bye. One herd at the crest of a particularly gruesome hill includes an elusive white reindeer that prances like a ghost in the dark shadows of the forest.

Reindeer wander onto the road during the last big ride day of the epic.

By late morning, clouds are swiftly moving in from the east. To lighten my load, I have packed only enough food for a meager lunch. Unfortunately, the ride through the fells is more taxing than I anticipated. Once again, I grind up long grades, coast, then pedal like crazy to gain enough momentum for the next hill. But the physics aren't working for me today. I end up walking the bike up the steepest hills. It is exhausting work, and my hunger returns with a vengeance. At one rest break, I paw through my front carrier, looking for gorp and granola, when I notice that the forest is bursting with ripe huckleberries. I park the bike and, like a hungry bear, I plunge into the woods, gorging on the succulent berries.

During the last 10 miles, I am vaguely aware that after today there will be no more long rides hauling a heavy wagon. My epic journey is over—and I've lived to tell the tale: I've ridden over 2,100 miles! I've accomplished what I set out to do, both physically and mentally. I removed myself from everyday life and had an adventure. By immersing myself in the land, I have learned much about Finland, a place I knew little about before I arrived.

Two months ago, when I imagined this day and Lapland seemed impossibly far away, I dreamt of sprinting the last few miles in one final adrenal celebratory rush. That will remain a dream. I want to, but can't. The cascade of events and the nonstop stimulus of adventure have worn out both my body and my brain. My legs ache. My saddle sores are back, and wasps are crawling down my shirt. My imagination, a fertile source of entertainment during the long solitary stretches, is no longer functioning with any degree of efficiency. I cannot sustain any thought for long, not even a decent daydream about how nice it would be to roll into Helsinki or sleep in my own bed and not worry about pedaling the next morning. What thoughts I have are fragments, and these are short-circuited by blankness. I have achieved a Zen state, not through practiced meditation but by exhaustion. I see, but I don't think.

Now, on these last miles, I see the asphalt, the trees, and the scuttling clouds against an unpolluted sky. I hear the distant rustle of the boughs. I observe that the yellowing tips of the birch branches have grown more pronounced each day, and my brain momentarily sparks to life, reminding me that winter is coming. I see other reminders of this. The purple fireweed blossoms, vibrant at the beginning of the epic, are now withered brown seed stalks. The pinks and blues of the lupine are a memory. Only the hearty yarrow, its tiny white blossoms defiant against the changing of the season, remains in bloom. The mosquitoes are dead. I outlasted the little buggers. The cold killed them off.

When I finally crawl into Sirkka, I know I have done it, but feel nothing except a vague sense of belonging to the earth, the wind, and the rain. I have become part of the whole. The trip will change me, probably in profound ways. This I know, but I cannot at this moment, as my long-suffering body pedals the last few revolutions, describe the nature of these changes. I have the rest of my life to figure that out. The only thing that is clear now is that the journey has sucked the emotional juices right out of my body. I need to rest.

In Sirkka, I rent an entire house: four bedrooms, sauna, fireplace, big kitchen, washer and dryer, big television, and enough room to rummage around in my leisure pants for a few days. The epic is over. After returning from the store with food and a couple of cans of Karjala beer, I unlock the door to my temporary home for the next three nights and try to put into perspective what has just happened.

Epilogue

A cyclist chases the wind on the beach near Oulu.

I ACTUALLY DID NOT DO THAT MUCH THINKING in my spacious Sirkka cabin because I was too busy eating, napping, and taking saunas. Three days later, I rode the bike to the town hotel, packed it up, and took a bus to Rovaniemi. From my upholstered seat, I marveled at how quickly the bus devoured the road, compared to my snail-like pace two weeks earlier when I was heading in the opposite direction. In Rovaniemi, I once again took advantage of Finland's marvelously efficient passenger train service, boarding a train to Oulu, a lovely city perched on the Gulf of Bothnia. I had hoped to attend the World Air Guitar Championships—one of the country's more bizarre festivals. But alas, when I arrived I discovered that the championships had been moved up a week. I kicked around Oulu for two days, then returned to Helsinki on September 1, where I spent the next three days terrorizing the city's buffets.

As I had suspected, the trip did promote some changes in me. I did not return to the nine-to-five routine of the work world. I doubt I ever will. A year after returning from the trip, I accepted a part-time position as the Chief Financial Officer of the Kitsap Regional Library System, a job that allowed me to write this book and still leave time to enjoy life. The exchange of income for more personal time was a no-brainer. I may be poorer financially, but I am richer in many other ways.

Once a week, I get on my road bike (Friday is still resting) in Seattle and ride the 11 miles to my office in east Bremerton. The trip involves an hour ferry ride and some mean fell-like hills, but after completing my Finnish epic—a trip I now sometimes have trouble believing I actually did—nothing much fazes me anymore.

Robert M. Goldstein
Seattle, Washington
August 2009

Endnotes

[1] *The Corruption Perceptions Index*, published by Transparency International, ranks countries according to data from various polls that measure the degree to which citizens feel that politicians and government workers in their home country are corrupt.

[2] The Sami were known as the Lapps by early explorers. The term Lapp is now considered derogatory by most Sami. The Sami language has similar linguistic roots to Finnish, but is considered a distinct language. The word *Lapp* means an old patch, something that is not useful and can be discarded. It also bears a resemblance to the Finnish word *lape,* which means periphery.

[3] Torvalds's basic operating system may be free, but stock options he received from United States companies that continued and enhanced its development vaulted him to millionaire status. Torvalds created Linux while a computer science student at the University of Helsinki. Married to six-time Finnish karate champion, Tove, Torvalds and his wife now live in Portland, Oregon. Torvalds's parents named him after the American Nobel Laureate in chemistry Linus Pauling, who, in a twist of geographical irony, was a professor at Oregon State University not far from where Torvalds now lives.

[4] Karelia is a distinct cultural region that today straddles Russia and Finland. In Finland, South Karelia generally extends from the extreme southeastern tip of Finland to Lake Saimaa. North Karelia begins north of Lake Saimaa and extends to Lapland. On the Russian side, the Karelian Peninsula extends from the Finnish border south of Lake Ladoga to the River Svir, which lies about 20 miles north of St. Petersburg.

[5] The wife of Czar Alexander III, Feodorovna's official title was Empress Consort after the death of her husband.

[6] The negotiations and subsequent breakdown have been a point of endless controversy among historians. Was the end result inevitable or could the Finns have avoided the ensuing war by accepting the Soviet demands? What is known is that during the course of negotiations, the Russians and Germans secretly reached the Molotov-Ribbentrop Pact. The agreement ceded Poland and other eastern European countries to Germany, while Finland fell under the Soviet sphere of influence. Knowing that Nazi Germany would not interfere with a Russian invasion of Finland no doubt had a strong influence on the Soviet decision to achieve their goals by force instead of negotiation.

[7] *Time*, World War—Northern Theatre "Hit Them in the Belly." Feb. 5, 1940, p 29.

[8] The quote from Mannerheim and the biblical reference by Kyösti Kallio is found in Vaino Tanner's detailed account of negotiations with the Soviet Union preceding the Winter War. (*The Winter War: Finland Against Russia 1939–1940.* Stanford University Press, 1957.)

[9] Official Soviet casualty reports are considered unreliable, but later reports indicate the Red Army lost up to 270,000, with 300,000 wounded.

[10] Shortly after the Continuation War began, British Prime Minister Winston Churchill sent a personal letter to Mannerheim noting that the "many friends of your country in England" were pained to see Finland enter the war against Russia, thus placing Finland on the side of the Nazis. Mannerheim replied, thanking Churchill for his thoughtful letter but explaining that he could not halt the offensive until Finland had regained territory lost during the Winter War. He added that he would be "deeply saddened if England felt herself forced to declare war on Finland." The British, as well as the other Allies, had no intention of going to war against Finland, but in order to satisfy Stalin, Great Britain formerly declared war on Finland a few days after Churchill received Mannerheim's response.

[11] Although no Finnish Jews where deported to Germany during the war, eight Jews who fled Austria and Poland and sought refuge in Finland were turned over to the Nazis in November of 1942. They subsequently perished in concentration camps. This incident was not publicly acknowledged by the Finnish government until November of 2000 when Prime Minister Paavo Lipponen apologized to the Jewish Community. When in Finland I was told that a rogue, anti-Semitic member of the Helsinki police department was largely responsible for the deportation. In 2003, the question of additional deportations surfaced with the publication of *The Extradited— Finland's Deportations to the Gestapo* by Finnish author and researcher Elina Sana, who wrote that Finnish officials also deported 3,000 foreigners, mostly captured Soviet soldiers, to Germany. Some were Jewish. In an article in the November 11, 2003, *Helsingin Sanomat International Edition*, Sana says that Finland was acting on orders from Hitler to deport Soviet political officers. Most of the extraditions occurred in 1941 and 1942. A week later, also in *Helsingin Sanomat*, Max Jakobson, Finland's former United Nations Ambassador and a respected member of the Jewish Community, provided further context for this unsettling time in Finnish history. Jakobson said the Finnish military agreed to place Jewish POWs in a separate camp, but political officers were exempt, which led to their deportation to Germany.

[12] The Soviets, invoking the Moscow Declaration of 1943, demanded that the Finns conduct trials of politicians who were responsible for the Continuation War and by inference cooperated with the Germans. The Finns generally regarded the proceeding and ensuing convictions of former President Risto Ryti, Prime Minister Johan Wilhelm Rangell, and Foreign Minister Väino Tanner, among others, as a kangaroo court sought to appease the Soviets. Mannerheim feared he would be prosecuted, but this never came to pass. There are rumors that Stalin himself, who would later confess to begrudging admiration for Finland's Marshal, intervened to keep Mannerheim from being charged by zealous Soviet officials. Ryti received the largest sentence, ten years, but was pardoned in 1949.

[13] Swedish and Finnish are the official languages of Finland. About six percent of the Finnish population speak Swedish as their first language, most living in the southwest near Turku or on the coast of Ostrobothnia. The Swedish spoken in Finland incorporates some Finnish words, making it distinct from that spoken in Sweden.

[14] Born into a Swedish-Finnish family, his original name was Axel Gallen, but as an adult he changed it to emphasize his Finnish roots. Gallen-Kallela became Mannerheim's aide-de-camp in 1919, and would later become one of Finland's greatest contemporary artists. Among his lesser-known works are the designs of flags and military uniforms for the new republic.

[15] This roughly comprised parts of modern-day Poland, Lithuania, Belarus, and Ukraine.

[16] A more detailed explanation of how the Goldsteins managed to get themselves from Czarist Russia to the New World can be found in my first book, *The Gentleman from Finland— Adventures on the Trans-Siberian Express*, pp 166–172.

[17] This detail and a following reference to the Gallen-Kallela funeral composition were gleaned from *Sibelius Eight, What Happened to it?* by Kari Kilpeläinen, published in the April 1995 edition of *Finnish Music Quarterly*.

[18] References to the burning of the manuscript and remembrances from associates who recalled Sibelius telling them that the completed symphony existed but was burned came from a Web-based article (www.sibelius.fi/english/elamankaari/sib) titled *Jean Sibelius, The Man, The War and the Destruction of the Eighth Symphony 1939–1945*. The article reports that Aino remembers a great burning party at Ainola in which Sibelius's manuscripts were used as kindling. Aino, whose initial reaction to the burning was shock, later told a grandson that the act seemed to calm her husband and restore his optimism.

[19] Finland's bike maps are called Pyöräily GT by Genimap, scale 1:200,000. The entire country is covered in six maps. My guess is that the other two languages are Finnish and Swedish or, given my ineptness with languages, Finnish and Navajo. To amplify the confusion that Finnish poses to the English speaker, the Lonely Planet guidebook vocabulary notes that the word for bicycle is polkupyörän. The dictionary I later acquired lists no translation for pyöräily, but says the root pyörä means "wheel."

[20] In 2004, the latest year for which statistics were available, the Finns paid 7.6 percent of Gross Domestic Product for health care, while Americans forked over double that amount. The Finns also operate a parallel private health provider network, which is partially subsidized by government health insurance. Transparency of fees is another wonder of the Finnish health care system. Standardized fees for service are clearly spelled out in a brochure issued by the Ministry of Social Affairs and Health. If you are having trouble believing the fee structure, I refer you to page 25 of the "Health Care in Finland" brochure, which states in clear English: "The daily charge is EUR 26 in a hospital and EUR 12 in a psychiatric hospital, covering examinations, treatment, medicine and meals."

[21] Born with the first name Karin, Månsdotter assumed the name Katrina when she was crowned queen. Catherine is the English equivalent.

[22] Details on Eric's imprisonment and the witch trials came from the impeccable Kastelhoms Museum and restoration displays. For the record, it is not clear whether Catherine Månsdotter accompanied her deranged husband to this castle. The museum only notes that the room where Eric was imprisoned was far too small to also hold his wife. As noted earlier, Catherine was confined for most of this time to Turku Castle and later released after her husband's death.

[23] The military action was related to the Crimean War, which pitted Britain, France, and Turkey against Russia.

[24] Vyborg was ceded by Finland to the Soviet Union as part of the armistice that ended the Winter War in 1940.

[25] The Finnish Civil War, like most civil wars, was a bloody affair. Even today, the accusations about executions in the aftermath of the White Army victory is a sensitive topic in Finland.

[26] Kati was true to her word. On July 24, 2008, a week after my appearance at the campground, the *Oriveden Sanomat*, now my favorite newspaper, published a front-page picture of the smiling and helmeted author under a headline that roughly translates as "Campsite for people who want to stay for longer or visit just for a rest." After a few introductory paragraphs, she writes, "A bicycle is turning a curve. A suitcase is traveling cleverly in the back of the bike. A man jumps down from his saddle and greets us happily in English. 'I have been interested in Finland for a long time. I have biked from Helsinki, and I'm going all the way to Lapland...,' says writer Robert M. Goldstein." Later, she writes, "People have been friendly to Goldstein, although he hasn't really missed having a true conversation with anybody. He enjoys the changing scenery and his own company. 'Could you please promise me that it's not going to rain tomorrow,' he asks and leaves to put up his tent."

[27] Aalto, Alvar., "Architecture in Central Finland." *Sisä-Suomi*, June 28, 1925.

[28] Thanks to the Alvar Aalto Museum in Jyväskylä for its informative displays that provided the details on Aalto's life and work.

[29] The literal translation of *mottis* describes timber chopped or sawed into segments.

[30] This remarkable story was gleaned from *The Troll Tale and Other Scary Stories*, collected and analyzed by Birke Duncan and Jason Marc Harris. Despite the title, the story is purported to be true and was recounted to the authors by Garrett Vance, who had been cycling through Sweden with his girlfriend in 1984. Vance related the story in an interview with Duncan, who was studying and analyzing the origins of folk tales.

[31] Mydans, Carl. *More Than Meets the Eye*. New York: Harper & Brothers, 1959, p 19.

[32] I'm not sure how Martiniére's publishers managed to get the full title on the book's spine, but for interested readers the book may be found under: *A new voyage into the northern countries being a description of the manners, customs, superstition, buildings, and habits of Norwegians, Laponians, Kilops, Borandians, Siberians, Samojedes, Zemblans, and Islanders: with reflexions* [sic] *upon an error in our geographers about the scituation* [sic] *and extent of Greenland and Nova Zembia.*

[33] The Siida is an excellent museum, but did not dwell on the less pleasant aspects of Sami history. The Sami who failed to embrace Christianity faced systematic persecution. One researcher claims that 20 percent of all witchcraft executions conducted by the Lutheran Church involved the Sami. Runes Hagen, a researcher at the University of Tromso, Norway, places the number of Sami executed during the witch trials at seventy-five. Threatened with death or eternal damnation unless they turned over their drums, the Sami had little practical choice other than to convert. Subsequently, the Sami adopted Lutheranism (the exception being the Skolt Sami who converted to Russian Orthodoxy), assimilating elements of their own historical culture and religion into their new faith. One cannot come away from reviewing contemporary Sami Web sites without feeling that an underlying tension still exists over the lingering affects of historical maltreatment.

[34] Missoulian.com, news on-line. "Indigenous Sami embraces their heritage." Oct. 20, 2007.

[35] The landmark's reference to the last fighting of the Lapland War is at odds with an account of the war's end in *Hitler's Arctic War—The German Campaigns in Norway, Finland and the USSR 1940–1945*. Authors Chris Mann and Christer Jörgensen state that the final battle occurred on November 28, 1944, at Karesuanto. However, the authors note that the Germans did not retreat from positions at Kilpisjärvi at the western extreme of the Finnish panhandle until April of 1945.

[36] *Hitler's Arctic War*, page 203. See previous reference.

[37] The "most-bombed" distinction is touted by Kirkenes, but Malta also claims that dubious title.

[38] Du Chaillu said: "I had always thought the Lapps had black eyes and dark hair, but these were fair-skinned and fair-haired, with blue eyes; the cheekbones were prominent—in two of the women not unpleasantly so—and the nose was peculiarly Lapp and *retroussé*. Measurements of the three women showed heights of four feet and one-quarter, four feet and three-quarters, and four feet six and three-quarters inches; the height of the two men ranged from four feet five to five feet and one-quarter inch."

[39] The story of the uprising is depicted in the *Kautokeino Rebellion,* a film released in 2008 and first screened in Inari at the Nightless Film Festival.

[40] At the behest of King Louis XV, Maupertuis went to Lapland as head of an expedition to take scientific measurements to prove that Earth was oblate (more or less squashed) rather than prolate.

[41] Acerbi's reference to Tornea is most likely the modern-day town of Tornio, Finland, which sits at the mouth of the Tornionjoki in the Gulf of Bothnia. The Tornionjoki provided the best water route into the interior of Finland, Sweden, and Lapland. The Muoniojoki is a tributary.

About the Author

ROBERT M. GOLDSTEIN WAS BORN IN LOS ANGELES, but grew up in Santa Clara, California, where he began his first bicycle forays. After graduating from Oregon State University in 1977 with a bachelor's degree in Technical Journalism, he worked as a newspaper reporter for the *Walla Walla Union Bulletin* and the *Bellevue Journal-American*. In the late 1980s, his career took a different direction after he received his master's degree in Public Administration from the University of Washington. Since that time, he has held a variety of administrative posts in California and Washington. He has traveled extensively and has published travel articles on Nepal, Bhutan, and China in the *Seattle Times* and the *Journal-American*. His critically acclaimed first book, *The Gentleman from Finland—Adventures on the Trans-Siberian Express*, chronicles a madcap journey across the Soviet Union. The book earned Goldstein the coveted Benjamin Franklin Award for best travel book published by a small publisher in North America in 2005. Currently, he is the chief financial officer of the Kitsap Regional Library. He lives in Seattle.

A rare sunny day near Nurmes, North Karelia

Bibliography

There are a plethora of books on Finland. The list below is a partial bibliography, consisting of sources I consulted in researching *Riding with Reindeer*. In addition, I consulted Internet sources, which are cited in the end notes for each chapter.

Acerbi, Giuseppe. *Travels through Sweden, Finland, and Lapland, to the North Cape, in the Years 1798 and 1799: Volumes 1 and 2.* Adamant Media Corp., 2001 (reprint of 1802 edition by Joseph Mawman, London).

Atatalo, Jaakko. *In a Nordic Village.* Benchmark Books, 2003.

Barnett, Andrew. *Sibelius.* Yale University Press, 2007.

Du Chaillu, Paul B. *The Land of the Midnight Sun* (2 volumes). Franklin Square, NY: Harper & Brothers, 1881.

Engle, Eloise, and Lauri Paanansen. *The Winter War: The Soviet Attack on Finland 1939–1940.* Stackpole Books, 1992.

Jägerskiöld, Stig Axel Fridolf. *Mannerheim: Marshal of Finland.* Hurst, 1986.

Lewis, Richard D. *Finland, Cultural Lone Wolf.* Intercultural Press, 2005.

Lundin, C. Leonard. *Finland in the Second World War.* Indiana University Press, 1957.

Mann, Chris, and Christer Jorgensen. *Hitler's Arctic War: The German Campaigns in Norway, Finland and the USSR 1940–1945.* St. Martin's Press, 2002.

Mannerheim, Carl Gustaf Emil. *Memoirs* (translated by Count Eric Lewenhaupt). Cassell, 1953.

Norrback, Martha, ed. *A Gentleman's Home: The Museum of Gustaf Mannerheim, Marshal of Finland.* Otava, 2001.

Rintala, Marvin. *Four Finns*. University of California Press, 1969.

Ross, Zoe, ed. *Insight Guides Finland*, 3rd ed. Singapore: Apa Publications GmbH & Co. Verlag KG, 2005.

Screen, John Ernest Oliver. *Mannerheim: The Finnish Years*. C. Hurst, 2000.

Screen, John Ernest Oliver. *Mannerheim: The Years of Preparation*. C. Hurst, 1970.

Tanner, Vaino. *The Winter War: Finland Against Russia 1939–1940*. Stanford University Press, 1957.

Trotter, William R. *A Frozen Hell: The Russo-Finnish Winter War of 1939–1940*. Algonquin Books of Chapel Hill, 1991.

Warner, O. *Marshal Mannerheim and the Finns*. London: Weidenfeld & Nicolson, 1967.

Acknowledgments

IN THIS DAY AND AGE OF DIGITAL HYPERSPEED, tweets, and sound bites, I remain in awe of the resources that must be mustered to produce a book—that is, a real book, the kind with paper pages. Riding a bike through Finland was only one of the critical tasks in seeing the completion of this project. Thanks to Mike and Caroline Ullmann for the initial and final reading of the manuscript and their usual keen insight. Karalynn Ott and Michele Whitehead of Verve Editorial were new to the Rivendell production team. Mardelle Kunz, team copyeditor, applied the final polish and style consistency while managing to check all of the Finnish place names, a mind-boggling task. Their thorough reading and thoughtful editing greatly improved this story. If you are in the market for good editors, try any or all of the above. Liz Kingslien who created the award-winning cover and interior design for *The Gentleman from Finland* and who was thankfully available for this new project, deserves special mention for producing the stylized maps (I love the little reindeers), the front and back covers, and the interior design. Bravo!

On the expedition support side, thanks to my talented sister Maria for the hand sewn expedition banner that ended up being more than just the metaphorical symbol of the expedition, and to Melinda Denson, who held down the home fort while I was away and who persevered through endless oral readings of the draft manuscript while held captive on a Trans-Canadian train trip (that's another story). Mark Hillman, whose family roots sink deep into Swedish-Finnish soil, gave generously of his time (and maps) to review with me critical route information and other pretrip morsels from his experiences of biking in Suomi, which greatly helped. Thanks to Anne Ross of the Kitsap Regional Library for writing the catalog in print information.

Lastly, I thank the people of Finland, Lapland, and Arctic Norway, whose hospitality, kindness, and resourcefulness lingers sweetly in my memory. I promise to return someday, perhaps when the weather is better.